AMERICA'S UNINSURED CRISIS
CONSEQUENCES FOR HEALTH AND HEALTH CARE

Committee on Health Insurance Status and Its Consequences

Board on Health Care Services

INSTITUTE OF MEDICINE
OF THE NATIONAL ACADEMIES

THE NATIONAL ACADEMIES PRESS
Washington, D.C.
www.nap.edu

THE NATIONAL ACADEMIES PRESS   500 Fifth Street, N.W.   Washington, DC 20001

NOTICE: The project that is the subject of this report was approved by the Governing Board of the National Research Council, whose members are drawn from the councils of the National Academy of Sciences, the National Academy of Engineering, and the Institute of Medicine. The members of the committee responsible for the report were chosen for their special competences and with regard for appropriate balance.

This study was supported by Contract No. 63982 between the National Academy of Sciences and the Robert Wood Johnson Foundation. Any opinions, findings, conclusions, or recommendations expressed in this publication are those of the author(s) and do not necessarily reflect the view of the organizations or agencies that provided support for this project.

Library of Congress Cataloging-in-Publication Data

America's uninsured crisis : consequences for health and health care / Committee on Health Insurance Status and Its Consequences, Board on Health Care Services, Institute of Medicine of the National Academies.
    p. ; cm.
  Includes bibliographical references.
  ISBN 978-0-309-12789-9 (pbk.)
  1. Medically uninsured persons—United States. I. Institute of Medicine (U.S.). Committee on the Consequences of Uninsurance.
  [DNLM: 1. Insurance, Health—trends—United States. 2. Medically Uninsured —United States. 3. Health Services Accessibility—economics—United States. W 250 AA1 A5125 2009]
  RA413.7.U53A44 2009
  362.1′04250973—dc22

                              2009016561

Additional copies of this report are available from the National Academies Press, 500 Fifth Street, N.W., Lockbox 285, Washington, DC 20055; (800) 624-6242 or (202) 334-3313 (in the Washington metropolitan area); Internet, http://www.nap.edu.

For more information about the Institute of Medicine, visit the IOM home page at: **www.iom.edu.**

Printed in the United States of America

The serpent has been a symbol of long life, healing, and knowledge among almost all cultures and religions since the beginning of recorded history. The serpent adopted as a logotype by the Institute of Medicine is a relief carving from ancient Greece, now held by the Staatliche Museen in Berlin.

Suggested citation: IOM (Institute of Medicine). 2009. *America's Uninsured Crisis: Consequences for Health and Health Care.* Washington, DC: The National Academies Press.

*"Knowing is not enough; we must apply.
Willing is not enough; we must do."*
—Goethe

INSTITUTE OF MEDICINE
OF THE NATIONAL ACADEMIES

Advising the Nation. Improving Health.

THE NATIONAL ACADEMIES

Advisers to the Nation on Science, Engineering, and Medicine

The **National Academy of Sciences** is a private, nonprofit, self-perpetuating society of distinguished scholars engaged in scientific and engineering research, dedicated to the furtherance of science and technology and to their use for the general welfare. Upon the authority of the charter granted to it by the Congress in 1863, the Academy has a mandate that requires it to advise the federal government on scientific and technical matters. Dr. Ralph J. Cicerone is president of the National Academy of Sciences.

The **National Academy of Engineering** was established in 1964, under the charter of the National Academy of Sciences, as a parallel organization of outstanding engineers. It is autonomous in its administration and in the selection of its members, sharing with the National Academy of Sciences the responsibility for advising the federal government. The National Academy of Engineering also sponsors engineering programs aimed at meeting national needs, encourages education and research, and recognizes the superior achievements of engineers. Dr. Charles M. Vest is president of the National Academy of Engineering.

The **Institute of Medicine** was established in 1970 by the National Academy of Sciences to secure the services of eminent members of appropriate professions in the examination of policy matters pertaining to the health of the public. The Institute acts under the responsibility given to the National Academy of Sciences by its congressional charter to be an adviser to the federal government and, upon its own initiative, to identify issues of medical care, research, and education. Dr. Harvey V. Fineberg is president of the Institute of Medicine.

The **National Research Council** was organized by the National Academy of Sciences in 1916 to associate the broad community of science and technology with the Academy's purposes of furthering knowledge and advising the federal government. Functioning in accordance with general policies determined by the Academy, the Council has become the principal operating agency of both the National Academy of Sciences and the National Academy of Engineering in providing services to the government, the public, and the scientific and engineering communities. The Council is administered jointly by both Academies and the Institute of Medicine. Dr. Ralph J. Cicerone and Dr. Charles M. Vest are chair and vice chair, respectively, of the National Research Council.

www.national-academies.org

COMMITTEE ON HEALTH INSURANCE
STATUS AND ITS CONSEQUENCES

LAWRENCE S. LEWIN (*Chair*), Executive Consultant, Chevy Chase, MD
JACK EBELER (*Vice Chair*), Consultant, Reston, VA
JOHN Z. AYANIAN, Professor of Medicine and Health Care Policy, Harvard Medical School, Department of Health Care Policy, Boston, MA
KATHERINE BAICKER, Professor of Health Economics, Harvard University School of Public Health, Boston, MA
CHRISTINE FERGUSON, Research Professor, George Washington University School of Public Health and Health Services, Washington, DC
ROBERT S. GALVIN, Director, Global Health, General Electric, Fairfield, CT
PAUL GINSBURG, President, Center for Studying Health System Change, Washington, DC
LEON L. HALEY, JR., Deputy Senior Vice-President Medical Affairs and Chief of Emergency Medicine, Grady Health System, and Associate Professor and Vice Chair, Clinical Affairs at Grady Department of Emergency Medicine, Emory University School of Medicine, Atlanta, GA
CATHERINE McLAUGHLIN, Senior Fellow, Mathematica Policy Research, Inc., and Professor, Health Management and Policy, University of Michigan School of Public Health, Ann Arbor
JAMES J. MONGAN, President and CEO, Partners HealthCare System, Boston, MA
ROBERT D. REISCHAUER, President, The Urban Institute, Washington, DC
WILLIAM J. SCANLON, Senior Policy Advisor, Health Policy R&D, Oak Hill, VA
ANTONIA VILLARRUEL, Professor and Associate Dean for Research at the University of Michigan School of Nursing, Ann Arbor
LAWRENCE WALLACK, Dean, College of Urban and Public Affairs, Professor of Public Health, Portland State University, Portland, OR

Study Staff

JILL EDEN, Study Director
LEA GREENSTEIN, Research Associate

Reviewers

This report has been reviewed in draft form by individuals chosen for their diverse perspectives and technical expertise, in accordance with procedures approved by the National Research Council's Report Review Committee. The purpose of this independent review is to provide candid and critical comments that will assist the institution in making its published report as sound as possible and to ensure that the report meets institutional standards for objectivity, evidence, and responsiveness to the study charge. The review comments and draft manuscript remain confidential to protect the integrity of the deliberative process. We wish to thank the following individuals for their review of this report:

GEORGES BENJAMIN, American Public Health Association
SHEILA BURKE, Malcolm Weiner Center for Social Policy, John F. Kennedy School of Government, Harvard University
MARSHALL H. CHIN, Department of Medicine, University of Chicago
MARY SUE COLEMAN, University of Michigan
SHERRY GLIED, Department of Health Policy and Management, Mailman School of Public Health, Columbia University
NEAL HALFON, Center for Healthier Children, Families & Communities, University of California, Los Angeles
KAREN IGNAGNI, America's Health Insurance Plans

ARTHUR L. KELLERMANN, Emory University School of Medicine
ERIC B. LARSON, Group Health, Center for Health Studies
MARTIN JOSE SEPULVEDA, International Business Machines
Corporation

Although the reviewers listed above have provided many constructive comments and suggestions, they were not asked to endorse the conclusions or recommendations nor did they see the final draft of the report before its release. The review of this report was overseen by **DON EUGENE DETMER,** American Medical Informatics, and **PATRICIA M. DANZON,** Health Care Management Department, The Wharton School, University of Pennsylvania. Appointed by the National Research Council and the Institute of Medicine, they were responsible for making certain that an independent examination of this report was carried out in accordance with institutional procedures and that all review comments were carefully considered. Responsibility for the final content of this report rests entirely with the authoring committee and the institution.

Foreword

The absence of health insurance is hazardous to your health. The Institute of Medicine (IOM) reviewed these hazards in a comprehensive six-part series of reports earlier in this decade. We return now to the issue, once again with the support of the Robert Wood Johnson Foundation, because as dire as were the consequences defined in our previous work, the situation is even more grim today. The costs of health care continue to escalate at rates well above wage or general economic growth and consume an ever increasing share of the American economy. As a result, health insurance becomes less affordable to a growing proportion of the population. The economy is now severely weakened, and even as the federal government takes steps to provide insurance to more children and to some who are unemployed, the gaps in health insurance in the United States call for a comprehensive solution.

The IOM has long recommended systemic health reforms coupled with comprehensive health insurance. Here, we report new, rigorous, and persuasive evidence that the lack of health insurance is injurious to health. This core finding applies to individuals of all ages. Gaining access to coverage improves health outcomes especially for those with chronic disease. Some evidence suggests that living in a community with large numbers of the uninsured may impair the quality of health care even for those individuals who have insurance.

The members of the committee that produced this report are distinguished individuals with diverse and pertinent expertise. Ably led by Lawrence S. Lewin, chair, and Jack Ebeler, vice chair, the committee worked diligently to critically assess the evidence about the value of health insurance. They were assisted greatly by excellent commissioned work by Embry Howell, Genevieve Kenney, Michael McWilliams, José Pagán, and Mark Pauly, and by the dedicated support of the IOM study team led by Jill Eden. For their important contributions, we thank all these individuals. Our thanks also go to the Robert Wood Johnson Foundation for its generous support.

We present this report in the earnest hope that it will contribute to comprehensive health insurance coverage in a new and successful effort to reform health care in America.

> Harvey V. Fineberg, M.D., Ph.D.
> President, Institute of Medicine
> February 2009

Preface

Some issues, like the problems of the uninsured in the United States, are with us for so long that we end up adapting to them as a seemingly inevitable chronic condition of our health care system. We become inured to another annual report on the number of people without health insurance coverage, and another report on the consequences—consequences that are often obscured for many of us and easiest to ignore. And we become cynical about yet another set of recommendations, and another debate on what to do.

That cycle must be broken. The lack of health insurance coverage for tens of millions of Americans cannot be ignored and should not be a chronic underpinning of American health care—it is in fact treatable and indeed preventable.

The Institute of Medicine (IOM) has spoken to this issue before. From 2000 to 2004, the IOM's Committee on the Consequences of Uninsurance issued a landmark series of six reports that reviewed and reported on the evidence on the effects of the lack of health insurance coverage. It confirmed that uninsured people, children as well as adults, suffer worse health and die sooner than those with insurance. It further identified consequences for families, communities, and the economy as a whole. The final report in the series, published in 2004, went on to set out a vision and principles for coverage, and made two recommendations for action: that the President and Congress develop a strategy to achieve universal coverage by 2010, and in the interim, that federal and state governments provide resources sufficient for Medicaid and State Children's Health Insurance Program coverage.

As of early 2009, no action has been taken. The IOM and the Robert Wood Johnson Foundation established another IOM panel to examine this critical issue because they concluded that sole reliance on the earlier IOM series of reports on the consequences of uninsurance would not meet the needs of the public and policy makers for an informed debate in 2009 and beyond. This panel, the Committee on Health Insurance Status and Its Consequences, was charged with identifying new insights not known or appreciated in the literature since the previous reports were published.

The committee found that private, employment-based coverage has continued to decline since the last report, and the number of uninsured has grown. All indicators point to a continuation of those trends, in light of health care cost growth that continues to exceed economic and wage growth, all of which is exacerbated by the economic recession the nation is now confronting. We found that the literature on health consequences is more robust than that available to the previous committee—lack of insurance coverage does have health consequences, and there is new literature to confirm an important but previously unanswered question: newly providing coverage to the previously uninsured does in fact improve things. Communities—including the insured population—may also be vulnerable to the deleterious effects of uninsurance.

Upon reviewing this evidence, we, like our predecessor committee, felt compelled to make a recommendation that is included in detail in the report: simply stated, we recommend with the strongest urgency we can convey that the President and Congress take action on coverage and costs.

Given the cycle of reports and inaction noted above, we grappled with a question that will be raised by many readers: what good is another report that coverage matters, and another recommendation for action? We, like many others, searched for some way we could identify a key finding, or describe the results in such a dramatic fashion, that it would break the cycle of inaction and compel action. But there isn't.

So why report again? The committee believes that the lack of action, frustrating though it is, cannot mean that we set the issue aside—because the consequences of inaction for the health of the uninsured are real. Instead, in light of the IOM mission as advisor to the nation to improve health, we call for renewed attention to the population without health insurance. There are many reasons that this debate is complicated and difficult to resolve, with legitimate, competing arguments from political and economic perspectives about whether and how to proceed. The one argument that the committee finds has no place whatsoever in a legitimate debate about this subject is that the lack of coverage doesn't matter for health. It does.

We would like to thank our committee for its insights and deliberations within an unusually short time frame; the researchers and other experts whose work we used; and the staff of the Board on Health Care Services who prepared the report. Our most ardent wish is that this is the final IOM report calling for action, and that the next IOM work in this area will comment on the implementation of exciting new directions for the nation.

Lawrence S. Lewin, *Chair*
Jack Ebeler, *Vice Chair*

Acknowledgments

The committee and staff are indebted to a number of individuals and organizations for their contributions to this report. We extend thanks to the following individuals who were essential sources of information, generously giving their time and knowledge to further the committee's efforts.

Jessica S. Banthin, Director of Modeling and Simulation, Center for Financing, Access and Cost Trends (CFACT), Agency for Healthcare Research and Quality (AHRQ)

Robert Blendon, Professor, Department of Health Policy and Management, Harvard School of Public Health and Kennedy School of Government

David Blumenthal, Director, Institute for Health Policy, Massachusetts General Hospital, Partners HealthCare System, Inc.

Joel Cohen, Director, Division of Social and Economic Research, CFACT, AHRQ

Steve Cohen, Director, CFACT, AHRQ

Philip Cooper, Senior Economist, CFACT, AHRQ

Peter Cunningham, Senior Health Researcher, Center for Studying Health System Change

Michelle M. Doty, Director of Survey Research, The Commonwealth Fund

Paul Fronstin, Senior Research Associate, Employee Benefit Research Institute

Elise Gould, Economist, Economic Policy Institute

Jack Hadley, Professor and Senior Health Services Researcher, Department of Health Administration and Policy, George Mason University

Sabrina K. H. How, Senior Research Associate, The Commonwealth Fund

Arthur L. Kellermann, School of Medicine, Emory University

Ronda Kotelchuck, Executive Director, Primary Care Development Corporation

Carol Meyer, Interim Chief Network Officer, Los Angeles County Department of Health Services

Wilhelmine Miller, Associate Research Professor, The George Washington University School of Public Health and Health Services

David M. Mirvis, Professor, Department of Preventive Medicine, University of Tennessee Health Science Center

Len Nichols, Director, Health Policy Program, New America Foundation

Felix L. Nuñez, Vice President of Clinical Services, Community Clinic Association of Los Angeles County

Matt Rutledge, Graduate Student Instructor, University of Michigan

Steven Schroeder, Distinguished Professor of Health and Health Care, Director, The Smoking Cessation Leadership Center, Department of Medicine, University of California, San Francisco

Kenneth Thorpe, Robert W. Woodruff Professor and Chair, Department of Health Policy Management Emory University, Rollins School of Public Health

Reed Tuckson, Senior Vice President, Consumer Health and Medical Care Advancement, UnitedHealth Group

Don Voth, Executive Director, Memphis & Shelby County Mental Health Summit

Funding for this study was provided by the Robert Wood Johnson Foundation (RWJF). The committee appreciates the opportunity and support extended by RWJF for the development of this report. Andrew Hyman was a superb project officer.

Finally, many within the Institute of Medicine were helpful to the study staff. The staff would especially like to thank Clyde Behney, Patrick Burke, Bronwyn Schrecker Jamrok, William McLeod, Janice Mehler, Abbey Meltzer, Lauren Tobias, and Jackie Turner.

Contents

List of Boxes, Figures, and Tables

Summary

Boxes

Chapter 1

Boxes

Figure

Chapter 4

Summary[1]

From 2001 to 2004, the Institute of Medicine (IOM) issued a comprehensive series of six reports that reviewed and reported on the evidence on how children, adults, families, and communities are affected by the lack of health insurance.[2] The committee reported that the evidence showed that not having health insurance is harmful to the health and overall well-being of both children and adults (Box S-1). In addition, the committee established principles for expanding coverage for all and recommended in the 2004 report *Insuring America's Health* that the President and Congress act by 2010 to achieve universal coverage, noting:

> "The benefits of universal coverage would enrich all Americans, whether accounted for in terms of improved health and longer life spans, greater economic productivity, financial security, or the stabilization of communities' health care systems."

It is now 5 years since the IOM made its recommendation, and there has still been no comprehensive national effort to achieve coverage for all Americans. In 2007, 45.7 million people in the United States—17.2 percent of the nonelderly U.S. population—were without health insurance. A severely weakened economy, rising health care and health insurance costs, growing unemployment, and declining employment-based health insurance coverage are all evidence that the U.S. health insurance system is in a state

---

[1] This summary does not include references. Citations for the findings presented in the summary appear in the subsequent chapters of the full report.

[2] For copies of the previous IOM report series on the consequences of uninsurance, please visit www.nap.edu.

BOX S-1
Previous IOM Findings on the Consequences
of Uninsurance, 2004

The clinical literature overwhelmingly shows that uninsured people, children as well as adults, suffer worse health and die sooner than those with insurance. Families with even one member who is uninsured lose peace of mind and can become burdened with enormous medical bills. Uninsurance at the community level is associated with financial instability for health care providers and institutions, reduced hospital services and capacity, and significant cuts in public health programs, which may diminish access to certain types of care for all residents, even those who have coverage. The economic vitality of the nation is limited by productivity lost as a result of the poorer health and premature death or disability of uninsured workers.

---

of crisis. There is no evidence to suggest that the trends driving loss of insurance coverage will reverse without concerted action.

With a new administration and a new Congress in 2009, many citizens, policy makers, and opinion leaders anticipate renewed energy and interest in finding a way to reverse declines in health insurance coverage and, ultimately, to expand coverage to all in the United States. It is in this context that the Robert Wood Johnson Foundation asked the IOM to conduct the present study. In response to the Foundation's request, the IOM appointed the Committee on Health Insurance Status and Its Consequences in April 2008.

The committee's charge was to review and evaluate the research evidence on the health and other consequences of uninsurance that has emerged since the IOM's earlier series of reports that might help inform the health care reform efforts in 2009 (Box S-2). Whereas the previous IOM studies on uninsurance were broad and comprehensive in scope, the present study focuses more narrowly on the following critical questions: (1) What are the dynamics driving downward trends in health insurance coverage? (2) Is being uninsured harmful to the health of children and adults? (3) Are insured people affected by high rates of uninsurance in their communities?

FINDINGS

In executing its charge, the committee has studied the research literature since 2002 and applied rigorous scientific criteria to set the record straight on the issue of health insurance coverage. The committee reports findings in three key areas: (1) trends in health insurance coverage and forces driving

---

**BOX S-2
Charge to the IOM Committee on Health
Insurance Status and Its Consequences**

The overarching objective of this study is to help inform the health reform policy debate as it unfolds in 2009. The committee will assess the research evidence—that has emerged since the IOM's 2001 to 2004 series of reports on uninsurance—on the consequences of uninsurance. Rather than performing a comprehensive review, the committee is charged with reviewing the literature to identify new insights not yet known or appreciated when the IOM's earlier reports were developed.

The search for new evidence will include the published literature on the consequences of uninsurance for individuals, families, communities, specific population groups, and safety net and other providers. The consequences may be related to health outcomes, such as morbidity and mortality; access to health care services; and economic impacts such as affordability of health coverage and its associated financing burden.

---

them, (2) the health consequences of uninsurance for children and adults, and (3) the implications of high community-level rates of uninsurance on people with health insurance in those communities. The committee's findings are summarized below.

Caught in a Downward Spiral: Health Insurance Coverage Is Declining and Will Continue to Decline

The fear of being without health insurance coverage is a growing strain on American families' sense of health and well-being. Concerns about losing health insurance coverage are well founded. In 2007, 5.9 million more people were uninsured than when the IOM issued its initial report on uninsurance. The uninsured included 8.1 million children and 36.8 million adults ages 18 to 64. In 2007, nearly 1 in 10 children and 1 in 5 nonelderly adults in the United States were without health insurance.[3]

Over the last decade, health insurance coverage has declined and will continue to decline. The cost of health care is driving the downward trend in both the private and public sectors. Health care costs and insurance premiums are growing at rates greater than the U.S. economy and family incomes. From 2001 to 2006, U.S. per capita health care spending grew by 47 percent compared to the 34 percent increase in gross domestic prod-

---

[3] The vast majority of the population age 65 and older has health insurance coverage through Medicare or other sources. For that reason, this study focuses on uninsurance among children and nonelderly adults.

uct. This trend shows no signs of abating. According to the Centers for Medicare & Medicaid Services, total U.S. health care spending may nearly double between 2008 and 2017.

The rapid growth in health care costs is making it increasingly difficult for U.S. employers to offer health insurance coverage to their workers. In addition, many employers have replaced permanent, full-time jobs with contract, part-time, and temporary positions that do not come with health benefits. And, early retirees are less likely to be offered retiree health insurance benefits than in the past.

Furthermore, even when employers are able to offer health insurance to their employees, increasing numbers of employees are declining these offers because they cannot afford the premiums. Between 1999 and 2008, the average annual employee premium contribution for family coverage rose from $1,543 to $3,354, far outpacing the growth in family incomes. High premium costs are especially burdensome to lower wage workers, who are finding it more and more difficult to take up offers of coverage from their employers.

Individuals without employer-sponsored health insurance who are not eligible for public insurance must rely on a limited nongroup health insurance market to obtain coverage. The premium costs for nongroup coverage can be exceedingly high and individual subscribers must pay the entire cost without a contribution from an employer. In most states, the insurer may deny coverage completely, impose either a permanent or temporary preexisting condition limitation on coverage, or charge a higher premium based on health status, occupation, and other personal characteristics. Some state and federal regulations have been put in place to help promote access to nongroup coverage, but current data limitations frustrate research that might illuminate the impact of the regulations.

It is possible that additional millions of low-income Americans would be uninsured today were it not for recent state and federal efforts to expand coverage. States and the federal government have substantially increased health coverage among low-income children and, to a lesser degree, among adults in the last decade, by expanding eligibility, conducting outreach to people already eligible, and expediting enrollment in Medicaid and State Children's Health Insurance Program (SCHIP) programs. Given the severity of the current economic crisis, however, some states will be unable to sustain these expansions—just at the time that increasing numbers of Americans are losing their jobs, their employer-sponsored health coverage, or both.

The committee's key findings on recent trends in health insurance coverage are summarized in Box S-3. **In sum, health insurance coverage in the United States is declining and the situation will get worse. The crisis is** engulfing employer-sponsored insurance, the cornerstone of private health coverage, and also threatens expansions in public coverage.

Coverage Matters: Health Insurance Is Integral to Personal Well-Being and Health[4]

When policy makers and researchers consider potential solutions to the problem of uninsurance in the United States, the question of whether health insurance matters to health is often an issue. This question is far more than an academic concern. It is crucial that U.S. health care policy be informed with current and valid evidence on the consequences of uninsurance for health care and health outcomes, especially for the 45.7 million individuals without health insurance.

The committee found that the new research evidence on the consequences of health insurance for children and adults is of higher quality and stronger than ever before. This robust body of evidence demonstrates substantial health benefits of health insurance coverage.

Important insights into how children benefit when they acquire health insurance are provided by well-designed evaluations of enrollment in Medicaid and SCHIP programs. With health insurance, it is clear that children gain access to a usual source of care; well-child care and immunizations to prevent future illness and monitor developmental milestones; prescription medications; appropriate care for asthma; and basic dental services. With health insurance, serious childhood health problems are more likely to be identified early, and children with special health care needs are more likely to have access to specialists. With health insurance, children have fewer avoidable hospitalizations, improved asthma outcomes, and fewer missed days of school.

For adults, there are serious harms and sometimes grave consequences to being without health insurance. Men and women without insurance are much less likely to receive clinical preventive services that have the potential to reduce unnecessary morbidity and premature death. Chronically ill adults delay or forgo visits with physicians and clinically effective therapies, including prescription medications. Uninsured adults are more likely to be diagnosed with later stage cancers that are detectable by preventive screening or by contact with a clinician who can assess worrisome symptoms. Without health insurance, adults are more likely to die from trauma

---

[4] The findings on the health consequences of uninsurance are based on two background papers commissioned by the IOM committee: (1) Health Consequences of Uninsurance Among Adults in the United States: An Update by J. Michael McWilliams, M.D., Ph.D., Harvard Medical School, and (2) Health and Access Consequences of Uninsurance Among Children in the United States: An Update by Genevieve M. Kenney, Ph.D., and Embry Howell, Ph.D., The Urban Institute.

BOX S-3
Key Findings on Trends in Health Insurance Coverage

Health insurance coverage has declined over the last decade despite increases in public program coverage and will continue to decline. There is no evidence to suggest that the trends driving loss of insurance coverage will reverse without concerted action. High and rising health care costs threaten not only employer-sponsored coverage, but also recent expansions in public coverage.

Private Health Insurance

- The rising cost of health care is driving the decline in private health insurance coverage. Health care costs and insurance premiums are growing substantially faster than the economy and family incomes.
- As the costs of health care increase, the importance and value of coverage increases for individuals, while at the same time it becomes less affordable.
- Employment has shifted away from industries with traditionally high rates of coverage to jobs with historically lower rates of coverage. In some industries, employers have relied more heavily on jobs without health benefits, such as part-time and shorter-term employment and contract and temporary jobs.
- Fewer workers, particularly among those with lower wages, are being offered employer-sponsored coverage and fewer among them can afford the premiums. And, early retirees are less likely to be offered retiree health insurance benefits than in the past.

Nongroup Insurance

- For many without employer-sponsored group coverage, nongroup health insurance coverage is prohibitively expensive or unavailable.
  o Access to nongroup coverage is highly dependent on individual circumstances and geographic location.
  o People with preexisting health conditions who lose employer-sponsored insurance face significant barriers to coverage, including unaffordable premiums.

Public Health Insurance

- Long-term fiscal pressures on the federal budget threaten to undermine bedrock state and federal health care programs.
- With a severely weakened economy and rising health care costs, some states will not be able to sustain their recent expansions of public programs for low-income children and adults.
- Increases in unemployment will further fuel the decline in the number of people with employer-sponsored coverage and put additional stress on state Medicaid and SCHIP programs.

or other serious acute conditions, such as heart attacks or strokes. Adults with cancer, cardiovascular disease, serious injury, stroke, respiratory failure, chronic obstructive pulmonary disease or asthma exacerbation, hip fracture, seizures, and serious injury are more likely to suffer poorer health outcomes, greater limitations in quality of life, and premature death if they lack health insurance. New evidence demonstrates that gaining health insurance ameliorates many of these problems.

The committee's key findings on the health consequences of uninsurance are summarized in Box S-4. **In sum, despite the availability of some safety net services, there is a chasm between health care needs and access to effective health care services for uninsured children and adults. Health insurance coverage in the United States is integral to individuals' personal well-being and health.**

Communities at Risk: High Levels of Uninsurance in Communities May Undermine Health Care for the Insured Population

Many of America's towns and cities have high concentrations of children and adults under age 65 who lack health insurance. Thus, the question arises: What are the implications of high rates of uninsurance for affected communities and for insured people in those communities?[5]

It has been estimated that the annual cost of health services provided to uninsured people in the United States will total about $86 billion in 2008. Uninsured patients will pay approximately $30 billion for these services out of pocket and receive the other $56 billion worth of services as uncompensated care.[6] An estimated $43 billion (75 percent) of the $56 billion will be covered through various government subsidies. But government subsidies for uncompensated care are not necessarily distributed to health care providers in proportion to the uncompensated care they provide. Many hospitals and other local providers bear a disproportionate and substantial financial burden. The extent to which hospitals' unreimbursed costs are absorbed by hospitals or passed on in the form of higher charges to insured patients (as many believe to be the case) has not been adequately documented and should be the subject of further research.

There are stark differences in uninsurance rates across states, counties, and even zip codes within counties. Yet the problem of uninsurance may not affect all communities in the same way, even when rates of uninsurance are comparable. The dynamics are complex and not well understood. When a community has a high rate of uninsurance and subsidies fall short

---

[5] In the discussion in this report, the term community refers to a group of people who (1) live in a particular geographic area, and (2) have access to a common set of health resources.

[6] Uncompensated care is defined as all care not paid for out of pocket by the uninsured.

BOX S-4
Key Findings on the Health Effects of Uninsurance

Children benefit considerably from health insurance, as demonstrated by recent evaluations of enrollment in Medicaid and SCHIP programs:

- When previously uninsured children acquire insurance, their access to health care services, including ambulatory care, preventive health care (e.g., immunizations), prescription medications, and dental care improves.
- When previously uninsured children who are well or have special health needs acquire insurance, they are less likely to experience unmet health care needs. Uninsured children with special health care needs are much more likely to have an unmet health need than their counterparts with insurance.
- When previously uninsured children acquire insurance, they receive more timely diagnosis of serious health conditions, experience fewer avoidable hospitalizations, have improved asthma outcomes, and miss fewer days of school.

Adults benefit substantially from health insurance for preventive care when they are well and for early diagnosis and treatment when they are sick or injured:

- Without health insurance, men and women are less likely to receive effective clinical preventive services.
- Without health insurance, chronically ill adults are much more likely to delay or forgo needed health care and medications.
- Without health insurance, adults with cardiovascular disease or cardiac risk factors are less likely to be aware of their conditions, their conditions are less likely to be well controlled, and they experience worse health outcomes.
- Without health insurance, adults are more likely to be diagnosed with later-stage breast, colorectal, or other cancers that are detectable by screening or symptom assessment by a clinician. As a consequence, when uninsured adults are diagnosed with such cancers, they are more likely to die or suffer poorer health outcomes.
- Without health insurance, adults with serious conditions, such as cardiovascular disease or trauma, have higher mortality.
- The benefits of health insurance have been clearly demonstrated through recent studies of the experiences of previously uninsured adults after they acquire Medicare coverage at age 65. These studies demonstrate when previously uninsured adults gain Medicare coverage:
  - o Their access to physician services and hospital care, particularly for adults with cardiovascular disease or diabetes, improves.
  - o Their use of effective clinical preventive services increases.
  - o They experience substantially improved trends in health and functional status.
  - o Their risk of death when hospitalized for serious conditions declines.

of costs, the financial impact on providers may be large enough to affect the availability and quality of local health care services for everyone, even for the people who have health insurance. Recent empirical analyses of the spillover effects of community uninsurance, including a study commissioned by the committee,[7] suggest that when local rates of uninsurance are relatively high, *insured* adults are more likely to have difficulties obtaining needed health care and physicians may be more likely to believe that they are unable to make clinical decisions in the best interest of the patient without losing income.

The specific contribution of uninsurance to these problems is not known, but widespread problems in health care delivery in local communities, including disparities in the supply of physician services and other health care resources, may be exacerbated by the burden of uninsurance and have potentially grave implications for the quality and timeliness of care not only for people who lack health insurance, but also for people who have health insurance in those communities.

The committee's key findings on the community-level consequences of uninsurance are summarized in Box S-5. **In sum, local health care delivery appears to be vulnerable to the financial pressures associated with high community-level uninsurance rates. Analyses commissioned by the committee and other recent research strongly suggest that when community-level uninsurance rates are relatively high, *insured* adults are more likely to have difficulties obtaining needed health care.**

RECOMMENDATION OF THE COMMITTEE

The committee's findings demonstrate that the body of evidence on the health consequences of health insurance is stronger than ever before. There is a compelling case for urgent action. Simply stated: health insurance coverage matters. Expanding health coverage to all Americans is essential and should be done as quickly as possible. The President, Congress, and other leaders in the public and private sectors should act immediately to ensure that all individuals have health insurance. Without such action, preventable suffering due to the lack of health insurance promises to get worse rather than better.

The committee recommends that the President work with Congress and other public and private sector leaders on an urgent basis to achieve

---

[7] Mark Pauly, Ph.D., and José Pagán, Ph.D., conducted original analyses of the effects of uninsurance on privately insured persons and local communities at the committee's request. The complete text of the commissioned analysis is available on the IOM website for the Health Insurance Status and Its Consequences project at http://www.iom.edu/CMS/3809/54070.aspx.

BOX S-5
Key Findings on the Consequences of High Community Uninsurance for People with Health Insurance

Local health care delivery appears to be vulnerable to the financial pressures associated with higher uninsurance. Analyses commissioned by the committee and other recent research strongly suggest that when community-level uninsurance rates are relatively high, *insured* adults are more likely to have difficulties obtaining needed health care and physicians are more likely to believe that they are unable to make clinical decisions in the best interest of the patient without losing income.

The empirical evidence indicates that higher community uninsurance is negatively associated with several well-validated indicators of access to and satisfaction with health care for *privately insured adults*, including:

- Having a place to go when sick, having a doctor's visit, visiting a doctor for routine preventive care, and seeing a specialist when needed.
- Satisfaction with the choice of primary care physician, being very satisfied with health care received during the last 12 months, trust that one's doctors put medical needs above all other considerations, and being very satisfied with the choice of specialist.

The Center for Studying Health System Change has documented growing economic disparities among U.S. communities with respect to geographic distribution of health care services, including new diagnostic and therapeutic techniques and technologies. The precise contribution of uninsurance to this dynamic is neither well understood nor readily measured. However, widespread problems in local health care delivery—not necessarily attributable to uninsurance—can be intensified by higher uninsurance rates.

For example:

- Providers and capital investment tend to locate in well-insured areas (and away from communities with high uninsurance). It is common for hospitals and clinics to focus major investments in more affluent locations with well-insured populations.
- Newer facilities with the most up-to-date technologies are a magnet for physician and other health care providers—this poses additional obstacles for financially stressed hospitals trying to recruit on-call specialists in high uninsurance areas.
- A number of hospital-based emergency care problems have serious implications for the quality and timeliness of care for insured as well as uninsured patients, including limits on inpatient bed capacity, outpatient emergency services, and timeliness of trauma care.

health insurance coverage for everyone and, in order to make that coverage sustainable, to reduce the costs of health care and the rate of increase in per capita health care spending.

There always has been, and will continue to be, uncertainty and disagreement about the best way to address major issues of public policy. The issue of cost, in particular, is daunting. But the nation has successfully addressed other complex issues that are intertwined with deeply held interests and ideologies. There is never a perfect opportunity for reform. This is the time to act, emboldened by the knowledge and compassion of a society that truly cares about its members and that has a history of tackling difficult problems.

Paying for health insurance coverage for all Americans will be expensive. The committee believes that steps to reduce the costs of health care and the rate of increase in per capita health care spending are of paramount importance if coverage for all is to be achieved and sustained. The committee does not believe that action should be delayed pending the development of a long-term solution to curbing underlying health care costs. Given the demonstrated harms of not having health insurance for children and adults, the committee believes that action to achieve coverage for all should proceed immediately, coupled with concerted attention to the long-term underlying trends in health care costs to assure sustainability of the system for all.

Health insurance coverage is integral to personal well-being and health. Despite the availability of some safety net services, there is a chasm between health care needs and access to effective health care services for uninsured children, adolescents, and adults. The committee agrees with the conclusion of our colleagues in the 2004 IOM report *Insuring America's Health*:

> "...health insurance contributes essentially to obtaining the kind and quality of health care that can express the equality and dignity of every person. Unless we can ensure coverage for all, we fail as a nation to deliver the great promise of our health care system, as well as of the values we live by as a society. It is time for our nation to extend coverage to everyone."

1

Introduction

Abstract: This chapter describes the objectives, context, scope, and methods of this report. From 2001 to 2004, an earlier Institute of Medicine (IOM) committee undertook an exhaustive examination of the consequences of uninsurance and recommended that the nation move quickly to implement a strategy to achieve universal coverage. Five years later, the IOM Committee on Health Insurance Status and Its Consequences has reexamined the crisis of uninsurance in the United States, albeit with a more narrow focus. The objective of this report is to assess the more recent evidence on three fundamental questions: (1) What are the dynamics driving downward trends in health insurance coverage? (2) Is being uninsured harmful to the health of children and adults? (3) Are insured people affected by high rates of uninsurance in their communities?

In 2007, there were 45.7 million people without health insurance in the United States—nearly 1 in 5 adults under age 65 and more than 1 in 10 children (DeNavas-Walt et al., 2008). The fear of being without health insurance coverage is a growing strain on American families' sense of health and well-being (Schoen et al., 2008). Family concerns about losing health coverage are well founded.

Figure 1-1 shows changes in the percentage of nonelderly adults in the United States without health insurance from 1999-2000 to 2006-2007. In 2006-2007, in nine states (Arizona, Arkansas, California, Florida, Louisiana, Mississippi, New Mexico, Oklahoma, and Texas)—up from just two states in 1999-2000—the percentage of nonelderly adults who did not have health insurance was 23 percent or more (Commonwealth Fund, 2008). In

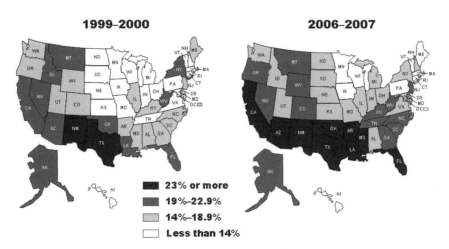

FIGURE 1-1 Comparison in the percentage of nonelderly adults without health insurance, by state, 1999-2000 and 2006-2007.
SOURCE: The Commonwealth Fund (2008). Reprinted, with permission, from The Commonwealth Fund, 2008. Copyright 2008 by The Commonwealth Fund (http://www.commonwealthfund.org).

13 states (Alaska, Colorado, Georgia, Kentucky, Montana, Nevada, New Jersey, North Carolina, Oregon, South Carolina, Tennessee, West Virginia, and Wyoming), the percentage of nonelderly adults without health insurance ranged from 19 to 23 percent. Only 10 states (Connecticut, Hawaii, Iowa, Maine, Massachusetts, Minnesota, Pennsylvania, Rhode Island, Vermont, and Wisconsin) had uninsurance rates for nonelderly adults below 14 percent. As described in this report, rising health care costs, stagnant family incomes, fiscal pressures on state budgets, and increased unemployment are likely to drive further coverage declines (Baicker and Chandra, 2006; Chernew et al., 2005; Cooper and Schone, 1997; Holahan and Cook, 2008).

With a new administration and a new Congress, many citizens, policy makers, and opinion leaders anticipate renewed energy and interest in finding a way to reverse the erosion of health insurance coverage and, ultimately, to expand coverage to all in the United States (Blendon et al., 2008; Bodaken, 2008; Lake et al., 2008; McInturff and Weigel, 2008; Oberlander, 2007).

OBJECTIVE OF THE STUDY

The Robert Wood Johnson Foundation (RWJF) asked the Institute of Medicine (IOM) to reexamine America's uninsured crisis in order to inform the health reform policy debate as it unfolds in 2009 and beyond. The objective of this report is to evaluate the research evidence on the consequences of uninsurance that has emerged since the IOM conducted its earlier examination of the issues.

The question of whether health insurance matters to health is far more than an academic concern. It is crucial that U.S. health care policy be informed with current and valid evidence, especially for the 45.7 million individuals without health insurance. In recent years, researchers have considerably strengthened the body of evidence on the consequences of uninsurance, especially the consequences of uninsurance for health outcomes. Better quality longitudinal data and quasi-experimental methods have been used to assess how uninsurance affects the health and mortality of adults (Card et al., 2007; Decker, 2005; Dor et al., 2006; Finkelstein and McKnight, 2007; Hadley and Waidmann, 2006; McWilliams et al., 2007; Polsky et al., 2006; Volpp et al., 2003, 2005). There is also new evidence on the benefits of coverage for children and adolescents from well-designed studies of enrollment in public health insurance programs, such as the State Children's Health Insurance Program (SCHIP) and Medicaid (Davidoff et al., 2005; Halterman et al., 2008; Howell and Trenholm, 2007; Kempe et al., 2005; Kenney, 2007; Szilagyi et al., 2006; Trenholm et al., 2005).

WHAT IS THE PURPOSE OF HEALTH INSURANCE?

The health insurance system in the United States, in contrast with health insurance in almost all other industrialized nations, is essentially a voluntary one. Most Americans with private health insurance obtain it through the workplace. Employers are free to choose whether and what kind of insurance to offer their employees, and individuals in the United States are usually free to accept or decline their employers' offer of coverage, to purchase individual coverage, or if they are eligible, to enroll in public programs such as Medicare, Medicaid, or SCHIP.

Health insurance pools risk across groups of individuals or firms and then shares the cost of payouts among them, thereby reducing the burden of catastrophic costs for individual participants. Insurance is most effectively pooled across large groups. When individuals, families, or small employers do not have access to large group coverage, they must apply for coverage in the individual or small group markets. People are more likely to purchase and maintain coverage if they expect to incur high costs—a phenomenon referred to as adverse selection. Insurers protect against adverse selection in the individual and small group health insurance markets by underwriting (i.e., assessment of applicants' health status and recent use of services). Thus, an insurer may completely deny coverage to applicants, impose permanent or temporary preexisting condition limitations on coverage, or charge a higher premium (depending on state insurance market regulations) on the basis of expected risk.

What is the purpose of health insurance? The answer depends on whose perspective is being considered:

- For consumers, health insurance often serves two purposes: (1) it provides a gateway to affordable health care through preferential pricing[1] of health care services and (2) it offers financial protection from unexpected health care costs.

- For clinicians, hospitals, and other health providers, health insurance ensures the financial stability of their operations. Indeed, health insurance as we know it today was first developed by Baylor University Hospital for exactly that purpose (Porter and Teisberg, 2006).

- With growing concern about the cost and quality of health care services, many large employers and purchasers of health benefits look to health insurance plans to encourage the use of beneficial, evidence-based services, particularly clinical preventive services such as childhood immunizations and certain adult cancer screening tests. Indeed, the quality of health insurance products is often assessed by measuring the extent to which the covered population receives such services (National Committee for Quality Assurance, 2008).

PREVIOUS IOM REPORTS ON UNINSURANCE

From 2001 to 2004, with the support of RWJF, the IOM issued a comprehensive series of six reports on the consequences of uninsurance for children, adults, families, communities, and the nation (IOM, 2001, 2002a,b, 2003a,b, 2004).[2] The series culminated with the publication in 2004 of *Insuring America's Health: Principles and Recommendations* (IOM, 2004). This report set out the IOM committee's vision and principles for health insurance coverage in the United States. It also included the committee's

---

[1] One recent analysis found that, for the same services, hospitals charge uninsured patients 2.5 times what they charge insurance companies and more than 3 times the hospital's Medicare-allowable costs (Anderson, 2007).

[2] For copies of the previous IOM report series on the consequences of uninsurance, please visit www.nap.edu.

BOX 1-1
The IOM's Past Findings and Recommendations Regarding Health Insurance Coverage in the United States, 2001-2004

In 2001, the IOM began a comprehensive 4-year study of the consequences of not having health insurance in the United States at the request of the Robert Wood Johnson Foundation.

From 2001 to 2004, the IOM published six reports that assessed the available evidence on how children, adults, families, communities, and the nation were affected by uninsurance. Among the principal findings in the earlier series of IOM reports on the consequences of uninsurance were the following:

- Children and adults without health insurance do not receive the care they need; they suffer from poorer health and development and are more likely to die early than children and adults who have coverage.
- Even one uninsured person in a family can put the financial stability and health of the whole family at risk.
- A high percentage of uninsured people within a community can adversely affect the overall health status of the community, its health care institutions and providers, and the access of its residents to key services.
- Recent federal initiatives to extend health insurance coverage have not closed the coverage gap.

The series concluded with the publication in 2004 of *Insuring America's Health: Principles and Recommendations.* In that report, the IOM Committee on the Consequences of Uninsurance recommended the following:

- The committee recommends that the President and Congress develop a strategy to achieve universal insurance coverage and to establish a firm and explicit schedule to reach this goal by 2010.
- The committee recommends that, until universal coverage takes effect, the federal and state governments provide resources sufficient for Medicaid and the State Children's Health Insurance Program (SCHIP) to cover all persons currently eligible and prevent the erosion of outreach efforts, eligibility, enrollment, and coverage.

SOURCE: IOM (2004).

---

recommendation that the nation move quickly to implement a strategy to achieve universal health insurance coverage. The key findings and recommendations of the 2004 report are provided in Box 1-1; the report's executive summary is presented in Appendix A.

As of early 2009, 5 years since the publication of the IOM's report *Insuring America's Health*, a comprehensive national plan to address America's uninsured crisis has yet to be enacted. A few states—most notably

Maine, Massachusetts, and Vermont—have achieved great progress to-wards the goal of universal health insurance coverage. Other states, including California, have attempted reforms but failed to move forward.

SCOPE AND METHODS OF THE STUDY

The scope of the earlier IOM series of studies on the consequences of uninsurance was broad and comprehensive: six published volumes assessed then-current evidence on the dynamics of health insurance coverage and the makeup of the uninsured population; effects of health insurance on health; implications for families including health and financial outcomes; impact on communities including the financing and delivery of health services, and community public health; economic and social implications such as spending and sources of spending on health care for the uninsured population including the estimated cost of expanding coverage, other costs including quality of life, family security, workforce participation and productivity; health systems impacts; and principles and strategies for extending coverage to all.

In contrast, the scope of this study is narrow and focuses on three essential questions (Box 1-2): (1) What are the dynamics driving downward trends in health insurance coverage? (2) Is being uninsured harmful to the health of children and adults? (3) Are *insured* people affected by high rates of uninsurance in their communities?

BOX 1-2
Charge to the IOM Committee on Health
Insurance Status and Its Consequences

The overarching objective of this study is to help inform the health reform policy debate as it unfolds in 2009. The committee will assess the research evidence—that has emerged since the IOM's 2001 to 2004 series of reports on uninsurance—on the consequences of uninsurance. Rather than performing a comprehensive review, the committee is charged with reviewing the literature to identify new insights not yet known or appreciated when the IOM's earlier reports were developed.

The search for new evidence will include the published literature on the consequences of uninsurance for individuals, families, communities, specific population groups, and safety net and other providers. The consequences may be related to health outcomes, such as morbidity and mortality; access to health care services; and economic impacts such as affordability of health coverage and its associated financing burden.

The IOM appointed the Committee on Health Insurance Status and Its Consequences to perform this study in April 2008. The 14-member committee included experts in analytic methods, public policy, vulnerable populations, employment-based health coverage, clinical medicine, health care delivery, health services research, health financing and economics, state health reform, and public health communication. Brief biographies of the committee members are presented in Appendix F.

The committee considered but excluded several topics from the study in order to optimize the depth and quality of its 6-month investigation into the three principal questions outlined above. Excluding these topics from this report should not be interpreted to mean they are unimportant. Indeed, these topics are inextricably linked with the nation's uninsured crisis and merit serious attention by policy makers. The omitted topics include the following: (1) The economic and financial impact of uninsurance. Health insurance has complex economic and financial implications for multiple aspects of American society—the productivity and financial stability of individuals, families, communities, health care systems and providers, American business, and local, state, and federal government. Related to these issues and also excluded from this study is the impact of uninsurance on household medical debt, the extent to which uninsurance affects the global competitiveness of American business, and whether providers shift the costs of uninsurance to private payers (a topic with only sparse and inconclusive evidence). (2) The effects of *under*insurance. Uninsurance and underinsurance involve distinctly different policy issues, and the strategies for addressing them may differ. Uninsurance—the focus of this study—refers to the lack of health insurance coverage. Underinsurance is defined with respect to health insurance coinsurance requirements and coverage limitations, e.g., excessive out-of-pocket expenditures and/or significant limits on health care benefits perceived as essential to health (Collins et al., 2008; Davis, 2007; Oswald et al., 2007; Schoen et al., 2005, 2008; Wender, 2007). However, there is no agreed upon definition of underinsurance and an inadequate evidence base for assessing its impact (Blewett et al., 2006; Ward, 2006). (3) The impact of discontinuities in health insurance. Employers switch health plans with relative frequency, a new job typically results in different health coverage, and low-income individuals cycle in and out of eligibility for public health insurance. Even minimal disruptions in coverage—such as switching between types of coverage—have been shown to affect use of health care services (Bindman et al., 2008; Federico et al., 2007; Lavarreda et al., 2008; Leininger, 2009). (4) The study sponsor asked the committee not to explore potential approaches to expanding health coverage.

As the committee's work progressed, the committee became aware of considerable misinformation about uninsurance and its consequences, so that setting the record straight became an important concern. Perhaps foremost among these misconceptions is that charity care and other safety net services ensure that the health of uninsured individuals is protected—a belief that finds no significant support in the research evidence (as Chapter 3 will show). The committee also became aware that the continuing erosion of health insurance coverage was creating urgent difficulties for individuals, their communities, and public agencies that pay for health insurance coverage. It believes that 2009 will open a window of opportunity for addressing the problem.

The committee deliberated during four in-person meetings and seven conference calls between May and November 2008. The committee's initial deliberations focused on clarifying the scope of its work. The research conducted for this study was accomplished with the assistance of several consultants.[3] Once the basic outline for the report was established, the committee commissioned two systematic reviews of research evidence on the consequences of not having health insurance for individuals: one review of the evidence on the consequences for children and adolescents and a second review on the consequences for adults. Both of these reviews of the research evidence focused on research published from 2002 to August 2008 in order to capture the evidence not available during the previous IOM examination of the relationship between health and health insurance. See Chapter 3 for details regarding the literature search strategy. The committee also commissioned original analyses of the Medical Expenditure Panel Survey, the household survey of the Community Tracking Study of the Center for Studying Health System Change, and the health insurance component of the Current Population Survey to examine trends in coverage and assess the impact of high rates of uninsurance on communities.

ORGANIZATION OF THE REPORT

This introductory chapter has described the context for this report, including the past IOM studies on uninsurance, the purpose of health insurance, the committee's charge, and the objectives, scope, and study methods for this report. Subsequent chapters address the following questions:

---

[3] J. Michael McWilliams, M.D., Ph.D., reviewed the research evidence on the consequences of not having health insurance for adults, and Genevieve Kenney, Ph.D., and Embry Howell, Ph.D., reviewed the child and adolescent literature. Mark Pauly, Ph.D., and José Pagán, Ph.D., conducted an original analysis of the effects of uninsurance on privately insured persons and local communities. Jessica Banthin, Ph.D., Steve Cohen, Ph.D., and Joel Cohen, Ph.D., staff at the Agency for Healthcare Research and Quality, conducted original analyses of how uninsured families are burdened by the lack of health coverage. Additional details on the literature reviews and analyses commissioned by the committee are provided in subsequent chapters.

- **Chapter 2—Caught in a Downward Spiral.** What are the dynamics driving downward trends in health insurance coverage?
- **Chapter 3—Coverage Matters.** Is being uninsured harmful to the health of children and adults? What are the consequences of not having health coverage on access to care and health outcomes? Does the health of individuals without coverage improve when they become insured?
- **Chapter 4—Communities at Risk.** Are insured people affected by high rates of uninsurance in their communities?
- **Chapter 5—Summary of Findings and Recommendation.** What are the committee's key findings and recommendation?

REFERENCES

Anderson, G. F. 2007. From "soak the rich" to "soak the poor": Recent trends in hospital pricing. *Health Affairs* 26(3):780-789.

Baicker, K., and A. Chandra. 2006. The labor market effects of rising health insurance premiums. *Journal of Labor Economics* 24(3):609-634.

Bindman, A. B., A. Chattopadhyay, and G. M. Auerback. 2008. Medicaid re-enrollment policies and children's risk of hospitalizations for ambulatory care sensitive conditions. *Medical Care* 46(10):1049-1054.

Blendon, R. J., D. E. Altman, C. Deane, J. M. Benson, M. Brodie, and T. Buhr. 2008. Health care in the 2008 presidential primaries. *New England Journal of Medicine* 358(4):414-422.

Blewett, L. A., A. Ward, and T. J. Beebe. 2006. How much health insurance is enough? Revisiting the concept of underinsurance. *Medical Care Research and Review* 63(6):663-700.

Bodaken, B. G. 2008. Where does the insurance industry stand on health reform today? *Health Affairs* 27(3):667-674.

Card, D., C. Dobkin, and N. Maestas. 2007. Does Medicare Save Lives? National Bureau of Economic Research Working Paper 13668 (JEL No. H51,I11).

Chernew, M., D. M. Cutler, and P. S. Keenan. 2005. Increasing health insurance costs and the decline in insurance coverage. *Health Services Research* 40(4):1021-1039.

Collins, S. R., J. L. Kriss, M. M. Doty, and S. D. Rustgi. 2008. Losing ground: How the loss of adequate health insurance is burdening working families, http://www.commonwealthfund.org/usr_doc/Collins_losinggroundbiennialsurvey2007_1163.pdf?section=4039 (accessed August 2008).

Commonwealth Fund. 2008 (unpublished). *Percent of adults ages 18–64 uninsured by state.* New York: The Commonwealth Fund.

Cooper, P. F., and B. S. Schone. 1997. More offers, fewer takers for employment-based health insurance: 1987 and 1996. *Health Affairs* 16(6):142-149.

Davidoff, A., G. Kenney, and L. Dubay. 2005. Effects of the State Children's Health Insurance Program expansions on children with chronic health conditions. *Pediatrics* 116(1): e34-e42.

Davis, M. M. 2007. Reasons and remedies for underinsurance for child and adolescent vaccines. *JAMA* 298(6):680-682.

Decker, S. L. 2005. Medicare and the health of women with breast cancer. *Journal of Human Resources* 40:948-968.

DeNavas-Walt, C., B. D. Proctor, and J. Smith. 2008. *Income, poverty, and health insurance coverage in the United States: 2007.* Washington, DC: U.S. Census Bureau.

Dor, A., J. Sudano, and D. W. Baker. 2006. The effect of private insurance on the health of older, working age adults: Evidence from the Health and Retirement Study. *Health Services Research* 41(3p1):759-787.

Federico, S. G., J. F. Steiner, B. Beaty, L. Crane, and A. Kempe. 2007. Disruptions in insurance coverage: Patterns and relationship to health care access, unmet need, and utilization before enrollment in the State Children's Health Insurance Program. *Pediatrics* 120(4): e1009-e1016.

Finkelstein, A., and R. McKnight. 2007. What did Medicare do? The initial impact of Medicare on mortality and out of pocket medical spending, http://econ-www.mit.edu/files/1820 (accessed May 18, 2008).

Hadley, J., and T. Waidmann. 2006. Health insurance and health at age 65: Implications for medical care spending on new Medicare beneficiaries. *Health Services Research* 41(2):429-451.

Halterman, J. S., G. Montes, L. P. Shone, and P. G. Szilagyi. 2008. The impact of health insurance gaps on access to care among children with asthma in the United States. *Ambulatory Pediatrics* 8(1):43-49.

Holahan, J., and A. Cook. 2008. The U.S. economy and changes in health insurance coverage, 2000-2006. *Health Affairs* 27(2):w135-w144.

Howell, E. M., and C. Trenholm. 2007. The effect of new insurance coverage on the health status of low-income children in Santa Clara County. *Health Services Research* 42(2): 867-889.

IOM (Institute of Medicine). 2001. *Coverage matters: Insurance and health care.* Washington, DC: National Academy Press.

———. 2002a. *Care without coverage: Too little, too late.* Washington, DC: National Academy Press.

———. 2002b. *Health insurance is a family matter.* Washington, DC: The National Academies Press.

———. 2003a. *Hidden costs, value lost: Uninsurance in America.* Washington, DC: The National Academies Press.

———. 2003b. *A shared destiny: Community effects of uninsurance.* Washington, DC: The National Academies Press.

———. 2004. *Insuring America's health: Principles and recommendations.* Washington, DC: The National Academies Press.

Kempe, A., B. L. Beaty, L. A. Crane, J. Stokstad, J. Barrow, S. Belman, and J. F. Steiner. 2005. Changes in access, utilization, and quality of care after enrollment into a State Child Health Insurance Plan. *Pediatrics* 115(2):364-371.

Kenney, G. 2007. The impacts of the State Children's Health Insurance Program on children who enroll: Findings from ten states. *Health Services Research* 42(4):1520-1543.

Lake, C. C., R. A. Crittenden, and D. Mermin. 2008. Health care in the 2008 election: Engaging the voters. *Health Affairs* 27(3):693-698.

Lavarreda, S. A., M. Gatchell, N. Ponce, E. R. Brown, and Y. J. Chia. 2008. Switching health insurance and its effects on access to physician services. *Medical Care* 46(10):1055-1063.

Leininger, L. J. 2009. Partial-year insurance coverage and the health care utilization of children. *Medical Care Research and Review* 66(1):49-67.

McInturff, W. D., and L. Weigel. 2008. Deja vu all over again: The similarities between political debates regarding health care in the early 1990s and today. *Health Affairs* 27(3):699-704.

McWilliams, J. M., E. Meara, A. M. Zaslavsky, and J. Z. Ayanian. 2007. Health of previously uninsured adults after acquiring Medicare coverage. *JAMA* 298(24):2886-2894.

National Committee for Quality Assurance. 2008. *HEDIS & quality measurement,* http://ncqa.org/tabid/59/Default.aspx (accessed July 16, 2008).

Oberlander, J. 2007. Learning from failure in health care reform. *New England Journal of Medicine* 357(17):1677-1679.

Oswald, D. P., J. N. Bodurtha, J. H. Willis, and M. B. Moore. 2007. Underinsurance and key health outcomes for children with special health care needs. *Pediatrics* 119(2): e341-e347.

Polsky, D., J. A. Doshi, J. Escarce, W. Manning, S. M. Paddock, L. Cen, and J. Rogowski. 2006. *The health effects of Medicare for the near-elderly uninsured.* Cambridge, MA: National Bureau of Economic Research.

Porter, M. E., and E. O. Teisberg. 2006. *Redefining health care: Creating value-based competition on results.* Cambridge, MA: Harvard Business Press.

Schoen, C., M. M. Doty, S. R. Collins, and A. L. Holmgren. 2005. Insured but not protected: How many adults are underinsured? *Health Affairs* w5.289-w5.302.

Schoen, C., S. R. Collins, J. L. Kriss, and M. M. Doty. 2008. How many are underinsured? Trends among U.S. adults, 2003 and 2007. *Health Affairs* 27(4):w298-w309.

Szilagyi, P. G., A. W. Dick, J. D. Klein, L. P. Shone, J. Zwanziger, A. Bajorska, and H. L. Yoos. 2006. Improved asthma care after enrollment in the State Children's Health Insurance Program in New York. *Pediatrics* 117(2):486-496.

Trenholm, C., E. Howell, D. Hughes, and S. Orzol. 2005. The Santa Clara County Healthy Kids Program: Impacts on children's medical, dental, and vision care. *Mathematica Policy Research Report,* http://www.mathematica-mpr.com/publications/PDFs/santaclara.pdf (accessed September 2008).

Volpp, K. G. M., S. V. Williams, J. Waldfogel, J. H. Silber, J. S. Schwartz, and M. V. Pauly. 2003. Market reform in New Jersey and the effect on mortality from acute myocardial infarction. *Health Services Research* 38(2):515-533.

Volpp, K. G., J. D. Ketcham, A. J. Epstein, and S. V. Williams. 2005. The effects of price competition and reduced subsidies for uncompensated care on hospital mortality. *Health Services Research* 40:1056-1077.

Ward, A. 2006. The concept of underinsurance: A general typology. *Journal of Medicine & Philosophy* 31(5):499-531.

Wender, R. C. 2007. The adequacy of the access-to-care debate: Looking through the cancer lens. *Cancer* 110(2):231-233.

2

Caught in a Downward Spiral

Abstract: This chapter examines the dynamics underlying the continuing decline in health insurance coverage. Health care costs and insurance premiums are growing at rates greater than the economy and family incomes. Employment has shifted away from industries with traditionally high rates of coverage (e.g., manufacturing) to service jobs (e.g., in wholesale and retail trades) with historically lower rates of coverage. In some industries, employers have relied more heavily on jobs without health benefits, including part-time and shorter-term employment, and contract and temporary jobs. Overall, fewer workers, particularly among those with lower wages, are offered employer-sponsored coverage and fewer among those offered insurance can afford the premiums. For many individuals and families without employer-sponsored group coverage, nongroup coverage is prohibitively expensive. With a severely weakened economy and rising health care costs, some states will face pressures to cut their recent expansions of public programs for low-income children and adults. Large increases in unemployment will further fuel the decline in the number of people with employer-sponsored coverage and put additional stress on state Medicaid and State Children's Health Insurance Programs (SCHIP) programs.*

A number of ominous signs point to a continuing decline in health insurance coverage in the United States. Health care costs are rising, increases in health insurance premiums outpace the limited growth of typical family incomes, continuing changes in the workplace diminish the availability of employer-sponsored health insurance (ESI), unemployment is climbing, and severe pressures on state budgets threaten to reverse the recent expansion of public coverage for children and adults (Baicker and Chandra, 2006;

Bernstein, 2008; Chernew et al., 2005; Dorn et al., 2008; Gould, 2007; Holahan and Cook, 2008; Reschovsky et al., 2006; Smith et al., 2008). This chapter begins with a brief description of the uninsured population and then explores the forces underlying current trends in private and public health coverage.

SNAPSHOT OF TRENDS IN HEALTH INSURANCE COVERAGE[1]

Sources of Health Insurance

The workplace has been the source of health coverage for several generations of Americans. Today, most privately insured people continue to be insured through their job or the job of a family member (Figures 2-1 and 2-2). However, since around 2000, ESI coverage has been on the decline. Among adults, ESI coverage dropped by 5 percentage points between 2000 and 2007, from 69.3 percent to 64.3 percent. ESI coverage of children also fell during this time period—from to 65.9 to 56.8 percent—but the decline was offset by rising enrollment in Medicaid and the State Children's Health Insurance Program (SCHIP). During this period, many states expanded eligibility, ramped up outreach, or streamlined application processes to expedite eligible children's enrollment in these public health insurance programs (Coughlin and Zuckerman, 2008; Smith et al., 2008).

Approximately 2.9 percent of the nonelderly population is insured through the TRICARE or CHAMPVA[2] military-related health insurance programs (Fronstin, 2008a).

Only a small proportion of the population purchases private health insurance outside the job setting. In 2007, an estimated 6.8 percent of the nonelderly population had individually purchased health insurance coverage. This percentage has been relatively steady for more than a decade (Fronstin, 2008a).

Who Are the Uninsured?

In 2007, there were 45.7 million people without health insurance in the United States, 5.9 million more than when the IOM issued its initial

---

[1] Because nearly 98 percent of the U.S. adult population over age 64 has health insurance coverage through Medicare or other sources (DeNavas-Walt et al., 2007), this chapter focuses on trends in coverage for the nonelderly population. References in the text to "adults" refer to 18- to 64-year-olds; "children" refers to the under-18 population.

[2] TRICARE is a health benefits program sponsored by the Department of Defense for military retirees and families of active duty, retired, and deceased service members. CHAMPVA refers to the Civilian Health and Medical Program for the Department of Veterans Affairs, a program for disabled dependents of veterans and certain survivors of veterans.

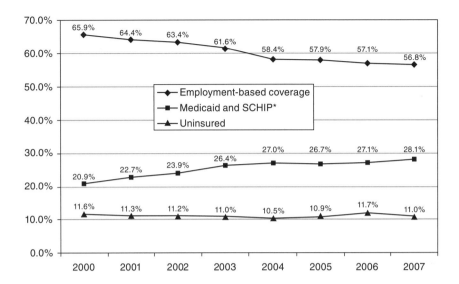

FIGURE 2-1 Percentage of U.S. children under age 18 with employment-based coverage, Medicaid or SCHIP coverage, and uninsured, 2000-2007.
*SCHIP = State Children's Health Insurance Program. Children who are otherwise eligible for Medicaid or have other insurance coverage are generally not eligible for SCHIP.
NOTE: This figure does not show individuals with sources of health insurance coverage other than employer-sponsored insurance, Medicaid, SCHIP, TRICARE, or CHAMPVA.
SOURCE: Fronstin (2008a). Reprinted, with permission, from *EBRI Issue Brief, 2008*. Copyright 2008 by Employee Benefit Research Institute.

report on uninsurance in 2001 (Box 2-1) (DeNavas-Walt et al., 2008; IOM, 2001). This includes 36.8 million nonelderly adults—nearly 1 in 5—and 8.1 million children—more than 1 in 10 (Table 2-1). These recent estimates show a small increase in the number and percent of Americans with health coverage from 2006 to 2007. However, the source of the increase was not a strengthening of private health insurance, but an expansion in government health insurance programs, including Medicaid, Medicare, and military health care. From 2006 to 2007, the proportion of the nonelderly adult population enrolled in a government-sponsored health plan increased from 27.0 percent to 27.8 percent (DeNavas-Walt et al., 2008). During the same period, the proportion of the population in a private health insurance plan fell from 67.9 percent to 67.5 percent. The decline in private coverage occurred in both employment-based and direct-purchase health plans.

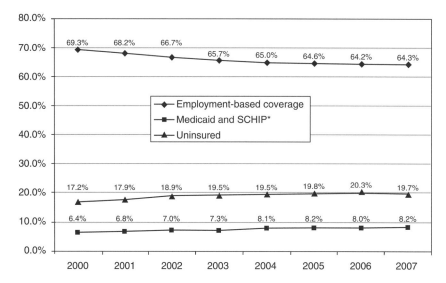

FIGURE 2-2 Percentage of U.S. adults ages 18-64 with employment-based coverage, Medicaid or SCHIP coverage, and uninsured, 2000-2007.
*SCHIP = State Children's Health Insurance Program. Adults are generally not eligible for SCHIP, but several states have been granted special federal approval to receive enhanced matching funds for coverage of parents of children enrolled in SCHIP and pregnant women.
NOTE: This figure does not show individuals with sources of health insurance coverage other than employer-sponsored insurance, Medicaid, SCHIP, TRICARE, or CHAMPVA.
SOURCE: Fronstin (2008a). Reprinted, with permission, from *EBRI Issue Brief, 2008*. Copyright 2008 by Employee Benefit Research Institute.

Uninsurance affects a broad swath of American households—as it did when the IOM first studied the topic. The uninsured population includes poor and middle-income people, members of one- and two-income families, white and black people, non-Hispanics and Hispanics, native-born and naturalized citizens and undocumented immigrants, children, adolescents, young adults, people reaching middle age, people approaching retirement, and early retirees. Statistics on the age, race and ethnicity, immigration status, household income, and work status of the uninsured, nonelderly population are presented in Appendix B.

Some low-income children and adults are eligible, but not enrolled in a public health insurance program (Table 2-2). Overall, an estimated 15.9 percent of the uninsured population is eligible for Medicaid or SCHIP

BOX 2-1
Estimates of the Uninsured U.S. Population
from Leading Federal Surveys

There is no question that tens of millions of people in the United States are uninsured, but there is some confusion about what appear to be conflicting counts of the uninsured population. The most prominent federal surveys used to develop estimates of the number of people without health insurance in the United States are described and compared below. Unless noted otherwise, estimates of the insured and uninsured population in this report are drawn from the health insurance component of the Annual Social and Economic Supplement of the Current Population Survey (CPS) conducted annually by the U.S. Census Bureau. Estimates of the number of uninsured people vary because the objectives and design of the surveys vary. Some of these differences are described below. In 2007, the CPS estimate was that 45.7 million people in the United States—or 17.2 percent of the nonelderly population—lacked health insurance.

- **Current Population Survey (CPS).** The CPS is the most widely cited source on health coverage. Every March, the U.S. Census Bureau asks respondents about their health coverage during the previous year in an annual supplement to a monthly labor force survey. The objective is to estimate the number of persons uninsured for *the entire previous year,* although most experts believe that many respondents provide answers that reflect their insurance status at the time of the interview. Compared with other federal surveys, the CPS tends to report the highest estimate of the number of people lacking coverage for a 1-year period.

- **Medical Expenditure Panel Survey (MEPS).** MEPS is a set of surveys of families and individuals and their medical providers and employers. MEPS is cosponsored by the Agency for Healthcare Research and Quality (AHRQ) and the National Center for Health Statistics (NCHS). In addition to collecting data on health coverage, MEPS collects a broad range of data on the cost and use of health care. Respondents are surveyed several times during the year and asked if they were uninsured *at any time since the previous interview* and then asked for *the time period without coverage.* MEPS can produce estimates for a point in time during the year, at any point in the year, and for the entire year. MEPS estimates the number of individuals without coverage for at least 1 month of the year. In 2006, 68 million or 26.7 percent of the nonelderly population met the MEPS definition of being uninsured.

- **National Health Interview Survey (NHIS).** The NHIS is a cross-sectional survey conducted by the NCHS to monitor trends in illness, injury, and disability and to track progress toward achieving national health objectives. Respondents are asked to report their health coverage *at the time of the survey* and *during the previous year.* The NHIS produces point-in-time estimates (uninsured at the time of the interview), intermittent estimates (uninsured part or all of the previous year), and long-term estimates (more than a year at the time of the interview). For the first 9 months of 2007, NHIS estimates of the uninsured nonelderly population in the United States were 43.4 million (16.7

BOX 2-1 Continued

percent) at the time of the interview; 54.1 million (20.8 percent) for sometime during the year; and 31.1 million (11.9 percent) for more than a year.

- **Survey of Income and Program Participation (SIPP).** SIPP is a longitudinal survey, conducted by the U.S. Census Bureau, in which the same group of respondents is asked approximately every 4 months about their health insurance coverage during the preceding 4 months. SIPP produces estimates of the number lacking insurance *at a particular point in time*, *for part of the year*, and *throughout the entire year*. SIPP also provides analyses of the distribution of income, wealth, and poverty, and of the effects of federal and state programs on the well-being of families and individuals. For 2005, SIPP estimates for the uninsured nonelderly population were 27.6 million (10.7 percent) uninsured for all 12 months, 65.9 million (25.6 percent) uninsured for at least 1 month, and 45.2 million (17.6 percent) uninsured in the month of December.

SOURCES: Chu and Rhoades (2008); Cohen et al. (2007); Congressional Budget Office (2003); Economic Research Initiative on the Uninsured (2006); State Health Access Data Assistance Center (2006).

TABLE 2-1 Number and Rate of Uninsurance Among Children and Adults, 2007

	Number (in millions)	Percent uninsured
Total	45.7	15.3
Nonelderly, under 65	45.0	17.2
Children ages 0-17	8.1	11.0
Adults ages 18-64	36.8	19.6
Adults over age 64	0.7	1.9

NOTE: Tabulations from the March 2008 Current Population Survey.
SOURCE: DeNavas-Walt et al. (2008).

---

health coverage (AHRQ Center for Financing Access and Cost Trends, 2008).

Most uninsured people in the United States are citizens. A substantial percentage of the uninsured population is made up of lower- to middle-income U.S. citizens who are not eligible for Medicaid or SCHIP. In 2005, citizens—with annual family incomes less than three times the federal poverty level (FPL) and ineligible for Medicaid or SCHIP—made up 41.4

TABLE 2-2 Comparison of the Uninsured and General U.S. Population Under Age 65 by Selected Categories, 2005

Category	Uninsured population (%)	General population (%)
People who are eligible for Medicaid or SCHIP	15.9	17.2
Noncitizens	17.7	7.0
U.S. citizens with family incomes greater than three times the federal poverty level (FPL)[a]	24.9	49.0
U.S. citizens with low- and middle-incomes who are not eligible for public coverage[b]	41.4	26.8
Low- and middle-income citizens ages 19–34 without children	13.7	5.8
Other low- and middle-income citizens	27.7	21.0
Total	100.0	100.0

NOTE: Each category is mutually exclusive. Tabulations are based on the January-June 2005 Medical Expenditure Panel Survey. Details may not sum to totals because of rounding.

[a] Citizens with "higher incomes" are those with family incomes that exceed three times the FPL. In 2005, the FPL was $21,386 for a family of four.

[b] Citizens with "low- and middle-incomes" are those with family incomes less than three times the FPL.

SOURCE: AHRQ Center for Financing Access and Trends (2008).

percent of the uninsured population, but only 26.8 percent of the general population. Some citizens—adults without children—are more likely to be uninsured because eligibility for public support is often linked with having a child.

Hispanics (of any race) and blacks are disproportionately uninsured compared to their numbers in the overall population. In 2007, blacks[3] made up 13.3 percent of the general population, but 16.7 percent of the uninsured population (DeNavas-Walt et al., 2008).

The Hispanic population was most likely to be uninsured. Hispanics made up 15.4 percent of the population but almost one-third (32.3 percent) of the uninsured population. Job differences explain some but not all of the disparity. Hispanic workers have the lowest rate of employer-sponsored coverage of any racial or ethnic group (Gould, 2008). In 2007, 67.4 percent of Hispanics over the age of 15 were in the civilian labor force, only slightly

---

[3] Includes multiracial blacks and blacks of Hispanic and non-Hispanic origin.

more than the overall population (U.S. Census Bureau, 2008).[4] Yet many Hispanic workers are employed in industries associated with low wages and limited health benefits, such as sales, building and grounds cleaning and maintenance, and food preparation and serving (Kochhar, 2005).[5] Rutledge and McLaughlin analyzed 20 years of pooled SIPP data to assess the trends in uninsurance among Hispanics (Rutledge and McLaughlin, 2008). They found that the decline in coverage among Hispanics occurred among both U.S. born and immigrants and was primarily driven by a decrease in private coverage.

THE FORCES BEHIND THE DOWNWARD SPIRAL IN HEALTH INSURANCE COVERAGE

Rising Costs Are Driving the Decline in Health Insurance Coverage

Most analysts agree that rising health care costs are the principal force driving the declines in health insurance coverage (Chernew et al., 2005; Cooper and Schone, 1997; Holahan and Cook, 2008). Health care costs—in both the private and public sectors—have been growing faster than the overall economy for decades. In 2006, health care spending averaged $7,026 per person in the United States (Catlin et al., 2008; Centers for Medicare & Medicaid Services Office of the Actuary, 2008b).

From 2000 to 2006, per capita health care spending grew by 47 percent compared to the 34 percent increase in gross domestic product (Centers for Medicare & Medicaid Services Office of the Actuary, 2008c). The trend is expected to continue (Congressional Budget Office, 2008; Ginsburg, 2008; Paulson et al., 2008; U.S. Government Accountability Office, 2008). The Centers for Medicare & Medicaid Services projects that total U.S. health care spending will almost double between 2008 and 2017 (Keehan et al., 2008).

Employer-Sponsored Insurance

Health insurance has been associated with the workplace ever since the 1930s when it was introduced as a fringe benefit of employment (Moran, 2005). However, the rapid growth in health care costs has made it increasingly difficult for employers to offer health coverage for their workers.

---

[4] This compares with 64.4 percent of the total U.S. population over age 15 in the civilian labor force.

[5] For additional research on health insurance trends in the Hispanic population, also see: Buchmueller et al. (2007); Fronstin (2008a,b); Hargraves (2004); Holahan and Cook (2005).

In addition, many workers with access to ESI have found it increasingly difficult to pay the employee premiums associated with taking up their employers' offers of coverage (Chernew et al., 2005; Cooper and Schone, 1997; Fronstin, 2008a; Holahan and Cook, 2008; U.S. Government Accountability Office, 2008).

Chernew and colleagues analyzed the decline between 1989 to 1991 and 1998 to 2000 in ESI in two cohorts of nonelderly Americans living in 64 large metropolitan statistical areas (Chernew et al., 2005). The researchers concluded that the rising cost of health insurance premiums was the principal factor underlying the decline in health insurance, leading to their conclusion that uninsurance will increase further if, as expected, health care costs continue to outpace income growth.

Growth in health insurance premiums for ESI coverage has far outpaced wage growth and family incomes. Between 1999 and 2008, the cumulative rate of increase in family premiums (119 percent) was substantially greater than the increase in workers' earnings (34 percent) (Kaiser Family Foundation and Health Research & Educational Trust, 2008a,b). Many employers and workers are finding that premiums are simply unaffordable. In 2005, nearly three-quarters of uninsured workers reported that they had declined employers' offers of employer-sponsored health insurance because of the high cost (Fronstin, 2008a).

As shown in Figure 2-3, the average annual single and family premiums for an employer-sponsored plan more than doubled from 1999 to 2008 (Kaiser Family Foundation and Health Research & Educational Trust, 2008a). Premiums for single individuals increased from $2,196 in 1999 to $4,704 in 2008, while family premiums increased from $5,791 in 1999 to $12,680 in 2008.

The aging of the so-called baby boom generation is likely to exacerbate the rising costs of health care (Congressional Budget Office, 2008). Many people born between 1946 and 1964 are now reaching the age when serious health problems emerge, the need for health care heightens considerably, and medical expenses climb. In 2007, 13.1 percent of 50- to 64-year-olds were uninsured—7.1 million individuals (Table 2-3) (Economic Research Initiative on the Uninsured, 2008). The rate of uninsurance among 50- to 64-year-olds is lower than most other age groups, but it is rising at a faster rate than other age groups. And, this is occurring as the sheer size of this population group reaches historic levels. Recent trends in employer-sponsored retiree health coverage are a contributing factor. In a 2008 survey, the Kaiser Family Foundation and Health Research & Education Trust found that large employers are increasingly unwilling to sponsor retiree health benefits for new employees (Kaiser Family Foundation and Health Research & Educational Trust, 2008a). Overall, fewer employers offer retiree ben-

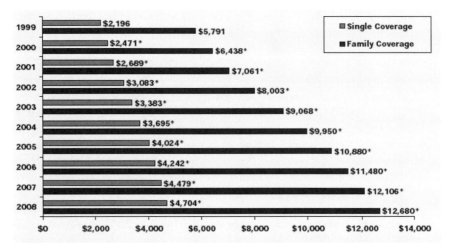

FIGURE 2-3 Average annual premiums for single and family employer-sponsored coverage, 1999-2008.
*Estimate is statistically different from estimate for the previous year shown (p < 0.05).
SOURCE: Kaiser Family Foundation and Health Research & Educational Trust (2008a). This information was reprinted with permission from the Henry J. Kaiser Family Foundation. The Kaiser Family Foundation is a nonprofit private operating foundation, based in Menlo Park, California, dedicated to producing and communicating the best possible information, research, and analysis on health issues.

TABLE 2-3 Changes in the Number and Percentage of Uninsured People in the Nonelderly U.S. Population by Age Group, 2000-2007

Age group	Year							
	2000	2001	2002	2003	2004	2005	2006	2007
Number uninsured (in millions)								
Under 18	8.4	8.2	8.2	8.1	7.7	8.1	8.7	8.1
18 to 29	11.7	12.1	13.1	13.7	13.6	14.0	14.5	14.0
30 to 49	13.1	13.9	14.9	15.4	15.7	15.7	16.2	15.7
50 to 64	5.0	5.2	5.6	5.9	6.0	6.6	7.1	7.1
Uninsured rate (in percent)								
Under 18	11.6%	11.3%	11.2%	11.0%	10.5%	10.9%	11.7%	11.0%
18 to 29	25.7	26.6	28.3	29.3	28.7	29.1	29.5	28.2
30 to 49	15.4	16.2	17.3	18.0	18.4	18.5	19.2	18.7
50 to 64	11.7	11.8	12.1	12.3	12.1	12.8	13.4	13.1

SOURCE: Economic Research Initative on the Uninsured (2008).

efits than in the past and, when retiree health benefits are offered, it is with higher premiums and higher patient cost sharing (Fronstin, 2008b).

Lower- and Middle-Income Workers

The rising cost of coverage is particularly burdensome for lower-income workers. Although employees' percentage share of ESI premiums has been stable, average employee premium costs have increased steadily. Between 1999 and 2008, the average annual employee premium contribution for family coverage rose from $1,543 to $3,354 (Kaiser Family Foundation and Health Research & Educational Trust, 2008a). Shen and Long studied the decline in ESI between 1999 and 2002—a period encompassing both economic growth and recession—in order to determine whether the downward trend in coverage was related to decreasing offers from employers or to increasing numbers of employees deciding not to take up offers of coverage (Shen and Long, 2006). They found that, in 2002, both changes were occurring—workers with family incomes lower than twice the FPL were far less likely to be offered an ESI plan than higher income workers earning two to four times the FPL (55.4 percent vs. 78.6 percent) and lower-income workers were less likely to take up an employer's offer of coverage (75.5 percent vs. 83.7 percent).

An analysis of data from MEPS provided to the committee by the AHRQ Center for Financing, Access, and Cost Trends indicates that the take-up of ESI coverage among lower-wage workers continued to decline through 2005 (AHRQ Center for Financing Access and Cost Trends, 2008; Cooper and Schone, 1997). Family take-up rates dropped from 75.8 percent in 1996 to 66.8 percent in 2005 for workers earning $7.00/hour or less and dropped from 86.1 percent in 1996 to 82.4 percent in 2005 for workers earning between $7.01/hour and $10.00/hour. Many middle-income workers, although not as vulnerable as lower-income workers, are also at risk of losing employer-sponsored coverage. In the Shen and Long study described above, both low- and middle-income workers experienced a 3 percentage-point drop in ESI coverage from 1999 to 2002 (Shen and Long, 2006).

The Changing Workplace

The American workplace has undergone significant change in the last decade. Since 2000, the occupation, firm size, and industry mix has changed; the gender and age distribution of the labor force has changed; and the importance of part-time, part-year, and contractual workers has changed (Bernstein and Shierholz, 2008; Gould, 2007; Haas and Swartz, 2007; Holahan and Cook, 2008; Reschovsky et al., 2006; Shen and Long, 2006). Health insurance coverage varies substantially across these different job categories, so these changes in job mix may have profound implications for health insurance coverage.

As shown in Table 2-4, the percentage of private sector workers covered by their employer's health plan varies markedly by occupation, firm size, and industry. In each year between 2002 and 2007, workers' coverage by their employer varied by at least 46 percentage points between industries, 32 percentage points between white collar and service workers, and 34 percentage points between large firms (500 or more employees) and small firms (less than 25 employees) (Gould, 2007, 2008). In 2007, for example, private sector employer coverage of white collar workers was more than double the rate for service workers, at 61.9 percent and 29.5 percent, respectively. The contrast between industries was similarly stark. More than 70 percent of mining and manufacturing workers were enrolled in their employer's health plan compared to less than 30 percent of agriculture, forestry, fishing, hunting, arts, entertainment, recreation, accommodation, and food service workers.

Table 2-4 also shows that the trends in private sector health insurance coverage differ by occupation, firm size, and industry. In all types of occupations (white collar, blue collar, service, and other), the percentage of private sector workers with ESI coverage was lower in 2007 than it was in 2000 (Gould, 2007, 2008). For blue-collar workers, however, the 5.0 percentage point decline between 2000 and 2007 exceeded the declines for white collar workers (3.0 percentage points) and service workers (4.4 percentage points). From 2000 to 2007, workers in firms of all sizes experienced declines in coverage, but the greatest decline (4.0 percentage points) occurred among workers with jobs in small firms.

The majority of states have enacted laws to promote small firms' access to small group health insurance coverage. From 1991 to 1996, for example, every state except Alaska, Michigan, and Pennsylvania enacted legislation to reform the small group health insurance market in some way (Simon, 2005). The reforms included various approaches, alone or in combination, such as limits on the methods insurers may use to set premiums for small group plans, requiring guaranteed issue of small group coverage, allowing insurers to sell "bare bones" small group coverage to first time buyers, limiting preexisting condition exclusions, and enhancing portability. There is no evidence, however, that the states' efforts have had a substantial positive impact (Simon, 2005, 2008).

Fewer Jobs with Health Benefits—More Part-Time and Short-Term Jobs

Rising health insurance premiums increase the ranks of both the uninsured and the unemployed. In addition, the compositions of the workplace and the workforce have undergone significant change (Bernstein and

Shierholz, 2008; Gould, 2007; Haas and Swartz, 2007; Holahan and Cook, 2008; Reschovsky et al., 2006; Shen and Long, 2006). Employers have increasingly replaced permanent, full-time jobs with contract, part-time, and temporary positions that do not come with health benefits. In an analysis of the impact of rising health insurance premiums on the labor market, Baicker and Chandra concluded that increasing premiums contribute to higher unemployment, reduced hours worked, and the greater likelihood that workers are employed part-time rather than full-time (Baicker and Chandra, 2006). The researchers estimated that a 10 percent increase in health insurance premiums reduces workers' likelihood of employment by 1.2 percentage points, reduces hours worked by 2.4 percent, and increases the odds of workers being employed only part-time instead of full-time by 1.9 percentage points.

Shen and Long's research suggests that low-wage workers are particularly at risk of uninsurance because only a small proportion (13 percent) of them have a spouse with access to ESI (Shen and Long, 2006). Because of the high cost of nongroup coverage, there are limited options for those workers not offered ESI. Particularly worrisome is that adults who decline offers of ESI are likely to remain uninsured and are more likely to be in poor health with high-cost medical conditions (Bernard and Selden, 2006; Glied and Mahato, 2008).

LIMITATIONS OF THE NONGROUP
HEALTH INSURANCE MARKET

People without access to ESI, other sources of group health insurance, or public insurance must turn to the nongroup health insurance market if they want to obtain health insurance. In 2007, only 6.8 percent of the non-elderly U.S. population was covered by a nongroup health insurance policy (Fronstin, 2008a). This percentage has been relatively steady for more than a decade, fluctuating between 6.5 percent and 7.2 percent. Meanwhile, the ranks of the uninsured have increased. Some state and federal regulations have been put in place to help promote access to nongroup coverage, but current data limitations undermine research to assess the outcome of the regulations (Simon, 2008).[6]

Access to nongroup health insurance coverage is highly dependent on individuals' circumstances and geographic location. Since states regulate the nongroup insurance market and health care costs vary substantially by location, the premiums for nongroup insurance policies are highly dependent on where one lives. Regardless of location, however, the premium

---

[6] The Kaiser Family Foundation maintains a website with extensive information on state and federal rules for the nongroup market (Kaiser Family Foundation, 2008).

TABLE 2-4 Percentage of Private Sector U.S. Workers with Access to and Coverage by Their Employers' Health Insurance, by Occupation, Firm Size, and Industry, 2000-2007[a]

	2000	2001	2002	2003	2004	2005	2006	2007
All workers[a]	58.9	58.2	57.3	56.4	55.9	54.9	55.0	55.4
Occupations								
White collar	65.0	64.5	63.1	62.4	62.4	61.2	61.4	61.9
Blue collar	59.0	58.1	57.1	56.4	54.8	53.9	53.4	53.9
Service	33.9	33.3	31.6	28.7	29.4	28.7	28.9	29.5
Other	26.7	27.9	30.4	25.8	23.9	24.7	25.4	22.2
Firm size								
24 or fewer[b]	36.2	34.9	35.0	34.4	33.6	32.6	32.6	32.1
Less than 100	43.9	43.4	42.6	42.0	41.0	40.4	40.1	40.1
100–499	65.9	64.8	64.8	63.7	63.2	61.7	62.0	63.1
500 or more	69.6	69.3	68.6	67.9	67.6	66.6	66.6	67.1
Industry[c]								
Agriculture, forestry, fishing, and hunting			37.1	29.1	25.8	26.1	29.5	27.1
Arts, entertainment, recreation, accommodation, and food services			32.5	30.4	30.5	30.6	29.7	31.9

Construction	47.5	44.8	42.4	42.4	44.1	44.1
Educational, health, and social services	59.4	59.4	60.2	57.5	58.4	60.2
Financial, insurance, real estate, and rental and leasing	65.8	65.5	65.2	64.4	65.4	65.1
Information	73.0	71.3	70.1	72.3	71.6	72.7
Manufacturing	72.7	73.0	71.8	71.2	70.9	70.2
Mining	78.4	76.8	79.1	73.4	74.3	73.9
Other services (except public administration)	40.1	38.9	39.2	39.5	35.9	37.4
Professional, scientific, management, administration, and waste management services	57.4	55.1	55.8	54.7	56.1	56.0
Transportation and utilities	66.9	65.7	66.8	63.6	61.6	63.0
Wholesale and retail trade	53.9	52.9	52.7	51.9	51.2	51.6

[a] Private-sector, wage and salary workers, ages 18 to 64, who worked at least 20 hours per week and 26 weeks per year and received employer-provided health insurance through their own job. The employer had to pay at least part of the insurance premium for the coverage to qualify as employer-provided coverage.

[b] Personal communication, E. Gould, Economic Policy Institute, November 7, 2008.

[c] Industry classifications changes make it impossible to compare 2006 with years earlier than 2002.

SOURCE: Gould (2007, 2008). Reprinted, with permission, from *EPI Briefing Paper, 2007*. Copyright 2008 by the Economic Policy Institute.

costs for nongroup coverage can be exceedingly high because the individual subscriber pays the entire cost without a contribution from an employer. Moreover, health insurers typically subject applicants for individual policies to underwriting (i.e., assessment of their health status and recent use of services) if they want coverage (Merlis, 2005). Individuals who apply for nongroup health insurance may be denied a policy because they or a family member have a preexisting condition or are employed in occupations viewed as high risk. In most states, the insurer may deny coverage completely, impose either a permanent or temporary preexisting condition limitation on coverage, or charge a higher premium based on health status, occupation, and other personal characteristics.

Individual medical insurability also depends on how recently one has been covered by a group health plan. Applicants with recent group coverage have some protections under the federal Health Insurance Portability and Accountability Act (HIPAA) (P.L. No. 104-191).[7] For example, HIPAA guarantees access to continued coverage for individuals with recent ESI coverage who change or lose jobs. HIPAA rules allow the states to specify some of the key terms of coverage (Kaiser Family Foundation, 2008). Most states offer HIPAA-eligible residents who are quoted high premiums access to a state high-risk pool; but the coverage can be expensive, include high cost-sharing requirements, and offer only limited benefits. HIPAA's rules do not protect individuals from future increases in premiums. As a consequence, someone who suffers serious medical condition or trauma may be charged extremely high premiums (Pauly and Lieberthal, 2008).

Beyond HIPAA-related rules, a few states have regulations that are designed to promote access to nongroup coverage by requiring guaranteed issue of nongroup policies, limits on preexisting condition exclusions, and caps on premiums (see Appendix C for details by state on regulations addressing access to individual health insurance policies). Six states, for example, require that all insurers offer all applicants a health policy regardless of health status: Maine, Massachusetts, New Jersey, New York, Vermont, and Washington (Kaiser Family Foundation, 2008). An additional six states have an insurer of last resort, Blue Cross Blue Shield, which must offer everyone a policy: District of Columbia, Michigan, North Carolina,

---

[7] Individuals eligible for coverage under HIPAA regulations are guaranteed the right to purchase individual coverage with no preexisting condition exclusion periods when they leave group coverage. To be eligible, the individual must have at least 18 months of prior coverage, uninterrupted by more than 63 consecutive days. The last day of prior coverage must be in a group plan and, upon leaving group coverage, the individual must elect and exhaust any available COBRA (Consolidated Omnibus Budget Reconciliation Act) continuation coverage or similar state continuation coverage. See Kaiser State Health Facts for more information about individual market guaranteed issue: http://www.statehealthfacts.org/comparetable. jsp?cat=7&ind=353.

Pennsylvania, Rhode Island, and Virginia. However, guaranteed issue requirements do not provide limits on the cost of policies—so, many are unaffordable.

ECONOMIC PRESSURES THREATENING
PUBLIC COVERAGE EXPANSIONS

It is possible that additional millions of low-income Americans would be uninsured today were it not for recent state and federal efforts to expand coverage. As noted previously, states and the federal government have substantially increased health coverage among low-income children and to a lesser degree among adults in the last decade, by expanding eligibility, conducting outreach to people already eligible, and expediting enrollment in Medicaid and SCHIP. And, as this report was being finalized, Congress reauthorized the SCHIP program (P.L. No. 111-3).

Every state has implemented an SCHIP program (Centers for Medicare & Medicaid Services Office of the Actuary, 2008a). The primary beneficiaries of SCHIP programs have been children, particularly those with family incomes between 100 percent and 200 percent of the FPL. State SCHIP programs have targeted benefits to these children because their family income is too high for them to qualify for Medicaid, but too low for their parents to afford private family health insurance coverage. According to estimates based on the NHIS, rates of uninsurance among children in low-income[8] families fell by more than one-third between 1997, the year before SCHIP was implemented, and 2005 (Ku et al., 2007). Recently, many states have moved to further expand enrollment in publicly subsidized programs. Between 2006 and 2007, 35 states enacted expansions in Medicaid or SCHIP eligibility for children and/or adults (Table 2-5). In 2008, 10 states implemented or authorized eligibility expansions for children (Ross and Marks, 2009).

It is now clear that some states may be unable to sustain recent expansions in Medicaid and SCHIP given the severity of the current economic crisis. During the last economic downturn, some states restricted enrollment procedures that led to steep declines in children's enrollment (Ross and Marks, 2009). When states face budget gaps, they must cut expenditures, raise taxes, or dig into state reserves. As of January 2009, state budget shortfalls were projected to total $350 billion through fiscal year 2011. At the time this report was being drafted, many states forecast budget deficits and were either putting expansion plans on hold or considering cuts to their Medicaid and SCHIP programs (Dorn et al., 2008; Johnson et al., 2009; Smith et al., 2008).

---

[8] Low income in this analysis was defined as less than 200 percent of the FPL.

TABLE 2-5 States Expanding Publicly Subsidized Coverage to Children or Adults, 2006-2007

	Children	Adults		Children	Adults
Number of states	26	18			
Alabama			Missouri	√	√
Alaska	√		Montana	√	
Arizona		√	Nebraska		
Arkansas			Nevada		√
California			New Hampshire		
Colorado	√		New Jersey		√
Connecticut		√	New Mexico	√	
DC	√		New York	√	√
Delaware		√	North Carolina	√	
Florida			North Dakota	√	
Georgia			Ohio	√	√
Hawaii	√		Oklahoma	√	√
Idaho			Oregon	√	
Illinois	√		Pennsylvania	√	
Indiana	√	√	Rhode Island		
Iowa	√	√	South Carolina	√	
Kansas		√	South Dakota		
Kentucky			Tennessee	√	√
Louisiana	√		Texas	√	√
Maine			Utah		
Maryland		√	Vermont		√
Massachusetts	√	√	Virginia		
Michigan			Washington	√	
Minnesota	√		West Virginia	√	
Mississippi			Wisconsin	√	
			Wyoming		√

SOURCE: McDonough et al. (2008). Copyrighted and published by Project HOPE/*Health Affairs* as McDonough et al., A Progress Report on State Health Access Reform, *Health Affairs*, 27(2): w105-w115, 2008. The published article is archived and available online at www.healthaffairs.org.

Nevertheless, states appear committed to the programs, especially with respect to expanded eligibility. As this report was prepared, few states had acted to reverse eligibility expansions for Medicaid or SCHIP (Johnson et al., 2009; Smith et al., 2008). Most states are looking for savings in a variety of other areas, such as provider reimbursements, pharmacy controls, and benefit reductions, or new sources of revenue such as patient cost-sharing and increasing the cost of premiums. Only two states reported new limits on eligibility for public insurance in 2008: Rhode Island lowered the maximum income eligibility for parents from 185 percent to 175 of the FPL

(Ross and Marks, 2009), and Maine established a waiting list for SCHIP coverage and froze enrollment for childless adults (Smith et al., 2008).

The U.S. Department of Labor announced in January 2009 that 2.6 million jobs had been lost in 2008 (U.S. Bureau of Labor Statistics, 2009). By the end of December 2008, the U.S. unemployment rate had reached 7.2 percent, bringing the total number of the unemployed to 11.1 million. Numerous studies show that rising unemployment, which causes people to lose their employer-based health insurance coverage, as well as to experience reductions in family incomes, leads to a rising demand for Medicaid and SCHIP coverage. Dorn and colleagues, for example, used 1990 to 2003 state-level data from the CPS and other sources to estimate the impact of unemployment on health insurance coverage. The researchers concluded that a 1 percentage point rise in the national unemployment rate would increase Medicaid and SCHIP enrollment by 1 million (assuming no cutbacks in eligibility) (Dorn et al., 2008). In addition, they found that a 1 percentage point rise in the national unemployment rate would increase the uninsured population by 1.1 million.

As shown in Figure 2-4, three states—Maine, Massachusetts, and

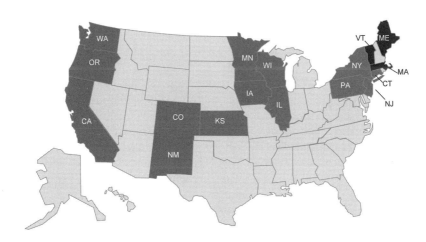

■ Enacted Universal Coverage (3 states)
■ Proposed Universal Coverage (14 states)

FIGURE 2-4 States moving toward comprehensive health care reform.
SOURCE: Kaiser Commission on Medicaid and the Uninsured (2008). This information was reprinted with permission from the Henry J. Kaiser Family Foundation. The Kaiser Family Foundation is a nonprofit private operating foundation, based in Menlo Park, California, dedicated to producing and communicating the best possible information, research, and analysis on health issues.

Vermont—have enacted and are implementing plans to achieve universal health coverage (Kaiser Commission on Medicaid and the Uninsured, 2008). In Massachusetts, 439,000 previously uninsured individuals had obtained health insurance as of March 2008. In Maine, 23,000 individuals and more than 725 small business had obtained coverage through Maine's initiative, "Dirigo Choice," as of February 2008. Vermont began implementation of "Catamount Health" in October 2007, and 5,704 individuals had enrolled as of September 2008. As this report was drafted in late 2008, an additional 14 states had reform plans under way: California, Colorado, Connecticut, Illinois, Iowa, Kansas, Minnesota, New Jersey, New Mexico, New York, Oregon, Pennsylvania, Washington, and Wisconsin (Figure 2-4). The downturn in the U.S. economy is likely to stymie many states' efforts to expand public health insurance coverage. In California, for example, the state assembly approved ambitious legislation to expand coverage in 2007, but soon after, the state senate rejected the bill.

CONCLUSION

Health insurance coverage has declined over the last decade despite increases in public program coverage, and will continue to decline. There is no evidence to suggest that the trends driving loss of insurance coverage will reverse absent concerted action. Rising health care costs and a severely weakened economy threaten not only employer-sponsored coverage, the cornerstone of private health coverage in the United States, but also threaten recent expansions in public coverage despite the recent reauthorization of SCHIP. Health care costs and insurance premiums are growing substantially faster than the economy and family incomes. Employment has shifted away from industries with traditionally high rates of coverage (e.g., manufacturing) to service jobs (e.g., in wholesale and retail trades) with historically lower rates of coverage. In some industries, employers have begun to rely more heavily on jobs without health benefits, such as part-time and shorter-term employment and contract and temporary jobs. Overall, fewer workers, particularly among those with lower wages, are offered employer-sponsored coverage and fewer among them can afford the premiums. And, early retirees are less likely to be offered retiree health insurance benefits than in the past. For many people without employer-sponsored health insurance, nongroup coverage is prohibitively expensive or unavailable. Some states are under extreme economic pressure to cut their recent expansions of public programs for low-income children and adults. Sharp increases in unemployment will further fuel the decline in the number of people with employer-sponsored coverage and add even greater stress on states' Medicaid and SCHIP programs.

REFERENCES

AHRQ Center for Financing Access and Cost Trends. 2008 (unpublished). *Tabulations from the January-June 2005 Medical Expenditure Panel Survey (MEPS) commissioned by the IOM Committee on Health Insurance Status and Its Consequences.*

Baicker, K., and A. Chandra. 2006. The labor market effects of rising health insurance premiums. *Journal of Labor Economics* 24(3):609-634.

Bernard, D. M., and T. M. Selden. 2006. Workers who decline employment-related health insurance. *Medical Care Trends in Medical Care Costs, Coverage, Use, and Access: Research Findings from the Medical Expenditure Panel Survey* 44(5):I-12–I-18.

Bernstein, J. 2008. *Income picture: Median income rose as did poverty in 2007,* http://www.epi.org/content.cfm/webfeatures_econindicators_income_20080826 (accessed September 29, 2008).

Bernstein, J., and H. Shierholz. 2008. A decade of decline: The erosion of employer-provided health care in the United States and California, 1995-2006. *EPI Briefing Paper* 209, http://www.epi.org/briefingpapers/209/bp209.pdf (accessed June 9, 2008).

Buchmueller, T. C., A. T. Lo Sasso, I. Lurie, and S. Dolfin. 2007. Immigrants and employer-sponsored health insurance. *Health Services Research* 42(1p1):286-310.

Catlin, A., C. Cowan, M. Hartman, S. Heffler, and The National Health Expenditure Accounts Team. 2008. National health spending in 2006: A year of change for prescription drugs. *Health Affairs* 27(1):14-29.

Centers for Medicare & Medicaid Services Office of the Actuary. 2008a. *Number of children ever enrolled year by program type, February 7, 2008,* http://www.cms.hhs.gov/NationalSCHIPPolicy/downloads/SCHIPEverEnrolledYEARFY2007FINAL.PDF (accessed October 5, 2008).

———. 2008b. *National Health Expenditure Projections 2007-2017,* http://www.cms.hhs.gov/NationalHealthExpendData/Downloads/proj2007.pdf (accessed September 5, 2008).

———. 2008c. *Table 1 National health expenditures aggregate, per capita amounts, percent distribution, and average annual percent growth, by source of funds: Selected calendar years 1960-2007,* http://www.cms.hhs.gov/NationalHealthExpendData/downloads/tables.pdf (accessed September 28, 2008).

Chernew, M., D. M. Cutler, and P. S. Keenan. 2005. Increasing health insurance costs and the decline in insurance coverage. *Health Services Research* 40(4):1021-1039.

Chu, M., and J. Rhoades. 2008. The uninsured in America, 1996-2007: Estimates for the U.S. civilian noninstitutionalized population under age 65. Statistical Brief 214 Agency for Healthcare Research and Quality, http://www.meps.ahrq.gov/mepsweb/data_files/publications/st214/stat214.pdf (accessed November 10, 2008).

Cohen, R. A., M. E. Martinez, and H. L. Free. 2007. Health insurance coverage: Early release estimates from the National Health Interview Survey. *Division of Health Interview Statistics, National Center for Health Statistics,* http://www.cdc.gov/nchs/data/nhis/earlyrelease/insur200806.pdf (accessed November 10, 2008).

Congressional Budget Office. 2003. *How many people lack health insurance and for how long?* http://www.cbo.gov/ftpdocs/42xx/doc4210/05-12-Uninsured.pdf (accessed August 1, 2008).

———. 2008. *The long-term budget outlook and options for slowing the growth of health care costs.* Testimony by Director Peter R. Orszag before the Senate Committee on Finance, http://cbo.gov/ftpdocs/93xx/doc9385/06-17-LTBO_Testimony.pdf (accessed August 7, 2008).

Cooper, P. F., and B. S. Schone. 1997. More offers, fewer takers for employment-based health insurance: 1987 and 1996. *Health Affairs* 16(6):142-149.

Coughlin, T. A., and S. Zuckerman. 2008. State responses to new flexibility in Medicaid. *Milbank Quarterly* 86(2):209-240.

DeNavas-Walt, C., B. D. Proctor, and J. Smith. 2007. *Income, poverty, and health insurance coverage in the United States: 2006.* Washington, DC: U.S. Census Bureau.

———. 2008. *Income, poverty, and health insurance coverage in the United States: 2007.* Washington, DC: U.S. Census Bureau.

Dorn, S., B. Garrett, J. Holahan, and A. Williams. 2008. Medicaid, SCHIP and economic downturn: Policy challenges and policy responses. http://www.kff.org/Medicaid/7770.cfm (accessed May 5, 2008).

Economic Research Initiative on the Uninsured. 2006. *Fast facts tables: SIPP 2005 data,* http://eriu.sph.umich.edu/fastfacts/index_w2.html (accessed October 11, 2008).

———. 2008 (unpublished). *Tabulations based on 2000-2007 Current Population Surveys commissioned by the IOM Committee on Health Insurance Status and Its Consequences.*

Fronstin, P. 2008a. Sources of health insurance and characteristics of the uninsured: Analysis of the March 2008 current population survey. EBRI Issue Brief 321, http://www.ebri.org/publications (accessed September 5, 2008).

———. 2008b. Trends in employment-based health benefits for workers and retirees. *Statement for the Senate Finance Committee,* http://finance.senate.gov/healthsummit2008/Statements/Paul%20Fronstin%20Statement.pdf (accessed January 30, 2009).

Ginsburg, P. B. 2008. Don't break out the champagne: Continued slowing of health care spending growth unlikely to last. *Health Affairs* 27(1):30-32.

Glied, S. A., and B. Mahato. 2008. *The widening health care gap between high- and low-wage workers.* Washington, DC: The Commonwealth Fund.

Gould, E. 2007. The erosion of employment-based insurance: More working families left uninsured. EPI Briefing Paper #203, http://www.epi.org/briefingpapers/203/bp203.pdf (accessed June 9, 2008).

———. 2008. The erosion of employment-based insurance: More working families left uninsured. EPI Briefing Paper #223, http://www.epi.org/briefingpapers/223/bp223.pdf (accessed November 15, 2008).

Haas, J., and K. Swartz. 2007. The relative importance of worker, firm, and market characteristics for racial/ethnic disparities in employer-sponsored health Insurance. *Inquiry* 44(3):280-302.

Hargraves, J. L. 2004. Trends in health insurance coverage and access among black, Latino and white Americans, 2001-2003. *Tracking Report: Results from the Community Tracking Study* 11, http://www.hschange.org/CONTENT/713/?topic=topic10 (accessed June 24, 2008).

Holahan, J., and A. Cook. 2005. *Are immigrants responsible for most of the growth of the uninsured?* http://www.kff.org/uninsured/upload/Are-Immigrants-Responsible-for-Most-of-the-Growth-of-the-Uninsured-issue-brief.pdf (accessed June 25, 2008).

———. 2008. The U.S. economy and changes in health insurance coverage, 2000-2006. *Health Affairs* 27(2):w135-w144.

IOM (Institute of Medicine). 2001. *Coverage matters: Insurance and health care.* Washington, DC: National Academy Press.

Johnson, N., P. Oliff, and J. Koulish. 2009. Facing deficits, two-thirds of states are imposing cuts that hurt vulnerable populations. Center on Budget and Policy Priorities, http://www.cbpp.org/3-13-08sfp.pdf (accessed January 27, 2009).

Kaiser Commission on Medicaid and the Uninsured. 2008. *States moving toward comprehensive health care reform,* http://www.kff.org/uninsured/upload/State%20Health%20Reform1.pdf (accessed September 1, 2008).

Kaiser Family Foundation. 2008. *Non-group coverage rules for HIPAA eligible individuals, 2007*, http://www.statehealthfacts.org/comparemap.jsp?ind=356&cat=7&sub=87&yr=1 8&typ=5 (accessed September 23, 2008).

Kaiser Family Foundation and Health Research & Educational Trust. 2008a. *Employer health benefits: 2008 annual survey (#7790)*, http://ehbs.kff.org/pdf/7790.pdf (accessed September 24, 2008).

———. 2008b. *Survey of employer health benefits, 2008*. Slide presentation, http://ehbs.kff. org/images/abstract/EHBS_08_Release_Adds.pdf (accessed September 24, 2008).

Keehan, S., A. Sisko, C. Truffer, S. Smith, C. Cowan, J. Poisal, M. K. Clemens, and The National Health Expenditure Accounts Projections. 2008. Health spending projections through 2017: The baby-boom generation is coming to Medicare. *Health Affairs* 27(2): w145-w155.

Kochhar, R. 2005. *The occupational status and mobility of Hispanics*, http://pewhispanic. org/files/reports/59.pdf (accessed October 7, 2008).

Ku, L., M. Lin, and M. Broaddus. 2007. *Improving children's health: A chartbook about the roles of Medicaid and SCHIP*. 2007 Edition. Washington, DC: Center on Budget and Policy Priorities.

McDonough, J. E., M. Miller, and C. Barber. 2008. A progress report on state health access reform. *Health Affairs* 27(2):w105-w115.

Merlis, M. 2005. Fundamentals of underwriting in the nongroup health insurance market: Access to coverage and options for reform. *National Health Policy Forum Background Paper*, April 13, 2005.

Moran, D. W. 2005. Whence and whither health insurance? A revisionist history. *Health Affairs* 24(6):1415-1425.

Paulson, H. M., M. O. Leavitt, E. L. Chao, and M. J. Astrue. 2008. *2008 annual report of the boards of trustees of the federal hospital insurance and federal supplementary medical insurance trust funds*, http://www.cms.hhs.gov/reportstrustfunds/downloads/tr2008.pdf (accessed June 10, 2008).

Pauly, M. V., and R. D. Lieberthal. 2008. How risky is individual health insurance? *Health Affairs* 27(3):w242-w249.

Reschovsky, J. D., B. C. Strunk, and P. Ginsburg. 2006. Why employer-sponsored insurance coverage changed, 1997-2003. *Health Affairs* 25(3):774-782.

Ross, D. C., and C. Marks. 2009. Challenges of providing health coverage for children and parents in a recession: A 50 state update on eligibility rules, enrollment and renewal procedures, and cost-sharing practices in Medicaid and SCHIP in 2009. *Kaiser Commission on Medicaid and the Uninsured*, http://www.kff.org/medicaid/upload/7855.pdf (accessed January 27, 2009).

Rutledge, M., and C. G. McLaughlin. 2008. Hispanics and health insurance coverage: The rising disparity. *Medical Care* 46(10):1086-1092.

Shen, Y.-C., and S. K. Long. 2006. What's driving the downward trend in employer-sponsored health insurance? *Health Services Research* 41(6):2074-2096.

Simon, K. 2005. Adverse selection in health insurance markets? Evidence from state small-group health insurance reforms. *Journal of Public Economics* 89(9-10):1865-1877.

———. 2008. Data needs for policy research on state-level health insurance markets. *Inquiry* 45(1):89-97.

Smith, V., K. Gifford, E. Ellis, R. Rudowitz, M. O'Malley, and C. Marks. 2008. *Headed for a crunch: An update on Medicaid spending, coverage and policy heading into an economic downturn results from a 50-state Medicaid budget survey for state fiscal years 2008 and 2009*, http://kff.org/medicaid/upload/7815.pdf (accessed October 2, 2008).

State Health Access Data Assistance Center. 2006. *Comparing federal government surveys that count uninsured people in America*, http://www.rwjf.org/files/publications/other/SHADAC_RWJ.pdf (accessed August 1, 2008).

U.S. Bureau of Labor Statistics. 2009. *Commissioner's statement on the employment situation*, http://www.bls.gov/news.release/pdf/jec.pdf (accessed January 27, 2009).

U.S. Census Bureau. 2008. 2007 American Community Survey. *S0201. Selected population profile in the United States. Population group: Hispanic or Latino (of any race)*, http://factfinder.census.gov/ (accessed November 20, 2008).

U.S. Government Accountability Office. 2008. *Long-term fiscal outlook. Action is needed to avoid the possibility of a serious economic disruption in the future*. Testimony by Director David M. Walker before the U.S. Senate Committee on the Budget. GAO-08-411T, http://www.gao.gov/new.items/d08411t.pdf (accessed August 7, 2008).

3

Coverage Matters

Abstract: If health insurance affects individuals' health, functioning, and quality of life, it is by enabling access to effective health care services, including preventive services, early detection of disease, diagnostic services, treatment, rehabilitation, and palliative care. Important new research has emerged since the Institute of Medicine last studied the question of whether health insurance matters to health. This chapter draws from two commissioned systematic reviews of the evidence that was published from 2002 through August 2008 on the relationships between (1) health insurance coverage and access to potentially beneficial health care services, (2) access to potentially beneficial health care services and health outcomes, and (3) the overarching link between health insurance coverage and health outcomes. The committee concludes that the existing body of evidence is stronger and of higher quality than in the previous study. The committee further finds that, in the United States, health insurance coverage is integral to health care access and health. For people without health insurance, there is a chasm between health care needs and access to needed services despite the availability of some safety net services. With health insurance, children are more likely to gain access to a medical home, well-child care and immunizations, prescription medications, appropriate care for asthma, and basic dental services. They are also more likely to have fewer avoidable hospitalizations, improved asthma outcomes, and fewer missed days of school. Uninsured adults face serious and sometime grave risk to their health. Without health insurance, adults have less access to effective clinical services including preventive care and, if sick or injured, are more likely to suffer poorer heath outcomes, greater limitations in quality of life, and premature death. When adults gain health insurance, they experience improved access to effective clinical services and better health outcomes.

When policy makers and researchers consider potential solutions to the problem of uninsurance in the United States, the question of whether health insurance matters to health is often an issue. This question is far more than an academic concern. It is crucial that U.S. health care policy be informed with current and valid evidence on the consequences of uninsurance for health care and health outcomes, especially for the 45.7 million individuals without health insurance.

Some people might think it is obvious that not having health insurance will have adverse consequences for individuals' health. On the other hand, some people believe that children and adults without health insurance have access to needed health care services at hospital emergency rooms, community health centers, or other safety net facilities offering charity care. And some observers note that there is a solid body of evidence showing that a substantial proportion of U.S. health care expenditures is directed to care that is not effective and may sometimes even be harmful. At least for the insured population, spending more and using more health care services does not always yield better health outcomes or increase life expectancy (Fisher et al., 2003; Fuchs, 2004; Wennberg and Wennberg, 2003; Wennberg et al., 2006).

Is having health insurance essential for gaining access to appropriate health care services? Or is there evidence that the uninsured population receives the health care services necessary to achieve health outcomes comparable to the insured population? This chapter provides a summary of the key findings from the research evidence on the relationships between health insurance and health outcomes that has emerged since the Institute of Medicine (IOM) released its last report on the issue in 2002 (IOM, 2002a). It is based on two systematic reviews of the literature on the consequences of uninsurance for individuals' health outcomes commissioned by the committee in 2008: one that evaluated the recent evidence pertaining to children and adolescents (Kenney and Howell, 2008) and a second that evaluated the evidence for adults (McWilliams, 2008).[1]

In 2002, the IOM judged the available evidence to be sufficiently strong and consistent to conclude that uninsured individuals do not receive needed health care services, and they suffer poorer health outcomes, including, for adults, greater risk of premature death (IOM, 2002a,b). Hadley drew similar conclusions in a comprehensive and rigorous literature review conducted shortly thereafter (Hadley, 2003). Freeman and colleagues, who conducted

---

[1] The commissioned reviews of the research evidence from 2002 to August 2008 on consequences of uninsurance for access and health were (1) Health Consequences of Uninsurance Among Adults in the United States: An Update, by J. Michael McWilliams, M.D., Ph.D., Harvard Medical School; and (2) Health and Access Consequences of Uninsurance Among Children in the United States: An Update, by Genevieve M. Kenney, Ph.D., and Embry Howell, Ph.D., The Urban Institute. Much of the discussion in this chapter is based on these reviews.

a more recent systematic review of the literature, reported in 2008 that the research consistently shows that health insurance increases the utilization of health care services and improves health outcomes (Freeman et al., 2008). Levy and Meltzer, on the other hand, have argued that the available evidence on the health effects of uninsurance on the general population is not convincing because of its reliance on observational research (Levy and Meltzer, 2008). These investigators do agree, however, that there is persuasive evidence that health insurance improves the health outcomes of certain vulnerable subgroups, such as infants, children, and adults with AIDS. They also believe that there is evidence that health insurance improves blood pressure control and other specific measures of health for a broader population of adults, particularly low-income adults.

CONCEPTUAL FRAMEWORK

The focus of this chapter is on how health insurance affects children's and adults' health outcomes. One would expect that the greatest effects of not having health insurance would be on the health outcomes of individuals who need health care the most, such as children with special health care needs and individuals who are acutely ill, suffer an injury or trauma, or have a chronic health condition. Of course, some health problems (e.g., obesity) may require a host of interventions beyond those provided through health insurance coverage (Forrest and Riley, 2004; Homer and Simpson, 2007).

The conceptual framework and focus of the committee in examining the potential effects of uninsurance on individuals' health outcomes is illustrated in Figure 3-1. If health insurance affects individuals' health status, functional status, and quality of life, it is by enabling access to potentially beneficial health care—that is, by enabling the timely use of personal health services to achieve the best possible health outcomes (IOM, 1993). As shown in Figure 3-1, health insurance is one of several factors that enable access to care, others being financial resources, geographic location, language and culture, and transportation. Potentially beneficial health services include clinical preventive services, early detection of disease, diagnostic services, treatment, rehabilitation, and palliative care. Rehabilitative and palliative care services are not addressed in this report because the relevant research is extremely limited.

Health insurance alone does not necessarily assure that individuals receive high-quality care (McGlynn et al., 2003). Other enabling factors, such as financial resources, geographic location, language and culture, and transportation, are also integral to health care access and outcomes, but are outside the scope of this study.

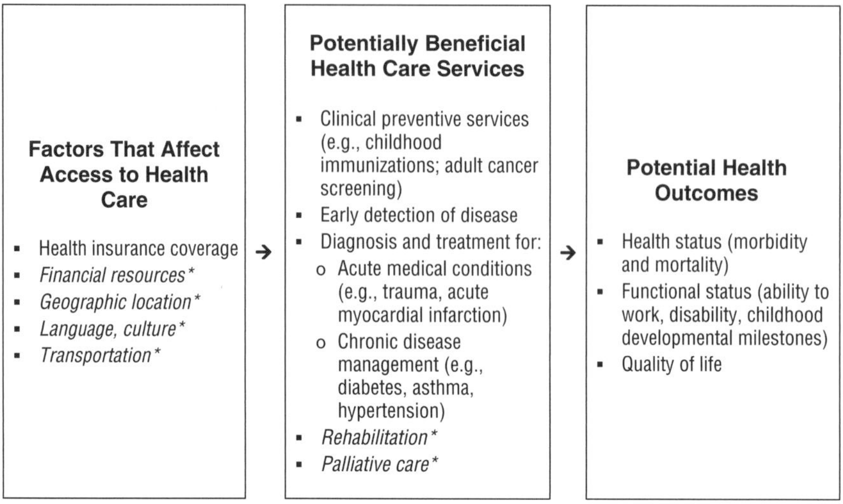

FIGURE 3-1 Conceptual framework and focus of the chapter.
*Items shown in italics are not addressed in this report.

METHOD OF THE REVIEW

As previously noted, this chapter is based on two systematic reviews of the research evidence on the consequences of uninsurance for individuals' health outcomes that were commissioned by the committee in 2008: one review of the evidence pertaining to children and adolescents (Kenney and Howell, 2008) and a second review of the evidence for adults (McWilliams, 2008). The authors of these reviews conducted comprehensive searches for evidence pertaining to the three important relationships illustrated in Figure 3-1: (1) the link between health insurance coverage and access to potentially beneficial health care services, such as clinical preventive services, early detection of disease, diagnostic services, and treatment; (2) the link between access to potentially beneficial health care services and health outcomes, such as health status, functional status, and quality of life; and (3) the overarching link between health insurance coverage and potential health outcomes.

Research Challenges in Assessing the Health
Consequences of Uninsurance

What constitutes valid research evidence on the consequences of not having health insurance? Definitions of some key concepts that are important to interpreting the research evidence on the health consequences of uninsurance are provided in Box 3-1. Conclusions about the links between health insurance and health outcomes must be drawn with caution from observational studies that compare health-related outcomes of insured and uninsured adults and use statistical techniques to adjust for differences in other predictors of health that may be related to health insurance status. Assessing the effect of uninsurance on health outcomes is a research challenge for two main reasons.

First, insured and uninsured adults may differ greatly in demographic or socioeconomic characteristics, environmental influences, clinical risk factors, health behaviors, preferences, or other predictors of health. It is virtually impossible to measure all systematic differences between these groups, some of which may be unobservable, let alone measure them all with precision. Moreover, most comparisons of insured and uninsured adults rely on previously collected data on a limited set of variables. As a result, important differences may remain after statistical adjustments that explain observed differences in health between insured and uninsured adults.

Second, not only might health insurance status affect health, but health may also affect health insurance status. Health declines, for example, lead to coverage gains through increased demand for private insurance or eligibility for public insurance, or lead to uninsurance through job loss, income reductions, or selection behaviors on the part of insurers. Thus, cross-sectional associations between health insurance status and health may be due to the effects of health on health insurance rather than the reverse.

Because of the limitations of observational comparisons, conclusions about the health consequences of uninsurance would ideally rely on experimental or quasi-experimental evidence (Levy and Meltzer, 2008). Without random assignment of insurance status, estimated effects cannot be characterized as causal with absolute certainty. The RAND Health Insurance Experiment, however, remains the only large experimental study of health insurance in which features of coverage were randomly assigned, and ethical and practical considerations make future trials of its kind unlikely. Furthermore, the RAND Health Insurance Experiment was conducted many years ago and did not include an uninsured group, thus its findings may not generalize to the current population of uninsured adults.

Given the limitations of observational studies and the dearth of experimental studies of the effects of health insurance, findings from quasi-experimental studies should be given greatest weight in formulating conclusions about the consequences of uninsurance (Levy and Meltzer, 2008). Still, the merits of observational studies should not be ignored. The results of quasi-experimental studies often cannot be generalized beyond a local or marginal group affected by a specific policy, and larger observational studies may support inferences about broader populations, particularly when

---

BOX 3-1
Key Concepts in Assessing Evidence on the
Health Consequences of Uninsurance

Endogenous variable. The dependent outcome variable in a study of cause and effect (e.g., mortality rates in studies of the impact of health insurance on mortality).

Exogenous variable. The independent explanatory variable in a study of cause and effect (e.g., health insurance coverage in a study of the effect of health insurance on mortality). The possibility that an endogenous variable, such as health insurance status, may be in fact endogenous, poses a challenge in determining cause and effect. Thus, for example, sicker people may be less likely to have health insurance because they are not working, in which case the lack of health insurance is due to poor health rather than the reverse.

Experimental study. A study in which the investigators actively intervene to test a hypothesis. In a randomized controlled trial of a drug, for example, participants are randomly assigned by the investigators to either the treatment group (which receives the drug) or the control group (which does not receive the drug). Such study designs can be used to draw firm conclusions about the effects of health insurance on health outcomes. The RAND Health Insurance study is an example, but ethical and practical considerations make future experimental studies on the effects of health insurance unlikely.

Natural experiment. A type of quasi-experimental study in which the circumstances in which different populations are exposed or not exposed to an intervention resemble those in an experimental study (in which study participants are randomly assigned to exposed and unexposed groups). Policy changes that expand eligibility for health insurance coverage to some people but leave a relatively similar group uncovered, such as the enactment of Medicare or the State

---

findings are consistent across observational and quasi-experimental analyses of similar outcomes. Observational analyses of detailed data may also allow testing of hypothesized confounders, and sensitivity analyses can be used to characterize the robustness of estimated associations. In this way, potentially causal pathways may be explored, paving the way for more definitive work.

For certain outcomes or populations, strong quasi-experimental designs may not be readily available, leaving observational evidence, albeit limited, as the sole source of information for policy makers. For example, although the research evidence on the health effects of health insurance is stronger and of higher quality than ever before, there are marked differences in the nature of the evidence for children and adults. As will be described later in the chapter, the research on children draws on strong, well-designed

Children's Health Insurance Program (SCHIP), can provide a natural experiment for assessing the effects of health insurance on health outcomes.

Observational study. A study in which investigators simply observe the course of events. Examples are cohort and cross-sectional studies. In **cohort studies**, groups with certain exposures or characteristics (e.g., no health insurance) are monitored over time to observe an outcome of interest (e.g., the quality of diabetes management over time). In **cross-sectional studies**, the prevalence of an outcome of interest (e.g., mortality among heart attack victims) is measured at a specific time or time period. Such observational studies are less definitive than experimental or quasi-experimental studies of the effects of health insurance on health outcomes.

Quasi-experimental study. A study in which empirical methods (e.g., difference-in-differences, interrupted time series, regression discontinuity, and instrumental variables methods) are applied to address the endogeneity of health insurance and health (i.e., bias from unmeasured confounding or reverse causality) by identifying the health effects of coverage changes or coverage differences that are possibly exogenous, or unrelated to health, and all observed or unobserved predictors of both coverage and health. In essence, quasi-experimental designs attempt to balance unobserved variables in studies using observational data.

Sensitivity analysis. An analysis of how "sensitive" a model is to changes to different sources of variation in the factors including in the model.

Study quality. For an individual study, study quality refers to all aspects of a study's design and execution including the extent to which bias is avoided or minimized.

SOURCES: IOM (2008); Levy and Meltzer (2008).

evaluations of children's participation in SCHIP, Medicaid, or county-based health insurance initiatives. These studies typically measure impacts on access to care and use basic statistical models to assess observational data and to control for confounding variables. Most of the research on children does not employ more sophisticated quasi-experimental techniques to balance unobserved characteristics between insured and uninsured groups in observational data. There are, however, several notable quasi-experimental studies of children that assess the health effects of coverage including asthma outcomes, timely diagnosis of serious conditions, and unnecessary hospitalizations (see later section on children's health outcomes for further details). In contrast, as this chapter will show, recent research has produced a robust quasi-experimental body of evidence on the effects of lacking insurance and gaining insurance on adult health.

Literature Search Strategy

As noted earlier, the committee commissioned systematic reviews of literature, published since 2002, on the health consequences of uninsurance for children and for adults in the United States. This section describes the search strategies for the two reviews. Box 3-2 provides the search terms used to identify the relevant literature. The searches were supplemented with known, relevant reports not identified through the electronic databases.

BOX 3-2
Literature Search Strategy

Systematic searches of the National Library of Medicine's MEDLINE and the American Economic Association's EconLit databases were conducted to identify potentially relevant studies published since 2002. Three Medical Subject Heading Terms from the National Library of Medicine's controlled vocabulary, "medically uninsured," "medical indigency," and "uncompensated care," were used to search MEDLINE. The searches in the EconLit database used keywords from a prior literature review and included "health insurance" or "payer source" in combination with the terms "asthma," "diabetes," and "obesity" for children, and "health status," "health outcomes," "mortality," "hypertension," "heart disease," "diabetes," "stroke," "cancer," "HIV," or "depression" for adults (Hadley, 2003).

Literature on Consequences for Children

The children's literature search was conducted in June 2008. It was limited to children ages 0 to 18 years. In addition to the searches described above, a supplementary MEDLINE search on children was conducted using the Medical Subject Heading term "insurance, health" and then limited further with several narrow terms, including "accidents," "adolescent," "ambulatory care," "asthma," "cancer," "dental care/dental caries," "diabetes," "emergency service, hospital," "immunization," "mental disorders," "mental health," "preventive health services," "SCHIP," "special health care needs," "wounds and injuries," and "medically uninsured." In total, the search of the children's literature generated 1,233 (MEDLINE) and 25 (Econlit) citations which were then screened for inclusion. Citations from selected author searches and bibliographies of more recent reviews were also screened.

Literature on Consequences for Adults

The adult search was conducted in August 2008. It was limited to studies that included adults ages 19 and older. In total, the search of the adult literature generated 755 (MEDLINE) and 192 (Econlit) citations which were then screened for inclusion. Citations from selected author searches and bibliographies of more recent reviews were also screened (Freeman et al., 2008; Levy and Meltzer, 2004, 2008).

Literature on the Effects of Uninsurance on Children

Studies on children were identified through systematic searches of the National Library of Medicine's MEDLINE and the American Economic Association's EconLit databases. The evidence base for establishing how and under what circumstances health insurance affects the health and functioning of children remains limited. The literature search identified many more studies examining the effects on children's access to care and service use than on their health status or functioning. Studies on children were included in this review if they estimated the effects of health insurance coverage on validated access measures (i.e., having a usual source of care, having a preventive visit or any ambulatory care visit, having unmet health needs, receiving recommended immunizations, having a usual source for dental care, having received a preventive dental visit or any dental care, and having an unmet need for dental care) or health outcomes. Ultimately, 57 studies on children were selected for inclusion in this review.

Literature on the Effects of Uninsurance on Adults

Studies on adults were similarly identified through systematic searches of the National Library of Medicine's MEDLINE database and the American Economic Association's EconLit database. A key requisite for inclusion in the review was the demonstration of a distinct contribution to the research reviewed in the IOM's previous report (IOM, 2002a). Potential contributions were considered in each of the following dimensions: (1) strength of study design and methodological rigor (e.g., quasi-experimental vs. observational design, inclusion of sensitivity analyses, handling of missing data); (2) quality of the data (e.g., longitudinal vs. cross-sectional, level of clinical detail, unique linkages); (3) importance of outcomes (e.g., validated measures of health vs. processes of care); and (4) external validity of results (e.g., findings generalizable to broader populations or previously unstudied diseases). Observational studies were excluded from the review unless they compared health outcomes for insured and uninsured adult subjects and investigated the sensitivity of results to statistical adjustments for observed demographic and socioeconomic characteristics. Ultimately, 42 studies on adults were selected for inclusion in this review.

FINDINGS

The results of the literature searches are summarized in this section. This new body of evidence on the beneficial consequences of health insurance and the harms of uninsurance is stronger than ever before. Health insurance coverage matters. Children and adults without health insurance have less access to beneficial health care services and poorer health outcomes than those who have health insurance.

Five tables summarizing the findings of recent studies on the impact of health insurance on children's access to and use of general health care services; children's access to and use of dental services, children's immunizations; children with special health care needs, and children's health status and related outcomes are presented in Appendix D. A single table that summarizes the findings of quasi-experimental studies of the effects of health insurance coverage on health outcomes for adults is presented in Appendix E.

Effects of Health Insurance on Access to Health Care Services

The new evidence on the effects of health insurance on children's and adult's access to health care services is summarized below. As detailed further below, there is solid evidence that health insurance improves children's access to beneficial preventive care and other effective health services. Children who obtain health insurance are more likely to gain access to a usual source of care or medical home, well-child care and immunizations to prevent illness and monitor developmental milestones, prescription medications, appropriate care for asthma, and basic dental services. Uninsured children with special health needs are much less likely to have access to specialists than their insured peers.

For adults, new evidence consistently and robustly demonstrates a wide range of positive effects of health insurance coverage on the receipt of beneficial preventive and other health care services. Without health insurance, adults have less access to effective clinical services including preventive care and, if sick or injured, are more likely to suffer poorer heath outcomes, greater limitations in quality of life, and premature death. When adults gain health insurance, they experience improved access to effective clinical services and better health outcomes. In sum, the best evidence that is available establishes important mediating links in the pathway from health insurance to health outcomes and suggests substantial potential for beneficial effects on adult health.

Effects on Children's Access to Health Care Services

Finding: Children benefit considerably from health insurance, as demonstrated by evaluations of enrollment in Medicaid and the State Children's Health Insurance Program (SCHIP).

Finding: When children acquire health insurance, their access to health care services, including ambulatory care, preventive health care (e.g., immunizations), prescription medications, and dental care, improves.

Finding: When children acquire health insurance, they are much less likely to experience unmet health care needs, both when they are well or when they have special health care needs.

Although children in the United States are typically perceived as in good health relative to adults, certain conditions including asthma, diabetes, and obesity have become relatively common among children. Further, there is a population of particularly vulnerable children with special health care needs that require ongoing medical attention and other health-related services. More than 10 million children in the United States meet the federal definition of children with special health care needs—i.e., children "who have or are at increased risk for a chronic physical, development, behavioral, or emotional condition and who also require health and related services of a type or amount beyond that required by children generally" (American Academy of Pediatrics, 2008). Such children with conditions such as asthma, arthritis or other joint problems, autism, blood problems, Down syndrome, mental retardation/developmental delays, depression, diabetes, heart problems, cystic fibrosis, cerebral palsy, or muscular dystrophy require health and related services of a type or amount beyond that required by children generally.

Research linking health insurance and children's access to care has flourished since the IOM's last study, particularly regarding the potential benefits of enrolling in a publicly sponsored health insurance program. New evidence from well-designed studies draws on state-level expansions of the SCHIP and Medicaid programs in 14 states and for local programs in three different California counties. The 14 states—California, Colorado, Florida, Illinois, Iowa, Kansas, Louisiana, Massachusetts, Missouri, North Carolina, New Jersey, New York, Tennessee, and Texas—account for over 60 percent of the nation's low-income children, represent all four census regions and major SCHIP program types, and vary with respect to program size and composition (Kenney, 2007).

The new evidence, discussed further below, strongly supports the finding that expansions in eligibility for Medicaid and SCHIP have produced gains in access to medical care for children targeted by the eligibility expansions, as well as the finding that positive spillover effects may arise for children who were already eligible for coverage. Well-designed evaluations of children's participation in SCHIP, Medicaid, or county-based initiatives have generated consistent and robust evidence showing that children's access to health care services improves after children enroll in a public health insurance program. Regardless of the state or locality, with health insurance, children's access to and use of preventive care (including immunizations), prescription medications, and dental care improves substantially. Importantly, these gains in children's access to health services do not seem to depend on the particular type of the public program in place or on the composition of the target population for the program. Thus, for example, similarly positive and significant effects were found in states that have different SCHIP models (e.g., Medicaid expansions vs. separate non-Medicaid programs vs. combination programs).

National studies examining the general impacts of eligibility expansions under Medicaid and SCHIP find that acquiring health coverage increases children's ambulatory care visits (Banthin and Selden, 2003; Currie et al., 2008; Davidoff et al., 2005). The study by Davidoff and colleagues also finds that eligibility expansions reduced children's unmet health needs (Davidoff et al., 2005).

Similarly, evidence from 14 state and local studies have found that acquiring public health insurance coverage increases the likelihood that children have a usual source of care and that children receive preventive or other ambulatory visits, including immunizations and dental visits, and reduces the likelihood that children experience unmet health needs (Damiano et al., 2003; Dick et al., 2004; Eisert and Gabow, 2002; Feinberg et al., 2002; Fox et al., 2003; Howell et al., 2008a,b; Kempe et al., 2005; Kenney, 2007; Kenney et al., 2007; Moreno and Hoag, 2001; Slifkin et al., 2002; Szilagyi et al., 2004; Trenholm et al., 2005).

Improvements in Children's Access to a Usual Source of Care. All but one study report significant improvements in having a usual source of care as a result of gaining public health coverage.[2] The magnitude of the impacts differs and ranges from increases of 20 to 30 percentage points or more (Howell et al., 2008b; Kenney, 2007; Kenney et al., 2007; Moreno and Hoag, 2001; Slifkin et al., 2002; Trenholm et al., 2005) to smaller increases in the likelihood of having a usual source of care (Damiano et al., 2003; Dick et al., 2004; Fox et al., 2003; Howell et al., 2008a; Szilagyi et al., 2004). Studies conducted with adolescents find that uninsured adolescents were significantly less likely to have a usual source of care and health care visits than insured adolescents and that the differences are larger than for younger children (Dick et al., 2004; Kenney, 2007; Klein et al., 2007; Probst et al., 2005; Slifkin et al., 2002). After enrolling in SCHIP, adolescents were more likely to have a range of ambulatory encounters, including preventive

---

[2] The term *significant* is used throughout the chapter to refer to statistically significant results.

visits, dental visits, and specialist visits. Kenney finds significant increases for adolescents in the likelihood of having a usual source of care after enrolling in SCHIP (Kenney, 2007).

Improvements in Children's Access to Preventive Care. Being enrolled in public coverage improves the likelihood that a child receives preventive care. The magnitude of the estimated impacts varied across the studies, though not as dramatically as the usual source of care estimates. Some studies (Fox et al., 2003; Howell et al., 2008b; Moreno and Hoag, 2001; Slifkin et al., 2002; Trenholm et al., 2005) find that coverage increases the likelihood of children's receiving a preventive visit by over 15 percentage points;[3] other studies find increases in the range of 8 to 13 percentage points (Dick et al., 2004; Eisert and Gabow, 2002; Kenney, 2007; Kenney et al., 2007; Szilagyi et al., 2004).[4] Insurance coverage also increases the likelihood that children have an ambulatory care visit (Howell et al., 2008a,b; Kenney, 2007; Kenney et al., 2007; Szilagyi et al., 2004; Trenholm et al., 2005).

Evidence on children's access to immunizations and dental visits further supports the positive relationship between health insurance and access to health care services. The majority of studies suggests a positive effect of insurance on immunization rates. Regardless of the immunization series examined, all but one of the studies finds that young uninsured children are less likely to be up-to-date on their immunizations than insured children, controlling for observed characteristics of the children (Allred et al., 2007; Dombkowski et al., 2004; Henderson et al., 2006; Joyce and Racine, 2005; Zhao et al., 2004).

Joyce and Racine controlled for selection into insurance by examining changes during the period of SCHIP implementation for all poor and near-poor children, compared to nonpoor children (Joyce and Racine, 2005). While immunization rates improved during the SCHIP implementation period for all children regardless of income, there was greater improvement for poor and near-poor children for the recently added varicella vaccine. No recent studies have shown that uninsured children have higher rates of preventable diseases, such as measles, compared to insured children. Still, the documented relationship between immunization and disease can be used to infer that children who lack timely immunizations are at greater risk of developing such diseases (Guerra, 2007).

---

[3] Moreno and Hoag examine whether preventive care visits were received on schedule.

[4] Kempe and colleagues also examine receipt of preventive care visits and report an odds ratio of 1.39 for receiving routine care associated with enrolling in public coverage (Kempe et al., 2005).

Improvements in Children's Access to Dental Care. The majority of studies on children's access to dental care showed significant improvements; with health insurance, use of dental services increased from 16 to 40 percentage points (Damiano et al., 2003; Fox et al., 2003; Howell et al., 2008a,b; Kenney, 2007; Kenney et al., 2007; Lave et al., 2002; Lewis et al., 2007; Mofidi et al., 2002; Selden and Hudson, 2006; Trenholm et al., 2005; Wang et al., 2007). These results mirror the findings on children's use of medical care, but the impact is sometimes greater for dental care access. Although the magnitude of effects varies somewhat depending on the study, the consistency of these findings across a range of studies—from local, to statewide, to national studies—increases their generalizability.

Reductions in Children's Unmet Health Needs. As just discussed, well-designed evaluations of children's participation in SCHIP, Medicaid, or county-based initiatives have generated consistent and robust evidence showing that children's access to health care services improves after children enroll in a public health insurance program. Thus, children and adolescents who gain health insurance are much less likely to have unmet health care needs than those who are uninsured.

Numerous studies conducted in recent years demonstrate that once children acquire health insurance through a public program, they are significantly less likely to have unmet health needs (Damiano et al., 2003; Dick et al., 2004; Feinberg et al., 2002; Fox et al., 2003; Howell et al., 2008b; Kenney, 2007; Kenney et al., 2007; Slifkin et al., 2002; Szilagyi et al., 2004; Trenholm et al., 2005).

Parents with children who have acquired health insurance are much less likely to report that their child has an unmet need for prescription drugs, mental health or specialty care, vision care, and preventive care. Gaining coverage was associated with 1- to 12-percentage-point declines in children's unmet need for prescription drugs (Damiano et al., 2003; Feinberg et al., 2002; Fox et al., 2003) and 10- to 14-percentage-point declines in unmet need for preventive care (Howell et al., 2008a; Szilagyi et al., 2004). After enrolling in SCHIP, adolescents experience declines in unmet needs for medical, specialist, hospital, and dental care, but not for mental and reproductive health care (Klein et al., 2007).

Uninsured children are generally at least twice as likely as children with dental insurance to have unmet need for dental care (Damiano et al., 2003; Davidoff et al., 2005; Feinberg et al., 2002; Fox et al., 2003; Howell et al., 2008a,b; Kenney, 2007; Kenney et al., 2007; Lave et al., 2002; McBroome et al., 2005; Mofidi et al., 2002; Szilagyi et al., 2004; Trenholm et al., 2005; Wang et al., 2007).

Nine studies of children with special health care needs indicate that uninsured children with special health care needs have higher unmet need

BOX 3-3
Ginny: A Girl with Special Health Care Needs Who Died
When She Lost Her Health Insurance Coverage

Ginny was born with a congenital cardiac anomaly that was repaired successfully when she was 5 years old and funded through her Medicaid insurance. She had steady follow up with her pediatric cardiologists, and as soon as she developed an arrhythmia at 11 years old, it was discovered and her regimen of anti-arrhythmic medication was titrated to perfectly control her heart's rhythm.

As the end of her Medicaid eligibility approached, Ginny scoured her small town for jobs, but none of the small businesses there would hire her. At the time of her 19th birthday, Ginny's Medicaid drug coverage stopped, and she was left without the means to buy her anti-arrhythmic medications and went without. Ginny died of a fatal arrhythmia 5 months later.

SOURCE: Garson (2007).

and lower use of critical services such as genetic counseling, mental health care, and specialist services than insured children with special health care needs (Busch and Horwitz, 2004; Davidoff et al., 2005; Dick et al., 2004; Jeffrey and Newacheck, 2006; Kenney, 2007; Mayer et al., 2004; Porterfield and McBride, 2007; Wang and Watts, 2007; Yu et al., 2006). Two studies demonstrate that uninsured children with special health care needs are six to eight times more likely to have an unmet need for health care than their insured counterparts (Mayer et al., 2004; Yu et al., 2006). For children with special health care needs, being uninsured can have disastrous consequences (Box 3-3).

Two studies have shown that following enrollment in SCHIP, children with special health care needs experienced greater reductions in unmet health needs than other children in SCHIP (Davidoff et al., 2005; Kenney, 2007). Kenney's evaluation of the effects of SCHIP in 10 states found that, after enrolling in SCHIP, children with special health care needs had significantly improved access to a wide range of health care services, including a usual source of care, preventive care, prescription medications, specialty and hospital care, and dental care (Kenney, 2007).

Effects on Adults' Access to Health Care Services

Finding: Adults benefit substantially from health insurance for preventive care when they are well and from early diagnosis and treatment when they are sick or injured.

Finding: Without health insurance, chronically ill adults are much more likely to delay or forgo needed health care and medications.

Finding: Without health insurance, adults are less likely to receive effective clinical preventive services.

Finding: The benefits of health insurance have been clearly demonstrated through recent studies of the experiences of previously uninsured adults after they acquire Medicare coverage at age 65. These studies demonstrate that when previously uninsured adults gain Medicare coverage:
- Their access to physician services and hospital care, particularly for adults with cardiovascular disease or diabetes, improves.
- Their use of effective clinical preventive services increases.

Table 3-1 shows data based on tabulations from the 2005 Medical Expenditure Panel Survey (MEPS) on the prevalence of serious medical conditions among uninsured adults in the United States (AHRQ Center for Financing Access and Cost Trends, 2008). The prevalence of chronic diseases reported by uninsured adults in the United States is high. More than 40 percent of uninsured adults ages 19 to 64 reported having one or more chronic conditions, such as asthma, hypertension, depression, diabetes, chronic obstructive pulmonary disease (COPD), cancer, or heart disease in 2005. Because uninsured adults seek health care less often than insured adults, they are often unaware of underlying health problems such as hyper-

TABLE 3-1 Prevalence of Serious Medical Conditions Among Uninsured Adults Ages 19-64, 2005

Condition	Percent with the condition
Any chronic condition	40.8
Asthma	3.4
Cancer	1.9
COPD	3.2
Depression	10.0
Diabetes	4.3
Heart disease	3.3
Hypertension	9.3
No chronic condition	59.2
Trauma-related disorders	16.5

SOURCE: AHRQ Center for Financing Access and Cost Trends (2008).

tension or hyperlipidemia (Ayanian et al., 2003). Nevertheless, uninsured adults report high rates of chronic disease (Table 3-1).

Data from the 2005 MEPS indicate that uninsured adults with chronic conditions are far less likely to use health care services than insured adults with the same chronic conditions. In 2005, as shown in Table 3-2, chronically ill adults who lacked health insurance had five to nine fewer health care visits per year than chronically ill adults who have health insurance. Uninsured adults with chronic illnesses were much more likely than their insured peers to go without any medical visits during the year—even when they were diagnosed with serious conditions such as asthma (23.4 of uninsured adults with no visits vs. 6.2 percent of insured adults), COPD (13.2 vs. 4.0 percent), depression (19.3 vs. 5.2 percent), diabetes (11.0 vs. 5.2 percent), heart disease (8.7 vs. 2.9 percent), or hypertension (12.7 vs. 5.3 percent).

Similarly, uninsured adults with asthma, cancer, COPD, diabetes, heart disease, or hypertension are at least twice as likely as their insured peers to say that they were unable to receive or had to delay receiving a needed prescription (Wilper et al., 2008).

Studies of the Effects of Health Insurance on Adults' Access to Care. Important new research has emerged since the IOM last studied the impact of uninsurance on adults in 2002 (IOM, 2002a). These include various quasi-experimental studies that have evaluated what effects gaining Medicare coverage at age 65 has on access to clinical preventive services and general health care services, including visits to physicians and hospitalizations, among adults who previously lacked health insurance or were members of groups that were more likely to be uninsured prior to age 65 (e.g., adults of lower socioeconomic status or racial and ethnic minorities).

Improved Access to Important Clinical Preventive Services for Adults. Five recent well-designed, quasi-experimental studies have estimated the effects of health insurance coverage on adults' use of important clinical preventive services (Busch and Duchovny, 2005; Card et al., 2004; Decker, 2005; McWilliams et al., 2003; Sudano and Baker, 2003).

In one of the quasi-experimental studies, Sudano and Baker used longitudinal survey data that provided detail on continuity of coverage and concluded that adults' rates of mammography, Pap testing, cholesterol testing, and influenza vaccination decreased in a stepwise fashion with increasing number of episodes of uninsurance over a 4-year period (Sudano and Baker, 2003). For women who reported 0, 1, 2, and 3 episodes of uninsurance, for example, rates of mammography screening were 76.7 percent, 62.0 percent, 53.4 percent, and 34.7 percent respectively, suggesting dose-response effects of coverage on use of recommended clinical services.

TABLE 3-2 Comparison of the Use of Health Care Services by Insured and Uninsured Adults with Serious Medical Conditions, 2005

Condition	No health care visit in past year (%)		Average number of visits in past year		Reported problems/ delays getting needed medical care (%)		Reported problems/ delays getting needed prescription (%)	
	Insured	Uninsured	Insured	Uninsured	Insured	Uninsured	Insured	Uninsured
Any chronic condition	8.1	20.0	10.4	7.1	6.2	18.7	5.2	14.3
Asthma	6.2	23.4	12.4	6.1	9.1	19.5	10.1	23.4
Cancer	3.1	3.5	17.6	8.7	8.5	14.1	7.0	15.8
COPD	4.0	13.2	12.4	5.8	8.7	23.7	6.8	20.3
Depression	5.2	19.3	15.6	10.0	10.8	24.0	9.7	18.2
Diabetes	5.2	11.0	14.4	7.6	7.1	19.3	8.9	19.8
Heart disease	2.9	8.7	14.2	8.6	9.1	20.6	8.5	18.3
Hypertension	5.3	12.7	11.6	6.9	6.8	19.4	6.9	15.9
No chronic condition	40.5	61.0	4.4	3.8	1.8	6.15	0.6	2.3
Trauma-related	6.6	21.5	12.0	7.3	7.6	18.2	5.8	10.6

NOTE: Visits include persons with one or more visits to an office-based, outpatient, or emergency services provider.
SOURCE: AHRQ Center for Financing Access and Cost Trends (2008).

In another study, Card and colleagues assessed changes in adults' use of preventive care services that were associated with gaining Medicare eligibility at age 65 (Card et al., 2004). Using a quasi-experimental approach, the researchers used age trends in adults' utilization of preventive care before age 65 to predict utilization of such care after age 65 and attributed any abrupt deviations from predicted trends occurring at age 65 to Medicare coverage. Several significant increases, ranging from 5 to 10 percentage points, in rates of influenza vaccination, cholesterol testing, mammography, or diagnosed hypertension occurred at age 65 for some groups of adults who were more likely to be uninsured before age 65 given their race, ethnicity, and educational attainment. However, the increases in the utilization of preventive care services were not consistently greater for all of these sociodemographic groups across all preventive services.

Decker, in a similarly designed analysis of a larger sample of over 250,000 women participating in the Behavioral Risk Factor Surveillance System surveys during 1991 to 2001, estimated rates of mammography more precisely and found increases at age 65 to vary significantly and more consistently across race, ethnicity, and educational attainment (Decker, 2005). The percentage of women reporting a mammogram in the prior 2 years increased by 2.6 and 4.8 percentage points among women with high school degrees and less than a high school education, respectively. Similarly, rates of mammography increased by 2.4 percentage points among white women, 4.4 percentage points among black women, and 7.5 percentage points among Hispanic women. In tests of differential effects, increases were significantly greater for women who were less educated or members of minority groups.

In another study, McWilliams and colleagues used longitudinal data from the Health and Retirement Study (HRS),[5] a nationally representative longitudinal survey of adults and their spouses over the age of 50 in the continental United States. The researchers assessed the receipt of basic clinical services before and after Medicare eligibility at age 65 for adults who were continuously uninsured, intermittently uninsured, or continuously insured from age 60 to 64 (McWilliams et al., 2003). Differences in use of cholesterol testing and mammography between continuously insured and continuously uninsured adults were significantly reduced after age 65 by 17.7 and 15.3 percentage points, respectively. Differential effects of gaining coverage on service use were positive but smaller for intermittently uninsured adults, and increases in cholesterol testing after age 65 were greatest for continuously uninsured adults with hypertension or diabetes, in whom such testing to guide cardiovascular risk reduction is particularly important.

---

[5] The HRS health status measures have been rigorously validated.

In the fifth study, Busch and Duchovny assessed the effects of state Medicaid eligibility expansions from 1995 to 2001 on Pap testing for previously uninsured mothers (Busch and Duchovny, 2005). They estimated that 29 percent of these uninsured mothers who had not been screened for cervical cancer were screened after they became eligible for Medicaid.

Improved Access to General Health Care Services for Adults. Three recent quasi-experimental analyses have examined the effects of health insurance coverage on adults' general use of health care and contribute noteworthy findings on the effects of health insurance coverage on adults' health outcomes (Card et al., 2004, 2008; Lichtenberg, 2002; McWilliams et al., 2007b). Sharing the same analytic strategy used in several analyses of preventive services, all three of the quasi-experimental studies of the effects of health insurance on the general use of care assessed the changes in health insurance coverage that occur after individuals reach age 65 due to nearly universal Medicare coverage among the U.S. elderly population.

In one of the three studies, Lichtenberg used cross-sectional data from the National Ambulatory Medical Care Surveys from 1973 to 1998 to examine annual per capita physician visits among adults (Lichtenberg, 2002). This study found an abrupt and persistent increase in use of physician visits among adults who were age 65 and older. A similar increase in hospital admissions among adults age 65 and older was also observed in data from the National Hospital Discharge Surveys during 1979 to 1992, but most of this surge in hospital admissions seemed to be due to the postponement of presumably elective admissions in the 2 years preceding Medicare eligibility.

In a second quasi-experimental study, Card and colleagues analyzed doctor visits reported in the National Health Interview Survey from 1997 to 2003 and hospital discharges from 1992 to 2002 in three states, disaggregated age profiles by sociodemographic predictors of coverage, and conducted more formal testing of trends (Card et al., 2004, 2008). Among individuals age 65 and older, the increase in routine doctor visits was especially pronounced among less educated adults and members of racial and ethnic minority groups who were more likely to be uninsured before age 65. Hospital admissions also increased sharply and persistently after age 65, but racial and ethnic differences in these increases varied by admission diagnosis and primary procedure performed.

McWilliams and colleagues, in a longitudinal analysis of the HRS from 1992 to 2004, found that near-elderly adults who were intermittently or persistently uninsured before reaching Medicare eligibility at age 65 reported significantly greater increases in doctor visits, hospital admissions, and total medical expenditures after age 65 than adults who had continuous private health insurance coverage before age 65 (McWilliams et al., 2007b). These investigators found that the differential increases in doctor visits, hospital admissions, and total medical expenditures were concentrated among adults who suffered from cardiovascular disease (hypertension, heart disease, or stroke) or diabetes—conditions for which there are many effective treatments to prevent costly complications. Moreover, previously uninsured Medicare beneficiaries with cardiovascular disease or diabetes reported relative increases in doctor visits (13 percent), hospitalizations (20 percent), and total medical expenditures (51 percent) compared with previously insured beneficiaries who were otherwise similar across observed characteristics at age 59 to 60 and had comparable generosity of coverage after age 65 (i.e., supplemental insurance and prescription drug coverage). These persistently elevated health care needs suggest that uninsured near-elderly adults with chronic conditions enter the Medicare program at age 65 with greater morbidity than they would if they had previously had health insurance.

In an observational study, Ward and Franks used longitudinal data on adults ages 21 to 64 from the 2000 to 2003 MEPS and found that total medical expenditures were higher for previously uninsured adults after they gained coverage but were not significantly different from expenditures among continuously insured adults (Ward and Franks, 2007). However, the sample of uninsured adults who experienced coverage gains was small (N = 385), and the changes in insurance status were voluntary and therefore could have been caused by changes in health.

Effects of Health Insurance on Health Outcomes

The new evidence on the effects of health insurance on a variety of health outcomes for children and adults is summarized below. Features of the key studies on children's health outcomes are summarized in Table D-5 in Appendix D; the key studies on adults' health outcomes are summarized in Table E-1, Appendix E. Although the evidence base demonstrating the link between health insurance and children's *access* to important health care services is quite strong, as discussed previously, the research on how children's *health* might benefit from gaining health insurance coverage is more limited. This is, in part, because many research studies of child health have not fully accounted for issues that are unique to children (IOM, 2004).[6] Moreover, most studies that evaluate the effects of health insurance on children cover too brief a time period (e.g., months or a year), to gauge

---

[6] In the report, *Children's Health, The Nation's Wealth: Assessing and Improving Child Health,* the IOM recommended that children's health be defined as the extent to which an individual child or groups of children are able or enabled to (1) develop and realize their potential; (2) to satisfy their needs; and (3) to develop the capacities that allow them to interact successfully with their biological, physical, and social environments (IOM, 2004).

longer term outcomes that might emerge in later childhood, adolescence, or adulthood (Forrest and Riley, 2004).

In contrast, the body of evidence on the effects of uninsurance on adults' health has strengthened considerably since 2002. Numerous studies have addressed some of the methodological shortcomings of past research. As discussed further below, 17 observational and 13 quasi-experimental rigorous analyses have reported significant findings related to health insurance and adults' health (Table 3-3) (McWilliams, 2008). The quality and

TABLE 3-3 Overview of Studies of the Impact of Health Insurance on Adults' Access to Health Care Services and Health Outcomes, 2002-2008

	Significant impact[a]		No impact or impact is not statistically significant[a]	
	Number of observational studies	Number of quasi-experimental studies	Number of observational studies	Number of quasi-experimental studies
Access to health services	2	9	1	1
Preventive services	2	5	4	1
General health services	0	4	0	0
Health outcomes (all)	17	13	2	7
General health and physical functioning	3	6	0	2
Mortality	2	2	0	2
Cardiovascular disease and diabetes	4	1	0	0
Cancer	6	0	1	2
Depression	0	1	0	0
Acute conditions[b]	2	3	1	1

NOTE: This table is based on a systematic review of research literature published between December 2001 and August 2008 on the consequences of uninsurance for adults. Altogether there were 42 studies. Several studies assessed more than one outcome or reported both significant and nonsignificant findings in separate analyses.

[a] Statistical significance is defined as $P \leq 0.05$.

[b] Acute conditions include acute myocardial infarction, congestive heart failure, COPD or asthma exacerbation, hip fracture, respiratory failure, seizure, and stroke.

SOURCE: McWilliams (2008).

consistency of the recent research findings is striking. As would be expected, health insurance is clearly most beneficial for adults who need medical attention, particularly for adults with common chronic conditions or acute conditions for which effective treatments are available. Furthermore, national studies assessing the effects of near-universal Medicare coverage after age 65 suggest that uninsured near-elderly adults who are acutely or chronically ill substantially benefit from *gaining* health insurance coverage.

Effects of Health Insurance on Children's Health Outcomes

Finding: With health insurance, children receive more timely diagnosis of serious health conditions, experience fewer avoidable hospitalizations, have improved asthma outcomes, and miss fewer days of school.

There are 13 recent studies on the health effects of health insurance coverage for children, including 5 studies that used quasi-experimental methods (Aizer, 2007; Bermudez and Baker, 2005; Cousineau et al., 2008; Currie et al., 2008; Howell et al., 2008a). These studies suggest that health insurance is beneficial for children in several ways, resulting in more timely diagnosis of serious health conditions, fewer avoidable hospitalizations, better asthma outcomes, and fewer missed school days (Aizer, 2007; Bermudez and Baker, 2005; Cousineau et al., 2008; Currie et al., 2008; Damiano et al., 2003; Fox et al., 2003; Froehlich et al., 2007; Howell and Trenholm, 2007; Howell et al., 2008a,b; Maniatis et al., 2005; Szilagyi et al., 2004, 2006).

The study by Maniatis and colleagues, for example, assessed children when first diagnosed with diabetes (Maniatis et al., 2005). They found that uninsured children were less likely to have their conditions diagnosed as early as insured children. Among the children diagnosed with diabetes, the uninsured children were more likely to present with severe and life-threatening diabetic ketoacidosis.

Three quasi-experimental studies found significant reductions in hospitalizations related to ambulatory care sensitive conditions (ACSC) for children enrolled in Medicaid or SCHIP (Aizer, 2007; Bermudez and Baker, 2005) or county-based health insurance programs (Cousineau et al., 2008). Aizer, in a quasi-experimental analysis of state hospital discharge files, Medicaid enrollment, and U.S. Census data, found that a 10-percentage-point increase in Medicaid enrollment led to about a 3-percentage-point reduction in ACSC admissions. Similarly, Szilagyi and colleagues reported improvements in asthma-related outcomes for New York children after they enrolled in SCHIP: the rate of asthma-related hospital stays for these children dropped from 11 percent to just 3 percent (Szilagyi et al., 2006). These investigators also reported significant declines in asthma-related emergency room visits among these children after they enrolled in SCHIP.

Effects of Health Insurance on Adults' Health Outcomes

Finding: Uninsured adults who acquire Medicare coverage at age 65, particularly if they have cardiovascular disease or diabetes, experience substantially improved trends in health and functional status.

Finding: Without health insurance, adults with cardiovascular disease or cardiac risk factors are less likely to be aware of their conditions, their conditions are less likely to be well controlled, and they experience worse health outcomes.

Finding: Without health insurance, adults are more likely to be diagnosed with later-stage breast, colorectal, or other cancers that are detectable by screening or by symptom assessment by a clinician. As a consequence, when uninsured adults are diagnosed with such cancers, they are more likely to die or suffer poorer outcomes.

Finding: Without health insurance, adults with serious conditions, such as cardiovascular disease or trauma, have higher mortality.

Finding: When previously uninsured adults gain Medicare coverage:
- They experience substantially improved trends in health and functional status.
- Their risk of death when hospitalized for serious conditions declines.

Improved Health and Physical Functioning of Adults. Several quasi-experimental studies have advanced our understanding of the effects of health insurance coverage on adults' overall health and physical functioning. Many of these studies were similar in their analytic approach, recognizing near-universal Medicare coverage after age 65 as a source of variation in insurance status that allows effects on health to be estimated more rigorously.

Card and colleagues, in a quasi-experimental analysis of cross-sectional data from the National Health Interview Survey during 1992 to 2001, found significant improvements in self-reported general health among adults in sociodemographic groups who experienced the largest gains in insurance coverage at age 65 (Card et al., 2004). The gap between more educated white adults and less educated black and Hispanic adults was narrowed after age 65 by a 12 percent relative reduction. In sensitivity analyses, Card and colleagues found no evidence for discontinuities in employment status, marital status, geographic location, or family income that might explain discontinuities in general health, suggesting these reduced disparities were due to increases in coverage after age 65 (Card et al., 2004).

In a related study, Decker and Remler used Canadian adults as international controls (Decker and Remler, 2004). Age profiles of general health status were constructed from National Health Interview Survey data for U.S. adults and from the National Population Health Survey for Canadian adults ages 55 to 74 and compared by income, country, and age (65 or older vs. under 65) in a quasi-experimental approach. Among the near-elderly age group, low-income adults in the United States were 15 percentage points more likely than high-income adults to be in fair or poor health, compared to an 8 percent absolute difference between low- and high-income adults in Canada. Among adults age 65 or older, this 7 percent international difference was reduced to 3 percent, suggesting that near-universal Medicare coverage reduced the excess risk of fair or poor health among low-income adults by 4 percent—or equivalently, that not having insurance explained more than half of the health disparity between low-income and high-income nonelderly adults in the United States.

In these studies of cross-sectional data, effects of Medicare coverage on other measures of health were not assessed, and uninsured adults, particularly those with specific conditions who might benefit most from coverage, could not be longitudinally followed as they became eligible for Medicare. Several subsequent studies used longitudinal data from the HRS to assess the effects of gaining Medicare coverage on the health of previously uninsured adults.

In an observational study, Baker and colleagues found that adults without health insurance for 1 to 2 years prior to age 65 were more likely to report a major decline in general health or a new functional limitation in their first interview after age 65 (Baker et al., 2006a). In subsequent interviews, after at least 2 years of Medicare eligibility, previously uninsured adults no longer reported significantly higher rates of these health declines.

In a quasi-experimental study, Polsky and colleagues used more recent data from the HRS to follow participants longer after age 65 and compared trajectories in self-reported general health between insured and uninsured near-elderly adults before and after age eligibility for Medicare (Polsky et al., 2006). Health declines became less frequent after age 65 for previously uninsured adults, such that the proportion of these adults reporting excellent or very good health after age 65 was nearly 8 percent higher than expected based on their trajectory before age 65. However, previously insured adults also reported a significant improvement in their health trajectory after age 65. This change in trajectory was slightly smaller, suggesting a net positive health effect for previously uninsured adults attributable to

Medicare coverage, but the differential effect was not significant. No other measures of health were included in this analysis.

Using the same data and similar quasi-experimental methods, McWilliams and colleagues compared changes in health trends reported by previously insured and uninsured adults after age 65 for a more comprehensive set of six self-reported general, physical, and mental health measures and a summary measure of these component items (McWilliams et al., 2007a). In comparison with adults who were continuously insured, adults who were intermittently or persistently uninsured from age 55 to age 64 reported significantly improved health trends after age 65 for the summary health measure and several component measures. Analyses of agility and mobility scores also suggested that gaining Medicare coverage improved trends in physical functioning for previously uninsured adults.

Two recent studies employed another quasi-experimental approach (instrumental variables methods) to estimate the effects of private health insurance on self-reported general health and physical functioning for near-elderly adults using data from the HRS (Dor et al., 2006; Hadley and Waidmann, 2006). Relative to no insurance coverage, both studies found statistically significant and substantial effects of private coverage on health that were much larger than those obtained from observational studies using more basic statistical models. In a third study that used instrumental variables techniques, Pauly analyzed the 1996 MEPS to assess the effects of health insurance coverage on medical expenditures, utilization, access to care, and general health status among nonpoor young women (Pauly, 2005). Although results were not statistically significant for the health status outcome, effects on expenditures, utilization, and access to care were significant and larger in magnitude than predicted by standard statistical comparisons commonly performed in observational studies.

Worse Outcomes for Adults with Serious Chronic and Acute Conditions. Uninsurance has profound health implications for the estimated 40 percent of uninsured adults age 19 to 64 who have chronic disease (Table 3-1). As discussed below, new studies provide compelling evidence demonstrating that health insurance is the most beneficial for adults who have chronic conditions such as hypertension, diabetes, and cancer, as well as serious injury, heart attack, stroke, and other acute conditions for which effective treatments are available (Table 3-4). Uninsured adults are more likely than insured adults to be unaware that they have an asymptomatic chronic condition, such as high blood pressure or early-stage cancer. Yet such underlying disease is often responsive to timely preventive and diagnostic services and appropriate management and treatment.

TABLE 3-4 Recent Research Findings on the Harmful Effects of Uninsurance for Adults with Selected Acute Conditions and Chronic Disease

Condition	Findings
Acute ischemic stroke	Uninsured adults are more likely than insured adults to suffer extremely poor outcomes, including neurological impairment, intracerebral hemorrhage, and death
Cancer	Uninsured adults are more likely than insured adults to be diagnosed at an advanced stage of cancer, especially if effective treatments are available and the condition can be detected early by screening (e.g., breast or colorectal cancer) or by clinical assessment of symptoms (e.g., melanoma, bladder cancer)
Congestive heart failure	Uninsured adults are at greater risk of death than insured adults
Diabetes	Uninsured adults have significantly worse glycemic control than insured adults
Heart attack	Uninsured adults are more likely than insured adults to die after heart attack
Hospital inpatients with serious acute conditions	Uninsured adults are at greater risk than insured adults of higher mortality in hospital and for at least 2 years after admission
Hypertension	Uninsured adults are less likely than insured adults to be aware of hypertension and, if hypertensive, more likely to have inadequate blood pressure control
Serious injury or trauma	After an unintentional injury, uninsured adults are less likely than insured adults to fully recover and more likely to report subsequent declines in health status. Uninsured adults in severe automobile accidents have a substantially higher mortality rate

SOURCES: Ayanian et al. (2003); Card et al. (2007); Doyle (2005); Fowler-Brown et al. (2007); Halpern et al. (2008); McWilliams (2008); Shen and Washington (2007); Volpp et al. (2005); Ward et al. (2008).

Delayed Diagnosis and Worse Health Outcomes for Adults with Chronic Conditions Such as Cardiovascular Disease or Diabetes. Ayanian and colleagues analyzed findings from the National Health and Nutrition Examination Survey (NHANES) III, a nationally representative assessment of the health and nutrition of 10,946 insured and uninsured adults ages 25 to 64 (Ayanian et al., 2003). They found that uninsured adults were much more likely than insured adults to have undiagnosed hypertension (high blood pressure) and hypercholesterolemia (high cholesterol), largely because of their limited access to health care services. A later analysis of NHANES III data analyzed outcomes for adults with diagnosed and treated hypertension (Duru et al., 2007). This study found that in comparison with insured adults, uninsured adults had substantially poorer blood pressure control even when treated.

The health implications of underdiagnosed and poorly managed hypertension can be profound. An observational analysis of longitudinal data from the Atherosclerosis Risk in Communities Study compared cardiovascular outcomes among insured and uninsured adults ages 45 to 64 in four U.S. communities from 1987 to 2000 (Fowler-Brown et al., 2007). Uninsured adults were more likely to be unaware of clinically determined hypertension, diabetes, and hypercholesterolemia, and those with hypertension were more likely to have inadequate blood pressure control—echoing the NHANES results described above. Uninsured adults had higher adjusted risks of stroke and death by 65 percent and 26 percent, respectively.

Uninsured adults who are hospitalized for acute ischemic stroke are far more likely than privately insured adults to suffer extremely poor outcomes. A recent observational analysis of the Nationwide Inpatient Sample found that among patients hospitalized for acute ischemic stroke, uninsured patients had higher levels of neurological impairment, a 24 percent higher mortality risk, and among those with intracerebral hemorrhage, 56 percent higher mortality risk (Shen and Washington, 2007). Because there are few therapeutic interventions for acute stroke, particularly acute intracerebral hemorrhage, these findings suggest that uninsured adults suffer more severe strokes because of poorer management of cardiovascular risk factors, such as hypertension (high blood pressure) and hypercholesterolemia (high cholesterol), and fewer preventive carotid endarterectomies when indicated for asymptomatic or symptomatic carotid stenoses.

Quasi-experimental research by McWilliams and colleagues has shown that previously uninsured adults report substantial improvements in cardiovascular health after turning age 65 and acquiring Medicare coverage (McWilliams et al., 2007a). The researchers analyzed data from the HRS during 1992 to 2004. Study participants were asked to rate their general health status, changes in general health, mobility, agility, pain, and symptoms of depression. The study compared the health status reports of previously insured and uninsured adults with cardiovascular disease or diabetes, finding that, by age 70, the disparities between the two groups had dropped by 50 percent. The previously uninsured adults reported significantly improved general, physical, and mental health as well as mobility and agility. Although these outcomes were not disease-specific, self-reported physical functioning correlates strongly with clinical complications of cardiovascular disease such as angina, dyspnea, neuropathy, visual impairment, myocardial infarction, and stroke (Guralnik et al., 1993; McHorney et al., 1993). Furthermore, previously uninsured adults also reported better outcomes related to myocardial infarctions, angina that limited activities, and hospitalization for congestive heart failure.

In addition, glycemic control was compared in two groups of diabetic adults: those under age 65 and those age 65 or older (with Medicare) (McWilliams et al., 2007a). Uninsured adults in the younger age group had significantly worse glycemic control compared to their insured counterparts. At age 65 or older, however, the outcomes were similar for the previously insured and previously uninsured adults. Finally, differential increases in doctor visits and hospital admissions after age 65 were also concentrated among adults with cardiovascular disease or diabetes (McWilliams et al., 2007b).

Thus there appear to be several ways in which acquiring Medicare coverage improves the health of uninsured adults with chronic disease, among them (1) improving access to prescription medications; (2) improving diabetes management, especially glycemic control; and (3) increasing access to outpatient and hospital care for adults with cardiovascular disease or diabetes. Access to prescription drugs appears to be especially important—previously uninsured adults who gained prescription drug coverage experienced the greatest health improvement. In sum, this body of observational and quasi-experimental research suggests that gaining health insurance coverage improves the health of previously uninsured adults with cardiovascular disease or diabetes, as improved access to care, greater use of effective procedures and medications, and better management of these conditions alleviates symptoms, maintains functioning, and prevents or postpones complications.

Delayed Diagnosis and Worse Health Outcomes for Adults with Cancer. A large body of observational research completed before 2002 demonstrated that uninsured adults with cancer are diagnosed at more advanced stages of disease, have poorer outcomes, and die sooner, even after adjusting for stage of disease (Box 3-4) (IOM, 2002a). These findings suggest deficits in screening and diagnostic services, as well as in curative and palliative procedures and therapies for uninsured adults with prevalent cancers, among them breast, cervical, colorectal, and prostate cancer and melanoma.

Two recent observational studies used data from the U.S. National Cancer Database to generalize these associations to the national population, as most prior studies of insurance coverage and cancer outcomes relied on state or regional cancer registries (Halpern et al., 2008; Ward et al., 2008). One study found that uninsured patients with cancers diagnosed between 1998 and 2004 were more likely than privately insured patients to be diagnosed at advanced stages of disease, particularly those with cancers that can be detected early by screening (e.g., breast or colorectal cancer)

BOX 3-4
Sheila: Unable to Obtain Breast Cancer Treatment
After She Lost Her Health Insurance

Sheila had been diagnosed with breast cancer and initially treated while her husband still received health insurance. But for 2 years after her mastectomy, she went without follow-up care because her husband lost his job and, as a result, she lost her insurance.

When she was finally seen by an oncologist, she learned that the tumor had recurred and metastasized widely. A new chemotherapeutic regimen was developed for her, but finding medical settings where she could receive it was difficult because she could not pay for the treatment, much less the other concomitant medical costs.

The emergency department (ED) was the only place Sheila could receive treatment without being turned away, though the cancer treatment was intermittent and haphazard at best. She would describe symptoms to get herself admitted to the hospital from the ED, at which point an oncologist would provide her treatment as long as she could stay. On her last trip to the ED, Sheila died of complications of her cancer.

SOURCE: Winokur (2007).

---

or by symptom assessment (e.g., melanoma or bladder cancer) (Halpern et al., 2008). In contrast, no significant differences in stage at diagnosis were found between insured and uninsured adults with cancers that typically become clinically apparent only at late stages and for which there are no effective screening tests (e.g., ovarian or pancreatic cancer).

Another study found that after adjusting for cancer stage, 5-year survival rates for uninsured adults were significantly lower than for privately insured adults diagnosed with breast or colorectal cancer—two prevalent cancers for which there are not only effective screening tests, but also treatments demonstrated to improve survival (Ward et al., 2008). Similar associations between insurance status, stage at diagnosis, and survival have also been demonstrated for laryngeal and oropharyngeal cancer in several recent observational studies using these data (Chen and Halpern, 2007; Chen et al., 2007a,b).

Increased Risk of Death Among Adults Hospitalized with Serious Conditions. Since 2002, three quasi-experimental studies have more rigorously assessed the effects of insurance coverage on mortality among adults with a variety of acute conditions, such as acute myocardial infarction, COPD or asthma exacerbation, hip fracture, respiratory failure, severe trauma, and stroke (Card et al., 2007; Doyle, 2005; Volpp et al., 2003).

Volpp and colleagues assessed mortality rates for insured and uninsured patients hospitalized for acute myocardial infarction in New Jersey before and after state market reforms in 1994 reduced subsidies for hospital care for the uninsured and changed the hospital payment system to price competition from one in which reimbursement was based on costs (Volpp et al., 2003). The research team performed difference-in-differences analyses of New Jersey hospital discharge data, in which discharge data from New York and the Nationwide Inpatient Sample were used to control for secular trends. While not directly addressing the effects of losing or gaining health insurance, this study sheds light on what happens to uninsured patients hospitalized with cardiovascular disease when changes in reimbursement policy restrict hospitals' ability to recoup the costs of providing care to uninsured adults.

Volpp and his colleagues found no significant changes in mortality from acute myocardial infarction for insured patients in New Jersey in comparison to patients in New York or the nation prior to 1994. In contrast, the absolute mortality rate increased differentially after the reform by 3.7 percent to 5.2 percent for uninsured patients in New Jersey compared to uninsured patients in New York, representing a 41 percent to 57 percent relative increase over their baseline death rate of 9.1 percent before the reform. Concurrent relative decreases in rates of cardiac procedures were also observed for these uninsured patients. These findings provide strong evidence that lack of health insurance coverage exposes uninsured patients with acute myocardial infarction to poorer quality of care and higher mortality risks when providers are reimbursed less for uncompensated care or are unable to use profits from insured patients to cover the costs.

In a similarly designed quasi-experimental analysis of discharge data in New York and New Jersey, Volpp and colleagues found relative increases in mortality for uninsured New Jersey patients admitted for congestive heart failure and stroke when compared to uninsured New York patients with these conditions (Volpp et al., 2005). On the other hand, they found mortality trends during the 1990 to 1996 period to be similar in New Jersey and New York for hospitalized patients with hip fracture, gastrointestinal bleeding, pulmonary embolism, or pneumonia, regardless of the patients' insurance status.

Card and colleagues, in another quasi-experimental study of state discharge data, assessed the effects of near-universal Medicare coverage after age 65 on mortality among acutely ill patients in California who were hospitalized between 1992 and 2002 (Card et al., 2007). To avoid a nonrepresentative sample of uninsured adults under age 65, the analysis focused on serious acute conditions or acute exacerbations of chronic conditions, including acute myocardial infarction, stroke, respiratory failure, COPD or asthma exacerbation, hip fracture, and seizure. A quasi-experimental analysis of mortality rates identified an abrupt decrease of 1 percentage point in 7-day mortality at age 65, suggesting that Medicare coverage reduced the overall death rate for these acutely ill patients by 20 percent. The mortality effect persisted for at least 2 years after admission, suggesting a lasting impact of increased use of beneficial procedures and medications. The decline in mortality was too large to be explained by changes in cross-sectional rates of uninsurance from age 64 to 65, suggesting that near-elderly adults who have limited public or private coverage may also benefit from Medicare coverage.

Doyle conducted an observational study of adults injured in severe automobile accidents in Wisconsin (Doyle, 2005). By focusing on seriously injured drivers who were unable to participate in their initial treatment decisions, this analysis successfully addressed any differences in care-seeking behaviors between insured and uninsured adults that might bias the findings. The study found that, compared to privately insured patients, the uninsured crash victims received 20 percent less care (i.e., especially more costly procedures and services) and had a substantially higher mortality rate—an increase of 1.5 percentage points above the mean rate of 3.8 percent. The study controlled for an array of potentially confounding factors and included sensitivity analyses to test the robustness of the results.

These studies of hospitalized patients suggest that health insurance coverage may not only affect patients' demand for health care services, but also provider behaviors in delivering care. Therefore, coverage expansion may not only improve outcomes for acutely ill patients by reducing delays before needed care, but also by allowing providers to offer effective but costly procedures and treatments at more equitable rates.

In another observational study, Hadley assessed insured and uninsured adults medical care and health status after unintentional injuries or newly diagnosed chronic conditions (Hadley, 2007). Using data from MEPS during 1997 to 2004, he found that, compared with insured adults, the uninsured adults received significantly fewer health care services, were less likely to fully recover, and more likely to report subsequent declines in health status.

Higher Mortality Rates Overall. Prior to 2002, two observational studies provided evidence that uninsured adults die at younger ages than their privately insured counterparts (IOM, 2002a). Of these two studies, the analysis that adjusted for more demographic, socioeconomic, and health characteristics estimated that the relative risk of death over 13 to 17 years was 25 percent greater for adults who were uninsured at baseline than for adults who were privately insured (Franks et al., 1993). Two subsequent observational analyses of data from the HRS estimated this increased relative risk to be 35 percent to 43 percent for uninsured near-elderly adults after controlling for even more predictors of mortality (Baker et al., 2006a; McWilliams et al., 2004). The association between uninsurance at baseline and subsequently higher mortality risk was particularly strong among near-elderly adults who were white, had low incomes, or had diabetes, hypertension, or heart disease (McWilliams et al., 2004). A sensitivity analysis demonstrated that the explanatory effect of an unmeasured predictor would have to be greater than the impact of smoking on mortality differences between insured and uninsured adults in the study for the increased risk among the uninsured to lose statistical significance. Another related study also found lack of health insurance was associated with major health declines, but not an increased risk of death within 2 years, suggesting that premature death is likely to be a long-term rather than short-term consequence of uninsurance among near-elderly adults (Baker et al., 2006b).

Because mortality generally represents a longer-term outcome for all but the severely or acutely ill, quasi-experimental analyses designed to identify abrupt discontinuities in mortality rates or even linear trends in mortality may not be suitable for estimating the effects of health insurance on mortality in the general population. Lichtenberg used life tables produced by the Social Security Administration and found a dramatic drop in the growth rate in annual probabilities of death for adults beginning at age 65 (Lichtenberg, 2002). However, in a subsequent analysis of National Center for Health Statistics Multiple Cause of Death files, Card and colleagues found no evidence of a deceleration in mortality rates at age 65 (Card et al., 2004). Similar assessments of the introduction of Medicare in 1965 found no discernable impact on mortality for beneficiaries (Card et al., 2004; Finkelstein and McKnight, 2005), although many subsequent medical advances have improved the effectiveness of health care for elderly adults in the United States.

Because of the often delayed effects of health services on survival, these null findings from some types of quasi-experimental studies should be interpreted with caution and are not necessarily inconsistent with positive findings from the observational comparisons described above. Indeed, in an instrumental variables analysis of longitudinal data, Hadley and Waidmann estimated that with universal health coverage, the absolute death rate for nonelderly adults could decrease from 6.7 percent to 3.9 percent (Hadley and Waidmann, 2006).

CONCLUSION

Important new research has emerged since the IOM last studied the question of what is known about the health consequences of health insurance for children and adults in 2002 (IOM, 2002a,b). These new findings convincingly suggest substantial health benefits of health insurance cover-

BOX 3-5
Summary of the Evidence on the Health Effects
of Uninsurance for Children and Adults

Children benefit considerably from health insurance, as demonstrated by recent evaluations of enrollment in Medicaid and the SCHIP program:

- When previously uninsured children acquire insurance, their access to health care services, including ambulatory care, preventive health care (e.g., immunizations), prescription medications, and dental care improves.
- When previously uninsured children who are well or have special health needs acquire insurance, they are less likely to experience unmet health care needs. Uninsured children with special health care needs are much more likely to have an unmet health need than their counterparts with insurance.
- When previously uninsured children acquire insurance, they receive more timely diagnosis of serious health conditions, experience fewer avoidable hospitalizations, have improved asthma outcomes, and miss fewer days of school.

Adults benefit substantially from health insurance for preventive care when they are well and for early diagnosis and treatment when they are sick or injured:

- Without health insurance, men and women are less likely to receive effective clinical preventive services.
- Without health insurance, chronically ill adults are much more likely to delay or forgo needed health care and medications.
- Without health insurance, adults with cardiovascular disease or cardiac risk factors are less likely to be aware of their conditions, their conditions are less likely to be well controlled, and they experience worse health outcomes.
- Without health insurance, adults are more likely to be diagnosed with later-stage breast, colorectal, or other cancers that are detectable by screening or symptom assessment by a clinician. As a consequence, when uninsured adults are diagnosed with such cancers, they are more likely to die or suffer poorer health outcomes.
- Without health insurance, adults with serious conditions, such as cardiovascular disease or trauma, have higher mortality.
- The benefits of health insurance have been clearly demonstrated through recent studies of the experiences of previously uninsured adults after they acquire Medicare coverage at age 65. These studies demonstrate when previously uninsured adults gain Medicare coverage:
  o Their access to physician services and hospital care, particularly for adults with cardiovascular disease or diabetes, improves.
  o Their use of effective clinical preventive services increases.
  o They experience substantially improved trends in health and functional status.
  o Their risk of death when hospitalized for serious conditions declines.

age. Important insights into how children benefit when they acquire health insurance are provided by well-designed evaluations of enrollment in Medicaid and the SCHIP program. And compelling findings on how adults are harmed by the lack of health insurance are available from new longitudinal analyses of previously uninsured adults after they acquire Medicare coverage at age 65 and other research.

The findings from the research described in this chapter are summarized in Box 3-5. With health insurance, it is clear that children are more likely to gain access to a usual source of care or medical home, well-child care and immunizations to prevent future illness and monitor developmental milestones, prescription medications, appropriate care for asthma, and basic dental services. With health insurance, serious childhood health problems are more likely to be identified early and children with special health care needs are more likely to have access to specialists. With health insurance, children have fewer avoidable hospitalization, improved asthma outcomes, and fewer missed days of school.

Without health insurance, several deleterious patterns emerge for adults. Men and women are much less likely to receive clinical preventive services that have the potential to reduce unnecessary morbidity and premature death. Chronically ill adults delay or forgo visits with physicians and clinically effective therapies, including prescription medications. Adults are more likely to be diagnosed with later-stage cancers that are detectable by screening or by contact with a clinician who can assess worrisome symptoms. Without health insurance, adults are more likely to die from trauma or other serious acute conditions, such as heart attacks or strokes. Adults with cancer, cardiovascular disease (including hypertension, coronary heart disease, and congestive heart failure), stroke, respiratory failure, COPD or asthma exacerbation, hip fracture, seizures, and serious injury are more likely to suffer poorer heath outcomes, greater limitations in quality of life, and premature death. New evidence demonstrates that gaining health insurance ameliorates many of these deleterious effects, particularly for adults who are acutely or chronically ill.

In sum, despite the availability of some safety net services, there is a chasm between the health care needs of people *without* health insurance and access to effective health care services. This gap results in needless illness, suffering, and even death. Health insurance coverage in the United States is integral to personal well-being and health.

REFERENCES

AHRQ Center for Financing Access and Cost Trends. 2008 (unpublished). *Tabulations from the 2005 Medical Expenditure Panel Survey (commissioned by the IOM Committee on Health Insurance Status and Its Consequences).*

Aizer, A. 2007. Public health insurance, program take-up, and child health. *The Review of Economics and Statistics* 89(3):400-415.

Allred, N. J., K. G. Wooten, and Y. Kong. 2007. The association of health insurance and continuous primary care in the medical home on vaccination coverage for 19- to 35-month-old children. *Pediatrics* 119(Suppl 1):S4-S11.

American Academy of Pediatrics. 2008. *Definition of children with special health care needs (CSHCN)*, http://www.medicalhomeinfo.org/about/def_cshcn.html (accessed January 5, 2009).

Ayanian, J. Z., A. M. Zaslavsky, J. S. Weissman, E. C. Schneider, and J. A. Ginsburg. 2003. Undiagnosed hypertension and hypercholesterolemia among uninsured and insured adults in the Third National Health and Nutrition Examination Survey. *American Journal of Public Health* 93:2051-2054.

Baker, D. W., J. Feinglass, R. Durazo-Arvizu, W. P. Witt, J. J. Sudano, and J. A. Thompson. 2006a. Changes in health for the uninsured after reaching age-eligibility for Medicare. *Journal of General Internal Medicine* 21:1144-1149.

Baker, D. W., J. J. Sudano, R. Durazo-Arvizu, J. Feinglass, W. P. Witt, and J. Thompson. 2006b. Health insurance coverage and the risk of decline in overall health and death among the near elderly, 1992-2002. *Medical Care* 44:277-282.

Banthin, J., and T. Selden. 2003. The ABCs of children's health care: How the Medicaid expansions affected access, burdens, and coverage between 1987 and 1996. *INQUIRY* 40(2):133-145

Bermudez, D., and L. Baker. 2005. The relationship between SCHIP enrollment and hospitalizations for ambulatory care sensitive conditions in California. *Journal of Health Care for the Poor & Underserved* 16(1):96-110.

Busch, S. H., and N. Duchovny. 2005. Family coverage expansions: Impact on insurance coverage and health care utilization of parents. *Journal of Health Economics* 24(5):876-890.

Busch, S. H., and S. M. Horwitz. 2004. Access to mental health services: Are uninsured children falling behind? *Mental Health Services Research* 6(2):109-116.

Card, D., C. Dobkin, and N. Maestas. 2004. *The impact of nearly universal insurance coverage on health care utilization and health: Evidence from Medicare.* Cambridge, MA: National Bureau of Economic Research.

———. 2007. *Does Medicare save lives?* Cambridge, MA: National Bureau of Economic Research.

———. 2008. The impact of nearly universal insurance coverage on health care utilization: Evidence from Medicare. *American Economic Review* 98(5):2242-2258.

Chen, A. Y., and M. Halpern. 2007. Factors predictive of survival in advanced laryngeal cancer. *Archives of Otolaryngology—Head & Neck Surgery* 133:1270-1276.

Chen, A. Y., N. M. Schrag, M. Halpern, A. Stewart, and E. M. Ward. 2007a. Health insurance and stage at diagnosis of laryngeal cancer: Does insurance type predict stage at diagnosis? *Archives of Otolaryngology—Head & Neck Surgery* 133:784-790.

Chen, A. Y., N. M. Schrag, M. T. Halpern, and E. M. Ward. 2007b. The impact of health insurance status on stage at diagnosis of oropharyngeal cancer. *Cancer* 110:395-402.

Cousineau, M. R., G. D. Stevens, and T. A. Pickering. 2008. Preventable hospitalizations among children in California counties after child health insurance expansion initiatives. *Medical Care* 46(2):142-147.

Currie, J., S. Decker, and W. Lin. 2008. Has public health insurance for older children reduced disparities in access to care and health outcomes? *Journal of Health Economics* 27(6):1567-1581.

Damiano, P., J. Willard, E. Momany, and J. Chowdhury. 2003. The impact of the Iowa S-SCHIP program on access, health status, and family environment. *Ambulatory Pediatrics* 3:263-269.

Davidoff, A., G. Kenney, and L. Dubay. 2005. Effects of the State Children's Health Insurance Program expansions on children with chronic health conditions. *Pediatrics* 116(1): e34-e42.

Decker, S. L. 2005. Medicare and the health of women with breast cancer. *Journal of Human Resources* 40:948-968.

Decker, S. L., and D. K. Remler. 2004. How much might universal health insurance reduce socioeconomic disparities in health?: A comparison of the US and Canada. *Applied Health Economics and Health Policy* 3:205-216.

Dick, A. W., C. Brach, R. A. Allison, E. Shenkman, L. P. Shone, P. G. Szilagyi, J. D. Klein, and E. M. Lewit. 2004. SCHIP's impact in three states: How do the most vulnerable children fare? *Health Affairs* 23(5):63-75.

Dombkowski, K. J., P. M. Lantz, and G. L. Freed. 2004. Role of health insurance and a usual source of medical care in age-appropriate vaccination. *American Journal of Public Health* 94(6):960-966.

Dor, A., J. Sudano, and D. W. Baker. 2006. The effect of private insurance on the health of older, working age adults: Evidence from the Health and Retirement Study. *Health Services Research* 41:759-787.

Doyle, J. J. 2005. Health insurance, treatment and outcomes: Using auto accidents as health shocks. *Review of Economics and Statistics* 87:256-270.

Duru, O. K., R. B. Vargas, D. Kermah, D. Pan, and K. C. Norris. 2007. Health insurance status and hypertension monitoring and control in the United States. *American Journal of Hypertension* 20:348-353.

Eisert, S., and P. Gabow. 2002. Effect of Child Health Insurance Plan enrollment on the utilization of health care services by children using a public safety net system. *Pediatrics* 110(5):940-945.

Feinberg, E., K. Swartz, A. Zaslavsky, J. Gardner, and D. K. Walker. 2002. Family income and the impact of a Children's Health Insurance Program on reported need for health services and unmet health need. *Pediatrics* 109(2):E29.

Finkelstein, A., and R. McKnight. 2005. *What did Medicare do (and was it worth it)?* Cambridge, MA: National Bureau of Economic Research.

Fisher, E. S., D. E. Wennberg, T. A. Stukel, D. J. Gottlieb, F. L. Lucas, and E. L. Pinder. 2003. The implications of regional variations in Medicare spending. Part 1: The content, quality, and accessibility of care. *Annals of Internal Medicine* 138(4):273-287.

Forrest, C. B., and A. W. Riley. 2004. Childhood origins of adult health: A basis for life-course health policy. *Health Affairs* 23(5):155-164.

Fowler-Brown, A., G. Corbie-Smith, J. Garrett, and N. Lurie. 2007. Risk of cardiovascular events and death—does insurance matter? *Journal of General Internal Medicine* 22:502-507.

Fox, M., J. Moore, R. Davis, and R. Heintzelman. 2003. Changes in reported health status and unmet need for children enrolling in the Kansas Children's Health Insurance Program. *American Journal of Public Health* 93(4):579-582.

Franks, P., C. M. Clancy, and M. R. Gold. 1993. Health insurance and mortality. Evidence from a national cohort. *JAMA* 270:737-741.

Freeman, J. D., S. Kadiyala, J. F. Bell, and D. P. Martin. 2008. The causal effect of health insurance on utilization and outcomes in adults: A systematic review of US studies. *Medical Care* 46(10):1023-1032.

Froehlich, T. E., B. P. Lanphear, J. N. Epstein, W. J. Barbaresi, S. K. Katusic, and R. S. Kahn. 2007. Prevalence, recognition, and treatment of attention-deficit/hyperactivity disorder in a national sample of US children. *Archives of Pediatrics & Adolescent Medicine* 161(9):857-864.

Fuchs, V. R. 2004. Perspective: More variation in use of case, more flat-of-the-curve medicine. *Health Affairs* 104.

Garson, A., Jr. 2007. Heart of the uninsured. *Health Affairs* 26(1):227-231.

Guerra, F. 2007. Delays in immunization have potentially serious health consequences. *Pediatric Drugs* 9(3):143-148.

Guralnik, J. M., A. Z. LaCroix, R. D. Abbott, L. F. Berkman, S. Satterfield, D. A. Evans, and R. B. Wallace. 1993. Maintaining mobility in late life. I. Demographic characteristics and chronic conditions. *American Journal of Epidemiology* 137:845-857.

Hadley, J. 2003. Sicker and poorer—the consequences of being uninsured: A review of the research on the relationship between health insurance, medical care use, health, work, and income. *Medical Care Research and Review* 60(2 Suppl):3S-75S.

———. 2007. Insurance coverage, medical care use, and short-term health changes following an unintentional injury or the onset of a chronic condition. *JAMA* 297:1073-1084.

Hadley, J., and T. Waidmann. 2006. Health insurance and health at age 65: Implications for medical care spending on new Medicare beneficiaries. *Health Services Research* 41:429-451.

Halpern, M. T., E. M. Ward, A. L. Pavluck, N. M. Schrag, J. Bian, and A. Y. Chen. 2008. Association of insurance status and ethnicity with cancer stage at diagnosis for 12 cancer sites: A retrospective analysis. *Lancet Oncology* 9:222-231.

Henderson, J. W., S. A. Arbor, S. L. Broich, J. M. Peterson, and J. E. Hutchinson. 2006. Immunization initiation among infants in the Oregon Health Plan. *American Journal of Public Health* 96(5):800-802.

Homer, C., and L. A. Simpson. 2007. Childhood obesity: What's health care policy got to do with it? *Health Affairs* 26(2):441-444.

Howell, E. M., and C. Trenholm. 2007. The effect of new insurance coverage on the health status of low-income children in Santa Clara County. *Health Services Research* 42(2):867-889.

Howell, E., L. Dubay, and L. Palmer. 2008a. The impact of the Los Angeles Health Kids Program on access to care, use of services, and health status. *Urban Institute Report*, http://www.urban.org/url.cfm?ID=411503 (accessed October 8, 2008).

Howell, E., D. Hughes, L. Palmer, G. Kenney, and A. Klein. 2008b. Final report of the evaluation of the San Mateo County Children's Health Initiative: Urban Institute Report.

IOM (Institute of Medicine). 1993. *Access to health care in America*. Washington, DC: National Academy Press.

———. 2002a. *Care without coverage: Too little, too late*. Washington, DC: National Academy Press.

———. 2002b. *Health insurance is a family matter*. Washington, DC: The National Academies Press.

———. 2004. *Children's health, the nation's wealth: Assessing and improving child health*. Washington, DC: The National Academies Press.

———. 2008. *Knowing what works in health care: A roadmap for the nation*. Washington, DC: The National Academies Press.

Jeffrey, A. E., and P. W. Newacheck. 2006. Role of insurance for children with special health care needs: A synthesis of the evidence. *Pediatrics* 118(4):e1027-e1038.

Joyce, T., and A. Racine. 2005. CHIP shots: Association between the State Children's Health Insurance Programs and immunization rates. *Pediatrics* 115(5):e526-e534.

Kempe, A., B. L. Beaty, L. A. Crane, J. Stokstad, J. Barrow, S. Belman, and J. F. Steiner. 2005. Changes in access, utilization, and quality of care after enrollment into a State Child Health Insurance Plan. *Pediatrics* 115(2):364-371.

Kenney, G. 2007. The impacts of the State Children's Health Insurance Program on children who enroll: Findings from ten states. *Health Services Research* 42(4):1520-1543.

Kenney, G., and E. Howell. 2008 (unpublished). *Health and access consequences of uninsurance among children in the United States: An update*. Report submitted to the Institute of Medicine Committee on Health Insurance Status and Its Consequences. The Urban Institute.

Kenney, G. M., J. Rubenstein, A. Sommers, S. Zuckerman, and F. Blavin. 2007. How are Medicaid programs working for children? Evidence from California and North Carolina. *Health Care Financing Review* 29(1).

Klein, J. D., L. P. Shone, P. G. Szilagyi, A. Bajorska, K. Wilson, and A. W. Dick. 2007. Impact of the State Children' Health Insurance Program on adolescents in New York. *Pediatrics* 119(4):e885-e892.

Lave, J. R., C. R. Keane, C. J. Lin, and E. M. Ricci. 2002. The impact of dental benefits on the utilization of dental services by low-income children in western Pennsylvania. *Pediatric Dentistry* 24(3):234-240.

Levy, H., and D. Meltzer. 2004. What do we really know about whether health insurance affects health? In *Health Policy and the Uninsured*, edited by C. G. McLaughlin. Washington, DC: Urban Institute Press. Pp. 179-204.

———. 2008. The impact of health insurance on health. *Annual Review of Public Health* 29:399-409.

Lewis, C. W., B. D. Johnston, K. A. Linsenmeyar, A. Williams, and W. Mouradian. 2007. Preventive dental care for children in the United States: A national perspective. *Pediatrics* 119(3):e544-e553.

Lichtenberg, F. R. 2002. The effects of Medicare on health care utilization and outcomes. In *Frontiers in Health Policy Research, Volume 5*, edited by A. M. Garber. Cambridge and London: MIT Press.

Maniatis, A. K., S. H. Goehrig, D. Gao, A. Rewers, P. Walravens, and G. J. Klingensmith. 2005. Increased incidence and severity of diabetic ketoacidosis among uninsured children with newly diagnosed type 1 diabetes mellitus. *Pediatric Diabetes* 6(2):79-83.

Mayer, M. L., A. C. Skinner, R. T. Slifkin, and The National Survey of Children with Special Health Care Needs. 2004. Unmet need for routine and specialty care: Data from the National Survey of Children With Special Health Care Needs. *Pediatrics* 113(2): e109-e115.

McBroome, K., P. C. Damiano, and J. C. Willard. 2005. Impact of the Iowa S-SCHIP program on access to dental care for adolescents. *Pediatric Dentistry* 27(1):47-53.

McGlynn, E. A., S. M. Asch, J. Adams, J. Keesey, J. Hicks, A. DeCristofaro, and E. A. Kerr. 2003. The quality of health care delivered to adults in the United States. *New England Journal of Medicine* 348(26):2635-2645.

McHorney, C. A., J. E. Ware, Jr., and A. E. Raczek. 1993. The MOS 36-Item Short-Form Health Survey (SF-36): II. Psychometric and clinical tests of validity in measuring physical and mental health constructs. *Medical Care* 31:247-263.

McWilliams, J. M. 2008 (unpublished). *Health consequences of uninsurance among adults in the United States: An update*. Report submitted to the Institute of Medicine Committee on Health Insurance Status and Its Consequences. Harvard Medical School.

McWilliams, J. M., A. M. Zaslavsky, E. Meara, and J. Z. Ayanian. 2003. Impact of Medicare coverage on basic clinical services for previously uninsured adults. *JAMA* 290:757-764.

———. 2004. Health insurance coverage and mortality among the near-elderly. *Health Affairs (Millwood)* 23:223-233.

McWilliams, J. M., E. Meara, A. M. Zaslavsky, and J. Z. Ayanian. 2007a. Health of previously uninsured adults after acquiring Medicare coverage. *JAMA* 298:2886-2894.

———. 2007b. Use of health services by previously uninsured Medicare beneficiaries. *New England Journal of Medicine* 357:143-153.

Mofidi, M., R. Slifkin, V. Freeman, and P. A. M. Silberman. 2002. The impact of a State Children's Health Insurance Program on access to dental care. *Journal of the American Dental Association* 133(6):707-714.

Moreno, L., and S. Hoag. 2001. Covering the uninsured through TennCare: Does it make a difference? *Health Affairs* 20(1):231-239.

Pauly, M. V. 2005. Effects of insurance coverage on use of care and health outcomes for non-poor young women. *American Economic Review* 95:219-223.

Polsky, D., J. A. Doshi, J. Escarce, W. Manning, S. M. Paddock, L. Cen, and J. Rogowski. 2006. *The health effects of Medicare for the near-elderly uninsured.* Cambridge, MA: National Bureau of Economic Research.

Porterfield, S., and T. McBride. 2007. The effect of poverty and caregiver education on perceived need and access to health services among children with special health care needs. *American Journal of Public Health* 97(2):323-329.

Probst, J. C., C. G. Moore, and E. G. Baxley. 2005. Update: Health insurance and utilization of care among rural adolescents. *Journal of Rural Health* 21(4):279-287.

Selden, T. M., and J. L. Hudson. 2006. Access to care and utilization among children: Estimating the effects of public and private coverage. *Medical Care Trends in Medical Care Costs, Coverage, Use, and Access: Research Findings from the Medical Expenditure Panel Survey* 44(5):I-19–I-26.

Shen, J. J., and E. L. Washington. 2007. Disparities in outcomes among patients with stroke associated with insurance status. *Stroke* 38:1010-1016.

Slifkin, R., V. Freeman, and P. Silberman. 2002. Effect of the North Carolina State Children's Health Insurance Program on beneficiary access to care. *Archives of Pediatric Adolescent Medicine* 156:1223-1229.

Sudano, J. J., Jr., and D. W. Baker. 2003. Intermittent lack of health insurance coverage and use of preventive services. *American Journal of Public Health* 93:130-137.

Szilagyi, P. G., A. W. Dick, J. D. Klein, L. P. Shone, J. Zwanziger, and T. McInerny. 2004. Improved access and quality of care after enrollment in the New York State Children's Health Insurance Program (SCHIP). *Pediatrics* 113(5):e395-e404.

Szilagyi, P. G., A. W. Dick, J. D. Klein, L. P. Shone, J. Zwanziger, A. Bajorska, and H. L. Yoos. 2006. Improved asthma care after enrollment in the State Children's Health Insurance Program in New York. *Pediatrics* 117(2):486-496.

Trenholm, C., E. Howell, D. Hughes, and S. Orzol. 2005. The Santa Clara County Healthy Kids Program: Impacts on children's medical, dental, and vision care. *Mathematica Policy Research Report,* http://www.mathematica-mpr.com/publications/PDFs/santaclara.pdf (accessed September 1, 2008).

Volpp, K. G., S. V. Williams, J. Waldfogel, J. H. Silber, J. S. Schwartz, and M. V. Pauly. 2003. Market reform in New Jersey and the effect on mortality from acute myocardial infarction. *Health Services Research* 38:515-533.

Volpp, K. G., J. D. Ketcham, A. J. Epstein, and S. V. Williams. 2005. The effects of price competition and reduced subsidies for uncompensated care on hospital mortality. *Health Services Research* 40:1056-1077.

Wang, G., and C. Watts. 2007. Genetic counseling, insurance status, and elements of medical home: Analysis of the National Survey of Children with Special Health Care Needs. *Maternal & Child Health Journal* 11(6):559-567.

Wang, H., E. C. Norton, and R. G. Rozier. 2007. Effects of the State Children's Health Insurance Program on access to dental care and use of dental services. *Health Services Research* 42(4):1544-1563.

Ward, E., M. Halpern, N. Schrag, V. Cokkinides, C. DeSantis, P. Bandi, R. Siegel, A. Stewart, and A. Jemal. 2008. Association of insurance with cancer care utilization and outcomes. *CA: A Cancer Journal for Clinicians* 58:9-31.

Ward, L., and P. Franks. 2007. Changes in health care expenditure associated with gaining or losing health insurance. *Annals of Internal Medicine* 146:768-774.

Wennberg, D. E., and J. E. Wennberg. 2003. Perspective: Addressing variations: Is there hope for the future? *Health Affairs* w3.614-w3.617.

Wennberg, J. E., E. S. Fisher, and S. M. Sharp. 2006. *The care of patients with severe chronic illness*. Lebanon, NH: The Dartmouth Atlas of Health Care.

Wilper, A. P., S. Woolhandler, K. E. Lasser, D. McCormick, D. H. Bor, and D. U. Himmelstein. 2008. A national study of chronic disease prevalence and access to care in uninsured U.S. adults. *Annals of Internal Medicine* 149(3):170-176.

Winokur, J. 2007. A losing battle. *American Journal of Nursing* 107(1):44-45.

Yu, H., A. W. Dick, and P. G. Szilagyi. 2006. Role of SCHIP in serving children with special health care needs. *Health Care Financing Review* 28(2):53-64.

Zhao, Z., A. H. Mokdad, and L. Barker. 2004. Impact of health insurance status on vaccination coverage in children 19-35 months old, United States, 1993-1996. *Public Health Reports* 119(2):156-162.

4

Communities at Risk

Abstract: When a community has a high rate of uninsurance and subsidies fall short of costs, the financial impact on health care providers may be large enough to affect the availability and quality of local health care services, even for people who are insured. This chapter reviews recent relevant research on this topic. There are stark differences in the burden of uninsurance across communities. Yet the problem of uninsurance may not affect all communities in the same way even when rates of uninsurance are comparable. The dynamics are complex and not well understood. Nevertheless, research on the potential spillover effects of community uninsurance suggests that when local rates of uninsurance are relatively high, insured adults are more likely to have difficulty obtaining needed health care and physicians may be more likely to believe that they are unable to make clinical decisions in the best interest of the patient without losing income. The precise contribution of uninsurance to this dynamic has not been fully defined. Nevertheless, well-documented fault lines in local health care delivery are particularly vulnerable to the financial pressures that may be exacerbated by higher uninsurance. These pressures contribute to the tendency of providers and capital investments in health care facilities and technology to be concentrated in well-insured areas, the reluctance of specialists to assume on-call responsibilities for emergencies, and a cascade of interrelated hospital-based problems such as insufficient inpatient bed capacity, strained emergency services, and barriers to timely trauma care. These problems can only worsen existing disparities between communities in the supply of provider services and other health care resources and may have potentially serious implications for the quality and timeliness of care for insured people, as well as uninsured people, in these communities. Unfortunately, the current economic crisis and associated *growth in unemployment will fuel further decline in the number of people with health insurance and likely intensify financial pressures on local health care delivery.*

Many of America's towns and cities have high concentrations of children and adults under age 65 who lack health insurance (DeNavas-Walt et al., 2008). Thus, two questions arise: What are the implications of high rates of uninsurance for affected communities and for insured people in those communities? Is the financial impact of uninsurance large enough to affect the availability and quality of local health care services for everyone in the community, even for the people who have health insurance?

In 2003, an earlier Institute of Medicine (IOM) committee warned of the potential harms of high rates of uninsurance for local health care, including reduced access to clinic-based primary care, specialty services, and hospital-based emergency medical services and trauma care (Box 4-1) (IOM, 2003). Such consequences reduce access to clinic-based primary care, specialty services, and hospital-based care, particularly emergency medical services and trauma care.

The prior IOM committee also observed that the evidence available in 2003 was observational and largely cross-sectional in design, making it difficult to infer causal relationships between uninsurance and these harms, and that there was a dearth of systematic data to measure the size, strength, and scope of community effects of uninsurance. Thus, the committee called for additional research to measure the size, strength, and scope of potential adverse community effects of uninsurance. As is explained later on in the chapter, sufficient evidence is still lacking and the methodologic obstacles to unraveling the dynamics of community effects remain very challenging.

This chapter reviews what is currently known about the impact of high community-level rates of uninsurance on people who have health insurance in affected communities, using the definition of community used in the 2003 IOM report (Box 4-2). The next section of the chapter provides some context for assessing the consequences of high uninsurance rates in communities. The third section discusses challenges in evaluating the impact of high community-level uninsurance rates and presents findings from recent studies of the spillover effects of uninsurance on communities including an analysis commissioned by the committee. The fourth section reviews recent evidence on a range of well-documented problems in local health care delivery that are vulnerable to financial pressures and may intensify when a large proportion of the community is uninsured. The final section of the chapter summarizes the committee's overall conclusions.

BOX 4-1
The IOM's Previous Findings on the Community
Effects of Uninsurance, 2003

One of the reports in the IOM's earlier series of reports on the consequences of uninsurance was a 2003 report entitled *A Shared Destiny: Community Effects of Uninsurance*. The following is an excerpt from that report.

The committee draws two conclusions based on its expert judgment and the sufficiency of the evidence base:

1. **A community's high uninsured rate has adverse consequences for the community's health care institutions and providers. These consequences reduce access to clinic-based primary care, specialty services, and hospital-based care, particularly emergency medical services and trauma care.**

2. **Research is needed to more clearly define the size, strength, and scope of adverse community effects that are plausible consequences of uninsurance. These include potentially deleterious effects on access to primary and preventive health care, specialty care, the underlying social and economic vitality of communities, public health capacity, and overall population health.**

What we don't know *can* hurt us. There is much that is not understood about the relationships between health services delivery and financing mechanisms and even less about how the current structure and performance of the American health care enterprise affect communities' economies and the quality of social and political life in this country. Because policy makers and researchers have not asked or examined these questions through comprehensive and systematic research and analysis, there is a limited body of evidence of mixed quality on community effects.

The committee believes, however, that it is both mistaken and dangerous to assume that the prevalence of uninsurance in the United States harms only those who are uninsured. It calls for further research to examine the effects of uninsurance at the community level but nonetheless believes there is sufficient evidence to justify the adoption of policies to address the lack of health insurance in the nation. Rather, the call for more research is to say that, as long as we as a nation tolerate the status quo, we should more fully understand the implications and consequences of our stalemated national health policy.

SOURCE: IOM (2003).

BOX 4-2
What Is a Community?

The term community, as used here, refers to a group of people who: (1) live in a particular geographic area, and (2) have access to a common set of health resources.

The term community can describe locations as small as neighborhoods and as large as metropolitan areas. How expansive a community is depends partly on the patterns of social, health care and economic interactions that are being analyzed. Thus, for example, the community that shares primary care resources such as physician practices and clinics may be relatively small and local, while the community sharing an advanced trauma care facility may encompass an entire metropolitan area and adjacent rural communities. The boundaries of a community can extend beyond where its residents live into where its residents work or routinely travel.

SOURCE: IOM (2003).

CONTEXT FOR ASSESSING COMMUNITY-LEVEL CONSEQUENCES OF UNINSURANCE

The Burden of Providing Care to Uninsured Patients

Although there is no definitive accounting of the financial burden of uninsurance at the local or national level, it has been estimated that the annual cost of health services provided to uninsured people in the United States will total about $86 billion in 2008 (Hadley et al., 2008). Uninsured patients will pay approximately $30 billion for these services out of pocket and receive the other $56 billion worth of services as uncompensated care.[1] An estimated $43 billion (75 percent) of the $56 billion will be covered through various government subsidies, including Medicare and Medicaid, disproportionate share hospital (DSH) payments, indirect medical education payments, direct care programs (e.g., community health centers), and state and local tax appropriations.

Payments for uncompensated care from the government are not necessarily distributed to health care providers in proportion to the uncompensated care they provide. Thus, many hospitals and other local providers bear a disproportionate and substantial financial burden due to their inability to receive adequate payment for the care they provide. Grady Memorial

---

[1] In this analysis, uncompensated care is defined as all care not paid for out of pocket by the uninsured.

BOX 4-3
Challenges at Grady Memorial Hospital in Atlanta

Grady Memorial Hospital is the only public hospital in Atlanta, Georgia, and the largest hospital in the state. An estimated one-third of Grady's patients are uninsured. The hospital receives substantial financial support from local Fulton and DeKalb counties and other public sources, but the subsidies fall short of the hospital's total costs for uncompensated care. Grady Memorial Hospital has run annual deficits for a decade. When this report was developed, the hospital estimated that its 2008 deficit would total $51 million.

Because of continual losses, Grady has delayed capital projects, postponed updating clinical technology, curtailed investment in information technology, and faced difficulties recruiting nurses and pharmacists. The hospital recently reported that it needed $370 million to overhaul operations; make capital improvements; and purchase basic diagnostic equipment, including X-ray machines, electrocardiogram and ultrasound devices, CT scanners, and MRI machines.

In 2006, Grady cared for 24 percent of Georgia's major trauma cases.* Many insured state residents may go elsewhere for routine health care services. But Grady is one of only four level-1 trauma centers in Georgia, and its service areas include a population of approximately 5.5 million people. Thus, when insured state residents experience severe trauma, they are likely to be transported to Grady.

---

* Personal Communication, G. Bishop, Bishop+Associates, October 29, 2008.
SOURCES: American College of Surgeons (2006); The Fulton-Dekalb Hospital Authority (2007); Grady Health System (2008a,b); Greater Grady Task Force (2007); Haley (2008).

Hospital illustrates how hospitals may be strained financially by the crisis in uninsurance and how financial burdens may threaten the quality of trauma and other care—even for patients who have health insurance (Box 4-3). The extent to which hospitals' unreimbursed costs are absorbed by hospitals or passed on in the form of higher charges to insured patients (as many believe to be the case) has not been adequately documented and should be the subject of further research.

Differences in Community-Level Uninsurance Rates

National trends in uninsurance rates, such as those discussed in Chapter 2, mask the tremendous variation in uninsurance rates across the United States. In 2007, for example, state-level uninsurance rates among the non-elderly population ranged from as low as 6 percent in Massachusetts to as high as 28 percent in Texas (U.S. Census Bureau, 2008a). Uninsurance rates in different counties within individual states also vary greatly, as shown in Figure 4-1.

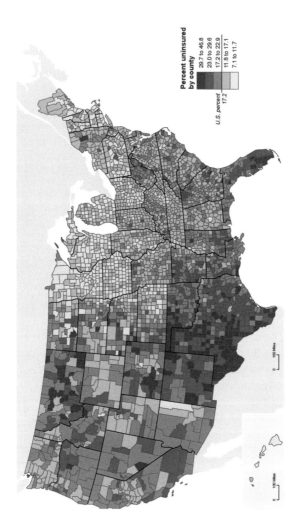

FIGURE 4-1 Percentage of the nonelderly U.S. population without health insurance, by county, 2005.

SOURCE: U.S. Census Bureau (2008b).

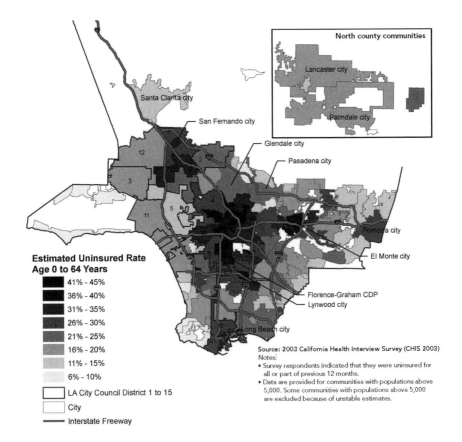

FIGURE 4-2 Variation in uninsurance rates among communities within Los Angeles County, 2003.
SOURCE: Yu et al. (2006). Reprinted, with permission, from *UCLA Health Policy Fact Sheet,* 2006. Copyright 2008 by the UCLA Center for Health Policy Research.

In fact, even within counties, there are enormous variations in uninsurance rates. Figure 4-2 shows, for example, that across zip codes within Los Angeles county, uninsurance rates among the nonelderly population in 2005 ranged from 6 percent to 45 percent (Yu et al., 2006).

HOW THE INSURED POPULATION IN A COMMUNITY MAY BE AFFECTED BY HIGH RATES OF UNINSURANCE

As noted earlier, there are considerable analytic challenges to evaluating the effects of community-level uninsurance rates on insured populations and health care delivery systems. The dynamics are complex and not well understood, in part because sufficient empirical data are simply not available. Teasing out the impact of uninsurance from other related dynamics is very difficult. Individual and family insurance status changes over time. Employers switch health plans and low-income families cycle in and out of eligibility for public health insurance (Federico et al., 2007). Even minimal disruptions in coverage—such as switching between types of coverage— have been shown to affect use of health care services (Bindman et al., 2008; Lavarreda et al., 2008; Leininger, 2009).

In addition, even when community rates of uninsurance are comparable, the problem of uninsurance may not affect communities the same way. Different communities' demographic makeup, employment patterns, residents' income distribution, and characteristics of the local health care system that may affect community-level health care utilization and outcomes directly, make it difficult to disentangle the spillover effects on health care utilization and outcomes due to uninsurance. And, to complicate matters even further, an extensive body of research has shown wide geographic variation in the quantity and quality of health care services provided even to the insured population, particularly the Medicare population (Fisher et al., 2003; Fuchs, 2004; Wennberg and Wennberg, 2003; Wennberg et al., 2006). Perhaps, as a consequence, the committee found only limited new research to inform its deliberations.

Nevertheless, important new data has emerged since the IOM last examined the community consequences of uninsurance—most notably, the survey and site visit data from the Community Tracking Study (CTS) of the Center for Studying Health System Change (HSC). HSC is a policy research organization in Washington, DC, that has been studying changes in the American health care system and the forces driving these changes since 1996 (HSC, 2006). The data that support much of HSC's research come from the CTS, which consists of periodic surveys of U.S. households and physicians. The household survey, among other things, tracks changes in health care access, utilization, insurance, perceptions of care quality, and problems paying medical bills (HSC, 2008). In the physician survey, practicing physicians across the country provide perspectives on how health care delivery is changing and answer questions about their practice arrangements and care practices. Other researchers have also produced valuable community-level research (Cook et al., 2007; Fairbrother et al., 2003; Gusmano et al., 2002; Hicks et al., 2006; Regenstein et al., 2004; Taylor et al., 2006).

For the first four rounds of the Community Tracking Household and Physician Surveys, conducted about every 2 years since 1996, the survey samples were clustered in 60 communities, randomly selected to provide a representative profile of change across the United States, and supplemented by a national sample (HSC, 2008). Among these communities are 48 "large" metropolitan areas (with populations greater than 200,000). Twelve of these communities (Boston; Miami; Orange County, California; northern New Jersey; Cleveland; Indianapolis; Phoenix; Seattle; Lansing; Greenville; Syracuse; and Little Rock) were randomly selected to be studied in depth using larger survey samples and site visits with health care leaders. These data can be used to draw conclusions for the nation and for individual communities.

Because of the paucity of research on how the insured population in a community is affected by high community-level rates of uninsurance, the committee asked Mark Pauly and José Pagán to conduct a special analysis of the CTS survey findings. If high rates of uninsurance affect the quality of care provided to the insured population, this should be evident in the CTS survey results (Pauly and Pagán, 2008).[2] Pauly and Pagán had previously used data from CTS surveys to develop an analytic model for assessing how the deleterious effects of uninsurance in a community "spill over" into the greater privately insured community (Pagán and Pauly, 2006; Pauly and Pagán, 2007).

The findings from the commissioned analysis by Pauly and Pagán, as well as from other studies of the spillover effects of uninsurance in communities with high levels of uninsurance, are presented below. These studies suggest that when local rates of uninsurance are relatively high, insured adults in affected communities are more likely than adults in other communities to have difficulties obtaining needed health care. As noted in Chapter 2, the current economic crisis and associated growth in unemployment will fuel further decline in the number of people with health insurance and likely further intensify financial pressures on local health care delivery.

Commissioned Analysis of the Spillover Effects of Community-Level Uninsurance

In the analysis commissioned by the committee, Pauly and Pagán used data from the 2003 Community Tracking Household Survey to assess the experiences of privately insured, working-age adults ages 18 to 64 in U.S. communities with high rates of uninsurance (Pauly and Pagán, 2008).[3] The 2003 CTS is described in Box 4-4. The household survey is particularly

---

[2] The complete text of the commissioned analysis of the effects of uninsurance on privately insured people and local communities by Mark Pauly, Ph.D., and José Pagán, Ph.D., is available on the IOM website for the Health Insurance Status and Its Consequences project at http://www.iom.edu/CMS/3809/54070.aspx.

[3] The CTS study population included privately insured, working-age adults ages 18 to 64. References in the text to "adults" refer to adults in this age group.

BOX 4-4
Uninsurance Rates Among Communities in the
2003 Community Tracking Study (CTS)

The 2003 CTS contained counties or groups of counties in metropolitan areas and rural areas randomly selected to ensure representation of the U.S. population. The CTS sample of 60 communities included 48 metropolitan areas with a population of more than 200,000; 3 communities with a population of less than 200,000; and 9 nonmetropolitan areas. Fifteen of the 60 communities with uninsured and underinsured rates in the lower 25th percentile were identified as "low medical cost burden" communities. Fifteen of the 60 communities with uninsured and underinsured rates in the upper 25th percentile were identified as "high medical cost burden" communities.

Uninsurance rates (percentage uninsured) among the 60 communities in the 2003 Community Tracking Household Survey ranged from a low of 5.0 percent in Bridgeport, Connecticut, to a high of 30.2 percent in Los Angeles, California. The following 7 communities had uninsurance rates between 20 and 30 percent in 2003:

Community	Uninsured rate (percentage uninsured)
Riverside, California	20.1
Houston, Texas	23.8
Shreveport, Louisiana	23.4
Orange County, California	24.9
West Palm Beach, Florida	26.1
Miami, Florida	26.7
Los Angeles, California	30.2

SOURCE: Cunningham (2007).

helpful for assessing the experiences of privately insured adults in communities with high rates of uninsurance because it determines respondents' health insurance status and asks respondents a series of well-validated survey questions related to individuals' access to care and satisfaction with the health care services they receive.[4]

Pauly and Pagán used multilevel logistic regression models to assess how higher rates of community-level uninsurance affect access to and sat-

---

[4] In 2007, the Community Tracking Household Survey was renamed the Health Tracking Household Survey. The survey design was scaled back to a national sample as a consequence of reduced funding and the new survey will not support community-level analyses the way the earlier Community Tracking Household Surveys did (personal communication, P. Ginsburg, Center for Studying Health System Change, December 2, 2008).

isfaction with care among privately insured, working-age adults, controlling for respondents' health status, age, education, race and ethnicity, marital status, gender, and income/family poverty level. As shown in Table 4-1, the results of this analysis suggest that higher rates of community uninsurance are negatively associated with several well-validated indicators of individuals' access to and satisfaction with health care. The access indicators include having a place to go when sick, having a doctor's visit, visiting a doctor for routine preventive care, and seeing a specialist when needed. The satisfaction measures include being very satisfied with the choice of primary care physician, being very satisfied with health care received during the last 12 months, trust that one's doctors put medical needs above all other considerations, and being very satisfied with the choice of specialists.

Using the findings of the regression analysis, Pauly and Pagán estimated the impact of a 10-percentage-point increase in community-level uninsurance rates (from the sample mean of 15.2 percent to 25.2 percent) on pri-

TABLE 4-1 Estimated Impact of Living in a Higher Uninsurance Community for Working-Age, Privately Insured Adults[a]

Effects on access to and satisfaction with care	Odds ratio[b]	95% confidence interval
Effect on access to care		
• Have a place to go when sick or in need of advice about health (n = 23,885)	0.63[c]	(0.60-0.68)
• Had doctor's visit in the past year (n = 23,956)	0.89[c]	(0.85-0.92)
• Had doctor's visit for routine preventive care (n = 23,956)	0.91[c]	(0.88-0.94)
• Saw specialist in the last 12 months when needed (n = 9,896)	0.85[d]	(0.76-0.95)
Effect on satisfaction with care		
• Very satisfied with choice of primary care physician (n = 22,062)	0.75[c]	(0.72-0.78)
• Very satisfied with health care (n = 22,791)	0.90[c]	(0.86-0.94)
• Trusts doctors (n = 20,815)	0.93[c]	(0.91-0.96)
• Very satisfied with choice of specialist seen (n = 9,586)	0.87[c]	(0.82-0.92)

[a] The study population included working-age, privately insured adults ages 18 to 64.

[b] Odds ratios less than 1.0 indicate that higher community uninsurance is associated with lower odds of the specific access or satisfaction variable for privately insured adults in the community. Thus, for example, the odds ratio of 0.63 (see above) indicates that privately insured adults in communities with higher uninsurance rates were less likely to "have a place to go when sick or in need of advice."

[c] Statistically significant difference, p < 0.001.

[d] Statistically significant difference, p < 0.01.

SOURCE: Pauly and Pagán (2008).

vately insured adults' reported access to and satisfaction with health care. The researchers found that higher community-level uninsurance rates were associated with small but significant declines in the measures of the privately insured adult population's access to care—including a 4.0-percentage-point decline (from 92.0 to 88.0 percent) in the probability of having a place to go when sick and a 2.2-percentage-point decline (from 64.8 to 62.6 percent) in the probability of having a routine preventive care visit. In addition, Pauly and Pagán found that higher community-level uninsurance rates were associated with small but significant declines in the measures of the privately insured adult population's satisfaction with care—including a 7.1-percentage-point decline (from 62.7 to 55.6 percent) in satisfaction with one's choice of primary care physician and a 2.7-percentage-point decrease (from 74.5 to 71.8 percent) in satisfaction with one's choice of specialist.

Other Research on Spillover Effects of High Community-Level Rates of Uninsurance

Other research is consistent with the findings of the 2008 Pauly and Pagán analysis commissioned by the committee. In 2006, Pagán and Pauly used the 2000-2001 Community Tracking Household Survey to assess the impact of community uninsurance on the medical needs of working-age, privately and publicly insured adults. They found that in communities with higher uninsurance rates, insured adults were more likely to report having an unmet medical need in the previous year (Pagán and Pauly, 2006). Insured adults in such communities were also more likely to report being in only fair to poor health.

In 2007, Pagán and colleagues used the 2000-2001 Community Tracking Physician Survey and the 2000-2001 and the 2003 Community Tracking Household Survey to assess the relationship between community uninsurance and primary care physicians' career satisfaction, perceptions about quality of care, and patients' trust in their physicians (Pagán et al., 2007).[5] The analysis included data from 4,920 primary care (i.e., specialists in internal medicine or general family practice) physician respondents who spent at least 20 hours per week in direct patient care.

---

[5] The 2000-2001 Community Tracking Physician Survey asked physicians about the extent to which they agree with the following statements: (1) I have the freedom to make clinical decisions that meet my patients' needs; (2) It is possible to provide high quality care to all of my patients; (3) I can make clinical decisions in the best interest of my patients without the possibility of reducing my income; (4) The level of communication I have with specialists about the patients I refer to them is sufficient to ensure the delivery of high-quality care; and (5) It is possible to maintain the kind of continuing relationships with patients over time that promote the delivery of high-quality care. The researchers developed dichotomous variables to capture whether a respondent agreed strongly or somewhat with each of the statements.

In this analysis, Pagán and colleagues found a significant negative relationship between higher rates of uninsurance and physicians' career satisfaction. They found that high uninsurance was negatively correlated with physicians' perceptions about quality of care. Higher community-level uninsurance rates were negatively related to the beliefs among physicians that they were able to make clinical decisions in the best interest of their patient without losing income or that they had sufficient communication with their patients' specialists. Furthermore, patients in communities with higher uninsurance rates were less likely to report trusting their physicians. In-depth site visits by HSC researchers have underscored these findings (Hurley et al., 2005; Lesser et al., 2005).

In a 2008 study, Pagán and colleagues used a multilevel logistic regression model to assess whether higher community-level rates of uninsurance affected mammography screening among insured women age 40 to 69, including not only privately insured women, but also women with Medicare or other sources of coverage (Pagán et al., 2008). They found that higher community-level uninsurance rates were associated with a significant decline in the insured women's access to care.

VULNERABILITIES IN LOCAL HEALTH CARE DELIVERY

Growing economic disparities between U.S. communities with respect to geographic distribution of health care services, including new diagnostic and therapeutic techniques and technology, have been well documented by HSC. As discussed below, the following widespread problems in local health care delivery not necessarily attributable to uninsurance are sensitive to financial pressures and may be exacerbated by higher community-level uninsurance rates:

- Health care providers and capital investment tend to locate in well-insured areas (and away from high uninsurance communities). It is common for hospitals to focus major investments in more affluent locations with well-insured populations.
- Physicians and other health care providers are drawn to newer facilities with the most up-to-date technologies. This phenomenon makes it especially challenging for financially stressed hospitals in communities with high uninsurance rates to recruit on-call specialists for emergencies.
- A range of hospital-based emergency care problems—including limits on inpatient bed capacity, outpatient emergency services, and timeliness of trauma care—have serious implications for the quality and timeliness of care for insured as well as uninsured patients.

The dynamics in communities with high or increasing uninsurance rates may thus make it increasingly difficult for people in those communities who have health insurance to obtain needed and high-quality health care services, and local primary care providers in those communities may find it more difficult to obtain consultations with specialists for their patients. The quality of care may be undermined not only in individual medical practices in the affected community, but also in the overall local health care delivery system. Consequently, patients in the affected community may lose faith in the ability of their physicians to act in their best interest (Pagán and Pauly, 2006). The precise contribution of uninsurance to this dynamic is neither well understood nor readily measured. Bazzoli and colleagues analyzed reductions in the services that hospitals provided between 1996 and 2002. The researchers found that non-safety net hospitals cut back maternity care, emergency department services, AIDS services, psychiatric emergency care, and substance abuse care—services commonly used by indigent patients (Bazzoli et al., 2005). However this research did not distinguish between high and low uninsurance communities.

Relocation of Health Care Services

Local health care delivery may be particularly vulnerable to the financial pressures associated with uninsurance. It is well established that people without health insurance see physicians far less often and use fewer health care services overall than their peers who have health insurance. This report has cited extensive evidence on the differences in health care utilization between insured and uninsured populations (see Chapter 3). The presence of a larger share of "low demanders" for health care services (i.e., uninsured individuals) could ultimately impact the quantity and quality of care available to everyone—including the insured—at the local level (Pauly and Pagán, 2007). Similarly, if a community has a high rate of uninsurance and government or other subsidies do not cover the costs of care provided to the uninsured, related financial pressures may motivate some providers to relocate to communities where patients are more likely to have health insurance.

There is growing evidence that hospitals and physicians operating in areas with high rates of uninsurance tend to focus more intensively on revenue-generating activities and to drop or limit unprofitable services (Cunningham et al., 2008). Health care providers can also limit the amount of charity care they provide. In communities with high rates of uninsurance, however, limiting charity care is hard to do.

Another alternative for health care providers is to extend or relocate services to more affluent areas where a higher percentage of patients is in-

---

BOX 4-5
Denver Hospitals Relocating to More Affluent Areas

Hospital relocations in Denver are an example of health care services moving away from high uninsurance communities to areas where a greater share of the patient population has health insurance. In 2004, 23.1 percent of the Denver county population was uninsured.

In 2007, two hospitals—the Denver Children's Hospital and the University of Colorado Hospital—moved to more affluent suburbs. A third Denver hospital, St. Anthony's Central Hospital, is building a new facility and plans to move out of the city in 2010.

The local press has reported that the state's largest safety net hospital and health care system, Denver Health, is attempting to absorb the patients left behind. In August 2007, the hospital reported diverting one of every five ambulances to more remote hospitals for lack of inpatient beds. In November 2008, Denver Health experienced a reported 19 percent increase in emergency department visits by uninsured patients compared to the previous year.

SOURCE: Abelson (2008); Colorado Health Institute (2006); Human (2007).

---

sured (Hurley et al., 2005). In 2005, HSC researchers conducted site visits and interviewed more than 1,000 respondents in randomly chosen markets from large, mid-size, and small metropolitan areas (Lesser et al., 2005). These researchers found growing economic disparities with respect to geographic distribution of health care services, including new diagnostic and therapeutic techniques and technology (Hurley et al., 2005). Although some institutions were upgrading existing facilities, many hospitals were focusing major investments in more affluent locations with well-insured populations. The newer facilities with the most up-to-date technologies become a magnet for physicians and other health care providers.

Hospital relocations in Denver illustrate this phenomenon of hospitals relocating to more affluent communities where people are more likely to have health insurance (Box 4-5). Such trends can only worsen existing disparities in the supply of physician services and other health care resources among U.S. communities.

Challenges in Hospitals' Recruitment of On-Call Specialists for Emergencies

Attracting specialty physicians to provide on-call coverage for hospital emergency departments has been a nationwide problem for more than a decade (IOM, 2007; O'Malley et al., 2007). In 2005, the American College of Emergency Physicians surveyed medical directors of hospital emergency departments. Emergency department directors in large and small hospitals across all geographic regions reported on-call coverage problems. Overall, almost three-quarters of the survey respondents (73 percent) reported difficulties staffing on-call specialists (American College of Emergency Physicians, 2006). Site visit reports by HSC researchers have documented the problem in hospitals in northern New Jersey, Seattle, Phoenix, Miami, and Little Rock (O'Malley et al., 2005).

Although staffing on-call physician specialists for hospital emergency departments may be a challenge faced by hospitals in all types of communities, hospitals already stressed by uninsurance are hard-pressed to cope with the added financial demands. In communities with higher rates of uncompensated care, local physician specialists may be increasingly reluctant to assume on-call responsibilities to cover emergencies.

Obstacles to obtaining specialty care on an emergency basis contribute to the crowding of hospital emergency departments and reduce the quality of care for everyone. When backup specialists are unavailable to perform emergency surgeries and provide other forms of definitive care, all patients are affected. Already stressed emergency departments may divert ambulances to more distant hospitals, leading to potentially dangerous delays in time-sensitive care for people who have conditions such as major trauma, myocardial infarction (heart attack), or stroke.

In fact, it appears that higher rates of uncompensated care associated with uninsurance are a major obstacle to resolving the problem (American Hospital Association, 2006). In many areas of the country, hospitals are able to recruit on-call medical staff only by paying large subsidies, particularly for neurosurgeons and orthopedists but also for specialists in other surgical specialties, neurology, and psychiatry (Burt and McCaig, 2006). Thus, for example, a hospital in the Phoenix area reported paying local neurosurgery groups a $10,000 weekly supplement to routine per patient reimbursements in order to ensure trauma care coverage (Hurley et al., 2005); a Little Rock hospital pays trauma surgeons an additional $1,000 per night; and a Miami hospital reports $10 million in annual payments to on-call specialists (O'Malley et al., 2007). In communities with high rates of uninsurance, hospitals may have great difficulty absorbing such costs.

Other Vulnerabilities in the Quality of Emergency Medical Services

Other problems in the quality of hospital-based emergency care include the crowding of hospital emergency departments, ambulance diversions, delays in patient care, and the "boarding" of critically ill patients (Olshaker and Rathlev, 2006; Vieth and Rhodes, 2006). "Boarding" occurs when an emergency department patient is admitted to the hospital without an available inpatient bed and, as a result, must remain in emergency room hallways or treatment rooms (IOM, 2007). These problems, although not directly attributable to uninsurance, may be exacerbated by high uninsurance rates. Recent research has documented that, conventional wisdom to the contrary, uninsurance is not a primary cause of emergency department overcrowding and uninsured patients are not more likely than insured patients to visit emergency departments for convenience and less acute conditions (Newton et al., 2008).

Financially stressed hospitals often limit the number of inpatient beds available for emergency admissions to minimize overhead costs and to maximize revenues from more profitable elective surgical admissions (O'Shea, 2007; U.S. Government Accountability Office, 2003). Generally, it is more efficient for hospitals to operate at or near full inpatient capacity than to staff beds for occasional increases in demand. However, shortages of inpatient beds, as well as shortages of on-call specialists, contribute to crowding of hospital emergency departments and longer waits for patients, the boarding of patients who need to be admitted, and ambulance diversions (IOM, 2007; O'Malley et al., 2005, 2007).

Longer waits are especially perilous for patients with time-sensitive life-threatening conditions, such as acute myocardial infarction, ischemic stroke, and severe sepsis or septic shock. As time elapses, there is a greater risk of irreversible damage and mortality. The Joint Commission has cited emergency department crowding as a cause of treatment delays for 31 percent of sentinel events involving death, serious physical injury including loss of limb or function, or psychological injury (The Joint Commission, 2002).

Treatment delays in hospital emergency departments also impede the responsiveness of community emergency medical services. Emergency medical services providers may be required to stay with critical patients waiting for care (Burt et al., 2006). A Los Angeles study, for example, found that ambulance crews had a median waiting time of 27 minutes in the emergency department; the longest wait was 6.75 hours (Eckstein and Chan, 2004).

More than one-third of hospitals reported going on ambulance diversion status at some point during the past year, according to the 2003-2004 National Hospital Ambulatory Medical Care Survey (Burt and McCaig, 2006). Ambulance diversions occur when hospital emergency rooms are so crowded that they cannot taken any more patients. These also delay patient care.

When hospitals are crowded and there are no inpatient beds available, critically ill emergency patients are boarded in emergency department hallways and treatment rooms (American College of Emergency Physicians, 2008; O'Shea, 2007; Trzeciak and Rivers, 2003). In particularly busy hospitals, some patients may be boarded for 1 or 2 days (IOM, 2007). The

Memphis Regional Medical Center, for example, has reported boarding patients for up to 48 hours (Wilson et al., 2005). Boarding may be harmful to critically ill patients and also diverts emergency department staff from attending to new incoming patients.

The problems of crowding of hospital emergency departments, ambulance diversions, delays in patient care, and patient boarding, which may be exacerbated by high uninsurance rates, have potentially grave implications for the quality and timeliness of care not only for uninsured patients, but for insured patients as well.

CONCLUSION

This chapter has examined what is known about the impact of uninsurance at the community level. There is no definitive accounting of the financial burden of uninsurance at the local or national level, but the total dollar value of services provided to uninsured people without reimbursement or subsidies nationwide was estimated to be $56 billion in 2008. In the aggregate, public subsidies cover a large share, but not all the costs of care provided to people without health insurance. Many local hospitals and other health providers who serve uninsured patients continue to bear a disproportionate and substantial burden of these costs. When a community has a high rate of uninsurance and subsidies fall short of costs, the financial impact on providers may be large enough to affect the availability, quality, and cost of local health care services for everyone, even for the people who have health insurance.

There are stark differences in community-level uninsurance rates across states, counties, and even areas within counties. In 2007, state-level uninsurance rates among the nonelderly ranged from 6 percent in Massachusetts up to almost 28 percent in Texas. Within Los Angeles county, uninsurance rates in the nonelderly population in 2005 ranged from 6 percent to 45 percent.

Evaluating the effects of community-level uninsurance rates on insured populations and health care delivery systems is challenging. Even when the rates of uninsurance are comparable, uninsurance may not affect all communities the same way. Community demographic characteristics, employment patterns, income, and the characteristics of the local health care system may affect health care utilization and outcomes directly, making it difficult to disentangle the spillover effects due to community-level uninsurance. Furthermore, an extensive body of research has shown wide geographic variations in the quantity and quality of health care services provided to the insured population. Nevertheless, an empirical study commissioned by the committee and other research on the potential spillover effects of community uninsurance suggests that when community-level rates of uninsurance are relatively high, *insured* adults in those communities are more likely to have difficulties obtaining needed health care and to be less satisfied with the care they receive. For example, privately insured, working-age adults in higher uninsurance areas are less likely to report having a place to go when sick, having a doctor's visit or routine preventive care, and seeing a specialist when needed. They are also less likely to be satisfied with their choice of primary care and specialty physicians or to feel trust in their doctor's decisions.

The Center for Studying Health System Change has documented growing economic disparities among communities with respect to the geographic distribution of health care services. The specific contribution of uninsurance to these problems is not known. The dynamics are complex and not well understood, in part because sufficient empirical data to inform the issue of how uninsurance affects communities are simply not available. But widespread problems in health care delivery in local communities, including disparities in the supply of physician services and other health care resources that are exacerbated by the burden of uninsurance, have potentially grave implications for the quality and timeliness of care not only for people who lack health insurance, but also for people who have health insurance.

REFERENCES

Abelson, R. 2008. Uninsured put a strain on hospitals. *The New York Times*, http://www.nytimes.com/2008/12/09/business/09emergency.html?pagewanted=2&_r=1&ei=5070&emc=eta1 (accessed December 9, 2008).

American College of Emergency Physicians. 2006. On-call specialist coverage in U.S. emergency departments. *ACEP Survey of Emergency Department Directors, April 2006*, http://www.acep.org/pressroom.aspx?id=25262 (accessed August 28, 2008).

———. 2008. *Emergency department crowding: High-impact solutions,* http://www.acep.org/workarea/showcontent.aspx?id=37960 (accessed August 28, 2008).

American College of Surgeons. 2006. *Resources for optimal care of the injured patient,* http://www.facs.org/trauma/hospitallevels.pdf (accessed October 13, 2008).

American Hospital Association. 2006. *Taking the pulse: The state of America's hospitals,* http://www.aha.org/aha/content/2006/PowerPoint/StateHospitalsChartPack2006.PPT (accessed October 16, 2008).

Bazzoli, G. J., R. Kang, R. Hasnain-Wynia, and R. C. Lindrooth. 2005. An update on safety-net hospitals: Coping with the late 1990s and early 2000s. *Health Affairs* 24(4):1047-1056.

Bindman, A. B., A. Chattopadhyay, and G. M. Auerback. 2008. Medicaid re-enrollment policies and children's risk of hospitalizations for ambulatory care sensitive conditions. *Medical Care* 46(10):1049-1054.

Burt, C. W., and L. F. McCaig. 2006. Staffing, capacity, and ambulance diversion in emergency departments: United States, 2003-04. *Advance Data from Vital and Health Statistics* No. 376: National Center for Health Statistics.

Burt, C. W., L. F. McCaig, and R. H. Valverde. 2006. Analysis of ambulance transports and diversions among U.S. emergency departments. *Annals of Emergency Medicine* 47(4):317-326.

Colorado Health Institute. 2006. *Profile of the uninsured in Colorado, an update for 2005.* Colorado Health Institute.

Cook, N. L., L. S. Hicks, A. J. O'Malley, T. Keegan, E. Guadagnoli, and B. E. Landon. 2007. Access to specialty care and medical services in community health centers. *Health Affairs* 26(5):1459-1468.

Cunningham, P. J. 2007. Overburdened and overwhelmed: The struggles of communities with high medical cost burdens. *The Commonwealth Fund* 28(pub. 1073).

Cunningham, P. J., G. J. Bazzoli, and A. Katz. 2008. Caught in the competitive crossfire: Safety-net providers balance margin and mission in a profit-driven health care market. *Health Affairs* w374-w382.

DeNavas-Walt, C., B. D. Proctor, and J. Smith. 2008. *Income, poverty, and health insurance coverage in the United States: 2007.* Washington, DC: U.S. Census Bureau.

Eckstein, M., and L. S. Chan. 2004. The effect of emergency department crowding on paramedic ambulance availability. *Annals of Emergency Medicine* 43(1):100-105.

Fairbrother, G., M. K. Gusmano, H. L. Park, and R. Scheinmann. 2003. Care for the uninsured in general internists' private offices. *Health Affairs* 22(6):217-224.

Federico, S. G., J. F. Steiner, B. Beaty, L. Crane, and A. Kempe. 2007. Disruptions in insurance coverage: Patterns and relationship to health care access, unmet need, and utilization before enrollment in the State Children's Health Insurance Program. *Pediatrics* 120(4): e1009-e1016.

Fisher, E. S., D. E. Wennberg, T. A. Stukel, D. J. Gottlieb, F. L. Lucas, and E. L. Pinder. 2003. The implications of regional variations in Medicare spending. Part 1: The content, quality, and accessibility of care. *Annals of Internal Medicine* 138(4):273-287.

Fuchs, V. R. 2004. Perspective: More variation in use of case, more flat-of-the-curve medicine. *Health Affairs* 104.

The Fulton-Dekalb Hospital Authority. 2007. *Combined financial statements for years ended December 31, 2005 and 2006.* Atlanta, GA.

Grady Health System. 2008a. Financial performance report: June 2008. *Financial Overview presented by CFO Mike Ayers to the Grady Memorial Hospital Corporation Board,* http://www.gradyhealthsystem.org/GMHC/Grady%20Financial%20Performance%20Report%20June%202008.pdf (accessed October 28, 2008).

———. 2008b. *Financial: Grady highlights at-a-glance,* http://www.gradyhealthsystem.org/financial.asp (accessed October 28, 2008).

Greater Grady Task Force. 2007. Greater Grady Task Force: Final report. *Metro Atlanta Chamber of Commerce,* http://www.metroatlantachamber.com/images/GGTFFinalReport.pdf (accessed October 6, 2008).

Gusmano, M. K., G. Fairbrother, and H. Park. 2002. Exploring the limits of the safety net: Community health centers and care for the uninsured. *Health Affairs* 21(6):188-194.

Hadley, J., J. Holahan, T. Coughlin, and D. Miller. 2008. Covering the uninsured in 2008: Current costs, sources of payment, and incremental costs. *Health Affairs* 27(5):399-415.

Haley, L. 2008. *Challenges in the safety net. Presentation to Robert Wood Johnson Health Policy Fellows,* Emory University, Atlanta, GA.

Hicks, L. S., A. J. O'Malley, T. A. Lieu, T. Keegan, N. L. Cook, B. J. McNeil, B. E. Landon, and E. Guadagnoli. 2006. The quality of chronic disease care in U.S. community health centers. *Health Affairs* 25(6):1712-1723.

HSC (Center for Studying Health Systems Change). 2006. *Community Tracking Study: Physician survey (2004-05).* Ann Arbor, MI: Inter-university Consortium for Political and Social Research.

———. 2008. *CTS surveys,* http://www.hschange.org/index.cgi?data=12 (accessed January 5, 2009).

Human, K. 2007. Denver hospitals see ER demand growing. *Denver Post*, September 24, 2007.

Hurley, R. E., H. H. Pham, and G. Claxton. 2005. A widening rift in access and quality: Growing evidence of economic disparities. *Health Affairs* w5-566–w5-576.

IOM (Institute of Medicine). 2003. *A shared destiny: Community effects of uninsurance.* Washington, DC: The National Academies Press.

———. 2007. *Hospital-based emergency care: At the breaking point.* Washington, DC: The National Academies Press.

The Joint Commission. 2002. Delays in treatment. *Sentinel Event Alert No. 26*, http://www.jointcommission.org/SentinelEvents/SentinelEventAlert/sea_26.htm (accessed September 5, 2008).

Lavarreda, S. A., M. Gatchell, N. Ponce, E. R. Brown, and Y. J. Chia. 2008. Switching health insurance and its effects on access to physician services. *Medical Care* 46(10):1055-1063.

Leininger, L. J. 2009. Partial-year insurance coverage and the health care utilization of children. *Medical Care Research and Review* 66(1):49-67.

Lesser, C. S., P. Ginsburg, and L. E. Felland. 2005. *Initial findings from HSC's 2005 site visits: Stage set for growing health care cost and access problems.* Washington, DC: Center for Studying Health System Change.

Newton, M. F., C. C. Keirns, R. Cunningham, R. A. Hayward, and R. Stanley. 2008. Uninsured adults presenting to US emergency departments: Assumptions vs data. *JAMA* 300(16):1914-1924.

Olshaker, J. S., and N. K. Rathlev. 2006. Emergency department overcrowding and ambulance diversion: The impact and potential solutions of extended boarding of admitted patients in the Emergency Department. *Journal of Emergency Medicine* 30(3):351-356.

O'Malley, A. S., A. M. Gerland, H. H. Pham, and R. A. Berenson. 2005. Rising pressure: Hospital emergency departments as barometers of the health care system. *Issue Brief: Findings from HSC No. 101*, http://www.hschange.com/CONTENT/799/799.pdf (accessed July 8, 2008).

O'Malley, A. S., D. A. Draper, and L. E. Felland. 2007. Hospital emergency on-call coverage: Is there a doctor in the house? *Issue Brief: Findings from HSC No. 115*, http://www.hschange.com/CONTENT/956/ (accessed August 1, 2008).

O'Shea, J. S. 2007. The crisis in America's emergency rooms and what can be done. *Backgrounder* No. 2092: Center for Health Policy Studies, http://www.heritage.org/research/HealthCare/upload/bg_2092.pdf (accessed October 14, 2008).

Pagán, J. A., and M. V. Pauly. 2006. Community level uninsurance and the unmet medical needs of insured and uninsured adults. *Health Services Research* 43(1).

Pagán, J. A., L. Balasubramanian, and M. V. Pauly. 2007. Physicians' career satisfaction, quality of care and patients' trust: The role of community uninsurance. *Health Economics, Policy and Law* 2:16.

Pagán, J. A., D. A. Asch, C. J. Brown, C. E. Guerra, and K. Armstrong. 2008. Lack of community insurance and mammography screening rates among insured and uninsured women. *Journal of Clinical Oncology* 26:6.

Pauly, M. V., and J. A. Pagán. 2007. Spillovers and vulnerability: The case of community uninsurance. *Health Affairs* 26(5).

———. 2008 (unpublished). *Spillovers of uninsurance in communities.* Report submitted to the Institute of Medicine Committee on Health Insurance Status and Its Consequences. Wharton School, University of Pennsylvania.

Regenstein, M., L. Nolan, M. Wilson, H. Mead, and B. Siegel. 2004. *Walking a tightrope: The state of the safety net in ten U.S. communities.* Washington, DC: Urgent Matters, Center for Health Services Research and Policy at the George Washington University School of Public Health and Health Services.

Taylor, E. F., P. Cunningham, and K. McKenzie. 2006. Community approaches to providing care for the uninsured. *Health Affairs* 25(3):w173-w182.

Trzeciak, S., and E. P. Rivers. 2003. Emergency department overcrowding in the United States: An emerging threat to patient safety and public health. *Emergency Medicine Journal* 20:402-405.

U.S. Census Bureau. 2008a. *Table HI05. Health insurance coverage status and type of coverage by state and age for all people: 2007*, http://pubdb3.census.gov/macro/032008/health/h05_000.htm (accessed November 20, 2008).

———. 2008b. *Percent uninsured under Age 65: 2005 SAHIE Program*, http://www.census.gov/hhes/www/sahie/data/2005/files/Under65_Pct_UI_2005.pdf (accessed November 2, 2008).

U.S. Government Accountability Office. 2003. *Hospital emergency departments: Crowded conditions vary among hospitals and communities*. GAO-03-460 Report to the Ranking Minority Member, Committee on Finance, U.S. Senate.

Vieth, T. L., and K. V. Rhodes. 2006. The effect of crowding on access and quality in an academic ED. *American Journal of Emergency Medicine* 24(7):787-794.

Wennberg, D. E., and J. E. Wennberg. 2003. Perspective: Addressing variations: Is there hope for the future? *Health Affairs* w3.614-w3.617.

Wennberg, J. E., E. S. Fisher, and S. M. Sharp. 2006. *The care of patients with severe chronic illness*. Lebanon, NH: The Dartmouth Atlas of Health Care.

Wilson, M. J., B. Siegel, and M. Williams. 2005. *Perfecting patient flow: America's safety net hospitals and emergency department crowding*. Urgent Matters Program, Washington, DC: National Association of Public Hospitals and Health Systems.

Yu, H., G. Frost, and E. R. Brown. 2006. *UCLA health policy fact sheet: Concentrations of uninsured residents in Los Angeles county communities*, http://www.healthpolicy.ucla.edu/pubs/files/LAC_lae_uninsured_042706.pdf (accessed August 8, 2008).

5

Summary of
Findings and Recommendation

From 2001 to 2004, the Institute of Medicine (IOM) Committee on the Consequences of Uninsurance issued a comprehensive series of six reports that reviewed and reported on the evidence on the effects of not having health insurance coverage. The final report in the series, *Insuring America's Health: Principles and Recommendations,* set out a vision and principles for health insurance coverage in the United States (IOM, 2004). In that 2004 report, the committee recommended action by the President and Congress to achieve universal coverage by 2010.[1] It stated:

> The benefits of universal coverage would enrich all Americans, whether accounted for in terms of improved health and longer life spans, greater economic productivity, financial security, or the stabilization of communities' health care systems.

It has now been 5 years since the IOM recommended action to achieve coverage for all Americans, and there has still been no comprehensive national effort to expand coverage to everyone. In 2007, 45.7 million people in the United States—or 17.2 percent of the nonelderly U.S. population—were without health insurance. A severely weakened economy, rising health care and health insurance costs, growing unemployment, and declining employment-based health insurance coverage are all evidence that the U.S. health insurance system is in a state of crisis. There is no evidence to suggest that the trends driving loss of insurance coverage will reverse without concerted action.

---

[1] The executive summary from the report is presented in Appendix A.

COMMITTEE'S RESOLUTION AND RECOMMENDATION

Resolution of the IOM Committee on Health Insurance Status and Its Consequences

In executing its charge, this committee has studied the available data and applied rigorous scientific criteria to set the record straight on the issue of health insurance coverage. The findings presented in the previous chapters and summarized below have expanded upon earlier IOM research on the consequences of being uninsured. The body of evidence on the health consequences of health insurance is stronger than ever before.

Lack of knowledge is not the problem. Preventable suffering related to uninsurance continues and promises to get worse rather than better. Inaction will lead to further erosion of coverage. There always has been, and will continue to be, uncertainty and disagreement about the best way to address major issues of public policy. The issue of cost, in particular, is daunting. But the nation has been successful with other complex issues that are intertwined with deeply held interests and ideologies. The opportunity to make the necessary difference is never the perfect one. Now is the time to act, emboldened by the knowledge and compassion of a society that truly cares about its members and that has a history of tackling difficult problems.

Recommendation

The committee recommends that the President work with Congress and other public and private sector leaders on an urgent basis to achieve health insurance coverage for everyone and, in order to make that coverage sustainable, to reduce the costs of health care and the rate of increase in per capita health care spending.

There is a compelling case for action. Simply stated: health insurance coverage matters. Expanding health coverage to all Americans is essential and should be done as quickly as possible. It is also of paramount importance that steps be taken to reduce health care expenditures and the rate of increase in per capita health care spending so that health insurance coverage for all can be achieved and sustained in an economically and politically viable manner. The committee does not believe that action should be delayed pending the development of a long-term approach to underlying health care costs. Given the demonstrated harms of not having health insurance for children and adults, the committee believes that actions to achieve coverage improvements should proceed immediately.

SUMMARY OF FINDINGS

On the basis of a careful review of the scientific literature since 2002, the committee reported findings in three key areas: trends in health insurance coverage, the health consequences of uninsurance for children and adults, and the implications of high community-level rates of uninsurance on people who have health insurance in affected communities. The committee's findings, which were discussed at length in previous chapters of this report, are summarized below.

Caught in a Downward Spiral: Uninsured Rates Are High and Getting Worse

Over the last decade, health insurance coverage has declined and will continue to decline. Health care costs and insurance premiums are growing at rates greater than the U.S. economy and family incomes. The situation is dire as it affects not only employer-sponsored coverage, the cornerstone of private health coverage in the United States, but also recent expansions in public coverage.

Overall, fewer workers, particularly those with lower wages, are offered employer-sponsored insurance, and fewer among the workers that are offered such insurance can afford the premiums. And, early retirees are less likely to be offered retiree health insurance benefits than in the past. Employment has shifted away from industries with traditionally high rates of coverage (e.g., manufacturing) to service jobs (e.g., in wholesale and retail trades) with historically lower rates of coverage. In some industries, employers have relied more heavily on jobs without health benefits, including part-time and shorter term employment, and contract and temporary jobs. Only a small percentage of Americans has nongroup private health insurance purchased in the individual insurance market. For many individuals and families without employer-sponsored group coverage, nongroup coverage is unaffordable.

States and the federal government have substantially increased health coverage among low-income children and, to a lesser degree, among adults in the last decade by expanding eligibility, conducting outreach to people already eligible, and expediting enrollment in Medicaid and State Children's Health Insurance Program (SCHIP) programs. As this report was being finalized, Congress reauthorized the SCHIP program (P.L. No. 111-3).[2] However, some states remain under extreme economic pressures to cut their recent expansions of public programs for low-income children and adults.

---

[2] Under this new legislation, the former SCHIP program is referred to as CHIP, the Children's Health Insurance Program.

Sharp increases in unemployment will further fuel the decline in the number of people with employer-sponsored coverage and add even greater stress on state health insurance programs.

Coverage Matters: Health Insurance Is Integral to Personal Well-Being and Health

Important new research has emerged since the IOM last studied the question of how health insurance affects health outcomes. This research clearly demonstrates that, despite the availability of care for the uninsured through safety net providers, insurance coverage makes a substantial difference in both access and outcomes. For children, well-designed evaluations of enrollment in Medicaid and SCHIP programs offer important insights into how children benefit when they acquire health insurance. For adults, new research—particularly recent longitudinal analyses of previously uninsured adults after they acquire Medicare coverage at age 65—has yielded compelling findings about how adults are harmed by not having health insurance.

Children with health insurance are more likely to gain access to a usual source of care or medical home, well-child care and immunizations to prevent future illness and monitor developmental milestones, prescription medications, appropriate care for asthma, and basic dental services. Serious childhood health problems are more likely to be identified early in children with health insurance, and insured children with special health care needs are more likely to have access to specialists. Children with health insurance have fewer avoidable hospitalizations, improved asthma outcomes, and fewer missed days of school.

Uninsured adults are much less likely to receive clinical preventive services that have the potential to reduce unnecessary morbidity and premature death. Chronically ill adults delay or forgo visits with physicians and clinically effective therapies, including prescription medications. Adults are more likely to be diagnosed with later stage cancers that are detectable by preventive screening or by contact with a clinician who can assess worrisome symptoms. Uninsured adults are more likely to die when hospitalized for trauma or other serious acute conditions, such as heart attack or stroke. Uninsured adults with cancer, cardiovascular disease (including hypertension, coronary heart disease, and congestive heart failure), serious injury, stroke, respiratory failure, chronic obstructive pulmonary disease or asthma exacerbation, hip fracture, seizures, and serious injury are more likely to suffer poorer health outcomes, greater limitations in quality of life, and premature death. New evidence demonstrates that gaining health insurance ameliorates many of these deleterious effects, particularly for adults who are acutely or chronically ill.

Communities at Risk: Higher Levels of Uninsurance in Communities May Undermine Health Care for the Insured Population

There are stark differences in the percentage of people without health insurance in different communities across the country. Many local health care providers in communities with high uninsurance rates bear a disproportionate and substantial financial burden due to America's uninsured crisis. Recent empirical evidence indicates that higher community-level uninsurance rates are negatively associated with several well-validated indicators of access to and satisfaction with health care among privately insured adults. Research commissioned by the committee suggests that when local rates of uninsurance are relatively high, insured adults are more likely to have difficulties obtaining needed health care and to be dissatisfied with their care. The precise contribution of uninsurance to this dynamic is not well understood.

There are also growing economic disparities between communities with respect to geographic distribution of physician services and other health care resources such as new diagnostic and therapeutic techniques and technology. Well-documented fault lines in local health care delivery—not necessarily attributable to uninsurance—are particularly vulnerable to the financial pressures associated with higher uninsurance and may be intensified by higher uninsurance rates. These include hospital-based emergency care problems, such as limits on inpatient bed capacity, outpatient emergency services, and timeliness of trauma care, that have potentially serious implications for the quality and timeliness of care for insured as well as uninsured patients.

CONCLUSION

For the aforementioned reasons, the committee concludes by joining the challenge put forth by our colleagues in the 2004 IOM report *Insuring America's Health*:

> ... health insurance contributes essentially to obtaining the kind and quality of health care that can express the equality and dignity of every person. Unless we can ensure coverage for all, we fail as a nation to deliver the great promise of our health care system, as well as of the values we live by as a society. It is time for our nation to extend coverage to everyone.

REFERENCE

IOM (Institute of Medicine). 2004. *Insuring America's health: Principles and recommendations*. Washington, DC: The National Academies Press.

Appendix A

Executive Summary of the 2004 IOM Report
Insuring America's Health: Principles and Recommendations

ABSTRACT

The lack of health insurance for tens of millions of Americans has serious negative consequences and economic costs not only for the uninsured themselves but also for their families, the communities they live in, and the whole country. The situation is dire and expected to worsen. The Committee urges Congress and the Administration to act immediately to eliminate this longstanding problem.

This report offers a framework for the public and policy makers to use as they weigh the pros and cons of various proposals. The framework consists of a set of principles informed by the research and analysis of the five previous reports in this series. The principles are applied to selected coverage prototypes to demonstrate the extent to which various proposals for extending coverage or designing new strategies to eliminate uninsurance would improve the current situation.

The lack of health insurance coverage for a substantial number of Americans has been a public policy problem throughout the past century and particularly over the past three decades. Three years ago, following a decade of strong economic growth but little progress reducing the number of the uninsured, the problem was urgent; 39 million people under age 65

NOTE: For a copy of the full report or any of the other five reports in the IOM series on the consequences of uninsurance, please visit www.nap.edu.

reported having been without insurance during the entire previous year.[1] In 2000, the Institute of Medicine (IOM) formed an expert Committee on the Consequences of Uninsurance to study the issue comprehensively, examining the effects of the lack of health coverage on individuals, families, communities, and the broader society.[2] Now, after a significant economic downturn, 17.2 percent of the population under age 65 is uninsured and the number has grown to over 43 million. One in three Americans were uninsured for a month or more during a two-year period (1996-1997) (Short, 2001). Fewer people have access to coverage at work, more people find the costs of private coverage too expensive, and others lose public coverage because of changed personal circumstances, administrative barriers, and program cutbacks. The situation is even more dire now than when the study began and it is expected to worsen in the foreseeable future because of federal and state budget constraints limiting public coverage programs, increasing costs of health care and insurance premiums, and continuing high rates of unemployment.

WHY SHOULD POLICY MAKERS AND THE PUBLIC CARE ABOUT COVERAGE?

The Committee has conducted an exhaustive review of the scientific evidence on the consequences of uninsurance and finds that having no insurance decreases access to health services and reduced access to health care among the uninsured is associated with the poorer health. The lack of coverage is not only associated with negative effects on the uninsured individual but also has implications for the entire family of the uninsured person and the community in which he or she lives, and economic costs to society nationally (IOM, 2001a, 2002a,b, 2003a,b). In short, in a series of five reports **the Committee concluded that:**

---

[1] The estimate of the uninsured is based on the Census Bureau's annual March Current Population Survey (CPS), as all annual estimates of the uninsured population of the United States presented in this report, unless otherwise noted. The CPS may overestimate the number of uninsured for the entire calendar year and does not account for all who are uninsured for shorter time periods (CBO, 2003). See Chapter 2 for a discussion of who is uninsured, why, and for how long.

[2] In this study, the focus is on people with no health insurance, such as "major medical" coverage for hospitalization and outpatient medical services, either for short or long periods. The Committee does not address *underinsurance*, that is, health plans that offer less than adequate coverage with excessive out-of-pocket payments, maximum benefit limits, or exclusion of specific services, such as mental health treatment. The problems of *underinsurance* are generally less severe than those of *uninsurance*, involve different policy issues and require the collection of different types of information. See further discussion in Chapter 2.

- The number of uninsured individuals under age 65 is large, growing, and has persisted even during periods of strong economic growth.
- Uninsured children and adults do not receive the care they need; they suffer from poorer health and development, and are more likely to die early than are those with coverage.
- Even one uninsured person in a family can put the financial stability and health of the whole family at risk.
- A community's high uninsured rate can adversely affect the overall health status of the community, its health care institutions and providers, and the access of its residents to certain services.
- The estimated value across the populations in healthy years of life gained by providing health insurance coverage is almost certainly greater than the additional costs of an "insured" level of services for those who lack coverage.[3]

GUIDING THE DEBATE

In this report, the sixth and last in the series, the Committee presents its conclusions and recommendations, based on the findings of its previous five reports. It calls for action on the problems of uninsurance and hopes to stimulate informed discussion of the various proposals that have been put forth to extend coverage. *By "extend coverage" we mean having more people gain coverage who previously had had none and reducing the uninsured rate.* To guide future discussion, the Committee offers principles, supported by the research, against which proposals for extending coverage can be assessed.

The Committee's review of clinical, epidemiological, and economic research for its earlier reports revealed certain features of health insurance that contribute to better health outcomes for those who have coverage. These insights into what accounts for the greater effectiveness of "insured" health care are reflected in the principles the Committee presents to guide policy makers and the public in analyzing proposals or developing new strategies. The Committee does not recommend or reject any specific proposal. Rather it demonstrates, through the use of the principles, how each of a wide range of proposals would improve the current situation.

---

[3] An "insured" level of services reflects the current average benefits under Medicaid or private health insurance for those under age 65.

ELIMINATING UNINSURANCE:
LESSONS FROM THE PAST AND PRESENT

Present-day efforts to reduce or eliminate uninsurance build on nearly a century of campaigns to bring about universal health insurance coverage. **Past campaigns have yielded both incremental changes and major reforms but not universal coverage, due to challenges to major structural changes posed by American political arrangements and the lack of political leadership strong and sustained enough to forge a workable consensus on coverage legislation. In addition, the opposition of provider, insurer, and business groups with economic interests potentially adversely affected by specific reform proposals has blocked universal coverage even though many have agreed with the general need for reform.**

In the early 1900s, health insurance was seen initially as a type of social insurance, justified as a means of protecting workers' lost income when disabled or ill (Starr, 1982). By the 1930s it became a way to make health services more affordable for individuals and thus encourage utilization. Opposition to compulsory public insurance at the national level fed the development of private-sector nonprofit and commercial health coverage organized through the workplace. Between 1940 and 1960, the proportion of the general population with private health insurance grew from 9 percent to 68 percent (Bovbjerg et al., 1993).

Reform efforts to extend public coverage to retirees and the poor, two groups unlikely to purchase private coverage and likely to have difficulty paying for health care, met with success in 1965 with the enactment of Medicare and Medicaid as amendments to the Social Security Act. These two new programs introduced tens of millions of newly insured persons, and billions of new public dollars, into the health care system. Campaigns for universal coverage in the 1970s and 1990s have been shaped by the tensions between the goals of enrolling greater numbers of people and controlling health care expenditures.

Recent Federal Incentives to Extend Coverage
Have Not Closed the Coverage Gap

Finding: Federal incremental reforms over the past 20 years have made little progress in reducing overall uninsured rates nationally, although public program expansions have improved coverage for targeted previously uninsured groups. Federal reforms of employment-based insurance have not included provisions for assuring affordability and, thus, have had limited effect.

Finding: Extensions of program eligibility for one group of uninsured often affect the coverage status of other population groups indirectly, for example, when State Children's Health Insurance Program enrollment efforts identify children who are eligible for but not enrolled in Medicaid.

Finding: Public programs fall short of their coverage goals when not all eligible persons enroll. When outreach and enrollment are made a priority, coverage levels rise. Public coverage programs sometimes employ administrative barriers to enrollment to contend with inadequate or unstable during periods of economic stress within states.

Health insurance coverage rates nationally reached their high point in 1980, when approximately 15 percent of the general population under age 65 was uninsured (Bovbjerg et. al., 1993). The percentage uninsured has not varied widely since then, but the number of uninsured people has grown substantially, to over 43 million, reflecting growth in the total population. Reforms since 1980 have made little progress in reducing the uninsured rate (Levit et al., 1992; Fronstin, 2002; Mills and Bhandari, 2003).

Since the mid-1980s, however, major federal initiatives to extend both public and private coverage, many modeled after successful state programs, have improved coverage rates among lower income children (in households earning less than 200 percent poverty) and boosted the numbers of lower income persons with public coverage. Between 1984 and 1990, Congress gradually expanded Medicaid for pregnant women, infants, and young children, delinking coverage from welfare eligibility. These Medicaid expansions were followed in 1997 by the creation of the State Children's Health Insurance Program (SCHIP), a 10-year, $40 billion allotment in federal matching and capped grants in aid to the states. The program reduced the number of uninsured children, though more than half of the remaining uninsured children are eligible but not enrolled (Broaddus and Ku, 2000; Dubay et al., 2002a; Kenney et al., 2003).

Federal initiatives to extend employment-based coverage have targeted improved portability and continuity of coverage through the Consolidated Omnibus Budget Reconciliation Act of 1985 (COBRA), the Health Insurance Portability and Accountability Act of 1996 (HIPAA), and the Trade Act of 2002 (TA). All three statutes attempt to preserve coverage for specific categories of transitioning and unemployed workers and their families, yet the lack of authority or resources under COBRA and HIPAA to make insurance premiums affordable has seriously limited their usefulness and impact. It remains to be seen whether the subsidized tax credit to be given to displaced workers and retirees under the TA's authority will make premiums affordable enough to increase coverage among the approximately 260,000 eligible persons (Healthcare Leadership Council, 2003).

State and Local Initiatives to Extend Coverage

Finding: The federal Employee Retirement Income Security Act of 1974 (ERISA) constrains the ability of states to mandate employment-based coverage, one strategy to extend private coverage within their boundaries.

Finding: Although some states have made significant progress in reducing uninsurance, even the states that have led major coverage reforms have large and persisting uninsured populations.

Finding: States do not have the fiscal resources to implement fully their existing public coverage programs and are further constrained from eliminating uninsurance within their boundaries by categorical limits on eligibility for federally supported public coverage programs.

Finding: Extensions of public or private coverage at the county level have focused on increasing coverage among targeted populations rather than the entire uninsured population locally. Despite the potential of local programs to fill targeted gaps, the lack of reliable funding source limits their scope and effectiveness.

Historically some states have taken the lead in extending coverage, but state efforts alone have been insufficient to eliminate uninsurance within their boundaries and have had little impact on the overall, national uninsured rate. This report highlights five states—Hawaii, Massachusetts, Minnesota, Oregon, and Tennessee—that have invested significant funds since the mid-1980s to expand their public programs and in some cases have also regulated the small group and nongroup insurance markets to create more affordable options. In 1994, these states began using Medicaid Section 1115 waivers, without additional federal dollars, to broaden eligibility, with all but Tennessee folding in their own separate coverage programs for persons ineligible for Medicaid. Though all have made progress in extending coverage, each state still has significant numbers of uninsured people.

All states are limited by ERISA, which does not permit direct state regulation of coverage plans sponsored by private employers.[4] States may not

---

[4] In 1983, Hawaii received an exemption from ERISA, under the condition that the provisions of the state's employer mandate not be updated.

tax employer-sponsored plans directly, require employers to offer coverage, or regulate what they do offer.

Addressing concerns about the substitution or crowding out of private coverage by new public programs has created administrative barriers to full enrollment of all eligible persons. The increasingly severe budget crises faced by the states beginning in 2001 have limited state reform and begun to erode coverage, although the prospect of losing federal revenue has motivated states to maintain much of their commitment to public coverage programs that receive federal matching funds (Smith et al., 2002; Boyd, 2003). State governments' capacity to finance health care and extend coverage tends to be weakest at times when demands for such support are likely to be the highest, for example, during an economic recession. Nonetheless, the growing unmet need for health insurance in recent years has catalyzed reform efforts in many states (IOM, 2003a).

Many states designate their counties as the providers of last resort for the underserved and the uninsured (IOM, 2003a). Across the nation, a handful of counties has experimented with innovative ways to improve access to care using insurance or an approach that resembles health insurance to reduce the impact of uninsurance on their communities. The Committee looked at the experiences of three urban counties that have led reform, Almeda County (CA), Hillsborough County (FL), and San Diego (CA). These counties have reformed the organization, financing, and delivery of local health services, combining outreach and enrollment activities with new sources of revenue to support coverage. Serious financial constraints limit the scope and effectiveness of these programs and keep them from fully reaching their goals.

Despite gradual expansions of public programs at the federal, state, and local levels and isolated efforts around the country to move toward the goal of universal coverage, the lack of political consensus has prevented a substantial reduction in uninsurance in the United States. Laudable efforts have been hindered by a lack of resources. The state and county programs described here are noteworthy but atypical; individual state and local efforts to extend health insurance will not achieve universal coverage nationally. In some states the size of the uninsured population is overwhelming and many states lack the resources to extend coverage substantially. The circumscribed nature of past and present initiatives suggests that attempts to provide universal coverage without a substantial infusion of new federal funds are unrealistic. Recognition of the need to treat the elimination of uninsurance as a national responsibility, as well as a state and local one, is essential to comprehensive reform of coverage.

Conclusion: The persistence of uninsurance in the United States requires a national and coherent strategy aimed at covering the entire

population. Federal leadership and federal dollars are necessary to eliminate uninsurance, although not necessarily federal administration or a uniform approach throughout the country. Universal health insurance coverage will only be achieved when the principle of universality is embodied in federal public policy.

A VISION OF UNIVERSAL COVERAGE

The Committee's previous reports detailed the negative effects on individuals' health, family stability, community health care institutions and access of residents, and the national economy associated with the existence of a large uninsured population. This report reviews a century of efforts aimed at reducing or eliminating uninsurance. This report also examines various approaches to providing health insurance because the Committee believes extending insurance coverage is a worthwhile and feasible endeavor. Imagine what the country would be like if everyone had coverage—people would be financially able to have health problems checked, to seek preventive and primary care promptly, and to receive necessary, appropriate, and effective health services. Hospitals would be able to provide care without jeopardizing their operating budget and all families would have security in knowing that they had some protection against the prospect of medical bills undermining their financial stability or creditworthiness. The Committee believes that this picture could become a reality and that it is an image worth pursuing because the costs of uninsurance to all of us—financial, societal, and in terms of health—are so great. The benefits of appropriate and timely health care are potentially even greater and can help motivate attaining this vision.

VISION STATEMENT

The Committee on the Consequences of Uninsurance envisions an approach to health insurance that will promote better overall health for individuals, families, communities, and the nation by providing financial access for everyone to necessary, appropriate, and effective health services.

PRINCIPLES TO GUIDE THE EXTENSION OF COVERAGE

The evidence reviewed and developed by the Committee in its first five reports contributes to the shared vision and the following five key principles. The first principle is the most basic and yet the most important. The remaining four principles are not ranked by priority. Selected pieces of evidence are provided in the following discussion of the principles. (See the Committee's earlier reports, *Coverage Matters, Care Without Coverage, Health Insurance Is a Family Matter, A Shared Destiny,* and *Hidden Costs, Value Lost,* and Chapter 2 in the full report, *Insuring America's Health,* for more detailed discussions of evidence.)

1. **Health care coverage should be universal.**
   - Everyone living in the United States should be covered by health insurance. Being uninsured can damage the health of individuals and families. Uninsured children and adults use medical and dental services less often than insured people and are less likely to receive routine preventive care (Newacheck et al., 1998b; McCormick et al., 2001; IOM, 2002b). They are less likely to have a regular source of care than are insured people (Zuvekas and Weinick, 1999; Weinick et al., 2000). Insurance coverage is the best mechanism for gaining financial access to services that may produce better health.
   - Uninsured people are less likely to receive high-quality, professionally recommended care and medications, particularly for preventive services and chronic conditions (Beckles et al., 1998; Cooper-Patrick et al., 1999; Powell-Griner et al., 1999; Ayanian et al., 2000; Breen et al., 2001; Goldman et al., 2001).
   - Uninsured children risk abnormal long-term development if they do not receive routine care; uninsured adults have worse outcomes for chronic conditions such as diabetes, cardiovascular disease, end-stage renal disease, and HIV (Hadley, 2002; IOM, 2002a,b).
   - Uninsured adults have a 25 percent greater mortality risk than do insured adults, accounting for an estimated 18,000 excess deaths annually (Franks et al., 1993a; Sorlie et al., 1994; IOM, 2002a).

2. **Health care coverage should be continuous.**
   - Continuous coverage is more likely to lead to improved health outcomes; breaks in coverage result in diminished health status (Lurie et al., 1984, 1986; Franks et al., 1993a; Sorlie et al., 1994; Baker et al., 2001).
   - Achieving coverage well before the onset of an illness would likely lead to a better health outcome because the chance of early detection would be enhanced (Perkins et al., 2001).
   - Interruptions in coverage interfere with therapeutic relationships, contribute to missed preventive services for children, and result in inadequate chronic care (Rodewald et al., 1997; Beckles et al., 1998; Burstin et al., 1998; Daumit et al., 1999, 2000; Hoffman et al., 2001).

3. Health care coverage should be affordable to individuals and families.

- The high cost of health insurance is the main reason people give for being uninsured (Hoffman and Schlobohm, 2000; IOM, 2001a). Nearly two-thirds of people with no coverage have incomes that are less than 200 percent of the federal poverty level (IOM, 2001a). Families in that income group have little leeway for health expenditures, making some form of financial assistance necessary for obtaining coverage (IOM, 2002b).
- Among families with no members insured during the entire year and incomes below the poverty level, more than a quarter paid out-of-pocket medical expenses that were more than 5 percent of income (Taylor et al., 2001).

4. The health insurance strategy should be affordable and sustainable for society.

- The Committee acknowledges that any health insurance strategy will likely face budgetary constraints on the benefits as well as on the administrative operations. Any major reform will need mechanisms to control the rate of growth in health care spending. There is no analytically derivable dollar amount of what society can afford; that will be determined through political and economic processes.
- The Committee believes that everyone should contribute financially to the national strategy through mechanisms such as taxes, premiums, and cost sharing because all members of society can expect to benefit from universal health insurance coverage.
- To help insure affordability, the reform strategy should strive for efficiency and simplicity.

5. Health insurance should enhance health and well-being by promoting access to high-quality care that is effective, efficient, safe, timely, patient-centered, and equitable.

- Insurance should be designed to enhance the quality of the health care system as specified above and recommended by the IOM's Committee on Quality of Health Care in America (IOM, 2001b).
- A benefit package that includes preventive and screening services, outpatient prescription drugs, and specialty mental health care as well as outpatient and hospital services would enhance receipt of appropriate care (Huttin et al., 2000; IOM, 2002a).
- Variation in patient cost sharing could be used as an incentive for appropriate service use because it can influence patient behavior (Newhouse and The Insurance Experiment Group, 1993).

USING THE PRINCIPLES

The Committee's research on the problems related to uninsurance demonstrates conclusively that there are benefits for the nation and all its residents from eliminating uninsurance and ensuring coverage for everyone. Based on review of past incremental and disjointed efforts to extend coverage, the limited progress made, and the remaining 43 million uninsured,

The Committee concludes that health insurance coverage for everyone in the United States requires major reform initiated as federal policy.

Achieving universal coverage across the country will require at a minimum federal policy direction and financial support. The new system would not necessarily be controlled wholly at the federal level or operated solely through a government agency. The Committee presents the preceding set of principles to be used in clarifying public debate about approaches to extending coverage. The principles provide objectives against which to measure various proposals. The Committee does not endorse or reject any particular approach to solving the problem of uninsurance, but recognizes that there are many pathways to achieving its vision.

The Committee recommends that these principles be used to assess the merits of current proposals and to design future strategies for extending coverage to everyone.

To illustrate how the principles should be used to evaluate reform proposals, the Committee sketches four prototypes for major reform in a simplified format so that the main incentives are clear. It then assesses each prototype against each of the principles, highlighting the model's strengths and weaknesses. These models all include aspects of strategies under discussion in the public debate but are not detailed legislative proposals or specific strategies favored by particular politicians or advocacy groups. Brief outlines of the prototypes (discussed fully in Chapter 5 of *Insuring America's Health*) are as follows

1. *Major public program extension and new tax credit:* No fundamental change in private insurance, Medicaid and SCHIP merged and expanded, Medicare extended to 55 year olds, a tax credit for moderate income individuals.
2. *Employer mandate, premium subsidy, and individual mandate:* Employers required to provide coverage and contribution to workers' premiums, subsidy for employers of low-wage workers, individuals required to accept employment-based insurance or obtain it privately, merged public program for those not covered at work.

3. *Individual mandate and tax credit:* Each person eligible for an advanceable, refundable tax credit and required to obtain coverage in the private market, Medicaid, and SCHIP eliminated.
4. *Single payer:* Administered federally, everyone enrolled, single benefit package, global budget, no Medicaid, SCHIP, or Medicare.

Each model meets some principles better than others and each principle may be more fully achieved by one prototype more than another. For example, the principle of universal coverage is more likely to be reached through any of the models with mandates than by the first prototype, which is entirely voluntary. Prototype 1 was included for completeness because it is an obvious approach currently under public consideration, although it would not achieve universality. The single payer model would most successfully eliminate gaps in coverage. The assessment of each model is fully discussed in Chapter 5 and summarized in Table ES.1.

The affordability to individuals and families of each prototype would depend on the size of the subsidies or tax credits and cost-sharing requirements, as well as eligibility levels for the public programs. The affordability and sustainability for society of each model would largely depend on the nature of cost controls in the system, sources of revenues, the amount of cost sharing, and the comprehensiveness of the benefit packages. Strong cost and utilization controls could affect access to services and health outcomes in ways yet to be determined. The Committee is mindful that defining a minimum benefit package for the uninsured would likely also affect some people who currently have a lesser insurance package, increasing their benefits and resulting in additional costs and probably increased access to services and drugs and improved health outcomes.

The potential of various models to enhance health through quality care would depend on the design of the benefit packages, the strength of the public programs, and effective consumer demand. There are shortcomings of each model, but each prototype could come closer to achieving the Committee's vision and be ameliorated with further refinement, and elements of different models could be combined to promote particular principles. Most importantly, **each prototype could more nearly achieve each principle than does the current system.**

NEXT STEPS

The Committee recognizes that it will take some time to develop, adopt, and implement a program of universal coverage and that it will require additional public resources to finance insurance. It will not be quick or easy to implement the necessary reforms and it will be preferable to phase in the changes according to a fixed schedule. Implementation should aim for a minimum number of transitional stages, each of which incorporates changes that are as coherent and simple as possible. Despite a long history of failed attempts to achieve insurance for everyone, the Committee believes that universal insurance coverage is an important and achievable goal for the country. Instead of considering the status quo as everyone's second choice when consensus on an approach to universal coverage fails to materialize, we should consider it the *last* choice. We cannot afford to ignore the problem of uninsurance.

The Committee recommends that the President and Congress develop a strategy to achieve universal insurance coverage and to establish a firm and explicit schedule to reach this goal by 2010.

The Committee recommends that, until universal coverage takes effect, the federal and state governments provide resources sufficient for Medicaid and SCHIP to cover all persons currently eligible and prevent the erosion of outreach efforts, eligibility, enrollment, and coverage.

The Committee is concerned that the current and growing economic pressures on state governments as well as at the federal level will have a negative impact on public programs and erode current coverage, making future coverage gains more difficult. Until everyone has financial access to health services through insurance, it is necessary to sustain current public coverage programs. It is also important to shore up the current capacity of health care institutions and providers who take a major responsibility for caring for the uninsured. Continuing support of service capacity, particularly in underserved areas, may be needed.

The Committee appreciates that making a national commitment to achieve universal insurance coverage will require strong bipartisan political support as well as broad-based and deep public support. We all bear the costs of the current nonsystem that leaves tens of millions without health coverage. Doing nothing and maintaining the status quo with over 43 million uninsured Americans is expensive. The nation suffers losses due to ill health, impaired development, early deaths, and lost productivity. The lack of health insurance is a destabilizing factor in families and for health care institutions that serve uninsured patients. In fact, the presence of uninsurance creates insecurity for everyone, even those with health insurance today, because losing that coverage tomorrow is so easy. Universal insurance coverage will benefit all Americans, enhance the great promise of our health care system, and reinforce our values as a democratic society. **It is time for our nation to extend coverage to everyone.**

TABLE ES.1 Summary Assessment of Prototypes Based on Committee Principles

Principles	Status Quo	Prototype 1 Major Public Program Expansion and Tax Credit
Coverage should be universal	Not universal; *43 million uninsured*	*Would not achieve universality because voluntary,* but would reduce uninsured population
Coverage should be continuous	*Not continuous;* income, age, family, job, and health-related *gaps in coverage*	Family- and job-related *gaps in coverage*
Coverage should be affordable for individuals and families	*Private coverage unaffordable* to many moderate- and low-income persons	*More affordable than current system* for those with low or moderate income
Strategy should be affordable and sustainable for society	*Not affordable or sustainable for society;* uninsurance is growing; cost of poorer health and shorter lives is $65 billion-$130 billion; some participants contribute; no limit on aggregate health expenditures or on tax political support; size of expenditures—spending is higher than other countries; sustainability of current public programs depends on economy and political support	All participants contribute; *aggregate expenditures not controlled; new public expenditures for only the public program expansion and tax credit;* sustainability public program depends on revenue sources and credit depends on political support
Coverage should enhance health through high quality care	*Quality of care* for the population *limited* because one in seven is uninsured	Opportunities to promote quality improvements *similar to current system*

Prototype 2	Prototype 3	Prototype 4
Employer Mandate, Premium Subsidy, and Individual Mandate	Individual Mandate and Tax Credit	Single Payer
Coverage likely to be high; depends on enforcement of mandates	*Depends on size of tax credit, enforcement,* and cost of individual insurance	*Likely to achieve universal coverage*
Brief gaps related to life and job transitions	*Minimal gaps*	*Continuous* until death or age 65
Yes for workers, assuming adequate employer premium assistance; *public program designed to be affordable* for all enrollees	Subsidy based only on income and family size leaves *older, less healthy, and those in expensive areas with less affordable coverage*	*Minimal cost sharing,* but could be problem for low income
All participants contribute; *basic package less costly than current employment coverage;* revenue from patients in public program; sustainability depends on revenue sources from employers' premium on assistance and public program	No limit on aggregate health expenditures or on tax expenditure, though federal costs relatively predictable and controllable through size of credit; *sustainable through federal income tax base;* size of credit depends on political support	Nearly all participants contribute; *aggregate expenditures controllable,* utilization not directly or centrally controlled; *high cost to federal budget;* administrative savings; sustainability depends on revenue source and political support
Could design quality incentives in expanded public program and basic benefit package; current employer incentives for quality remain	*Similar incentives to current private insurance* system; consumer could choose quality plans	*Potentially yes,* depends on proper design

Appendix B

Statistics on the Nonelderly U.S. Population Without Health Insurance, 2007

TABLE B-1 Age, Race, Hispanic Origin, and Immigrant Status of the Nonelderly U.S. Population Without Health Insurance Coverage, 2007

Characteristic	Uninsured population (in millions)	Proportion of the uninsured population (%)	Uninsured rate (%)
Total	45.7	100.0	15.3
Age			
All children, under age 18	8.1	17.8	11.0
All adults, ages 18-64	36.8	80.6	19.6
18 to 24 years	8.0	17.5	28.1
25 to 34 years	10.3	22.6	25.7
35 to 44 years	7.7	16.9	18.3
45 to 54 years	6.8	14.8	15.4
55 to 64 years	4.0	8.8	12.0
Race			
White[a]	34.3	75.1	14.3
White, not Hispanic	20.5	45.0	10.4
Black[b]	7.6	16.7	19.2
Asian	2.2	4.9	16.8
American Indian/Alaska Native[c]	0.9	1.9	32.9
Native Hawaiian/Pacific Islander[c]	0.1	0.3	19.5
Hispanic origin			
Hispanic	14.8	32.3	32.1
Not Hispanic	30.9	67.7	12.2
Immigrant status			
U.S. native	33.3	72.9	12.7
Naturalized citizen	2.7	5.8	17.6
Not a citizen	9.7	21.3	43.8

NOTE: Proportions may not total 100 percent because of rounding.

[a] Includes both Hispanic and non-Hispanic.

[b] Includes multiracial blacks and blacks of Hispanic and non-Hispanic origin.

[c] Indicates values from small sample sizes averaged over two years (2006-2007).

TABLE B-2 Household Income and Family Work Status of the
Nonelderly U.S. Population Without Health Insurance Coverage, 2007

Characteristic	Uninsured population (in millions)	Proportion of the uninsured population (%)	Uninsured rate (%)
Total	45.7	100.0	15.3
Household Income			
Poor, less than $25,000	13.5	29.6	24.5
Low income, $25,000 to $49,999	14.5	31.8	21.1
Middle income, $45,000 to $74,999	8.5	18.6	14.5
Higher income, greater than $75,000	9.1	20.0	7.8
Work status			
Total, 18 to 64 years old	36.8	100.0	19.6
Worked during year	26.8	72.8	18.1
Worked full-time	21.1	57.3	17.0
Worked part-time	5.8	15.8	23.4
Did not work	10.0	27.2	25.4

NOTE: Proportions may not total 100 percent due to rounding.

REFERENCE

DeNavas-Walt, C., B. D. Proctor, and J. Smith. 2008. *Income, poverty, and health insurance coverage in the United States: 2007*. Washington, DC: U.S. Census Bureau.

Appendix C

State Regulations Promoting Access to Individual Health Insurance Policies, 2007

TABLE C-1 State Regulations Promoting Access to Individual Health Insurance Policies, 2007

State	All insurers must guaranteed issue all products (6 states)	All insurers must guaranteed issue some products (8 States)	Insurers of last Resort (6 states)	High-risk pool for medically eligible (31 states)
Alabama	No	No	No	No
Alaska	No	No	No	Yes
Arizona	No	No	No	No
Arkansas	No	No	No	Yes
California	No	Yes[a]	No	Yes
Colorado	No	No	No	Yes
Connecticut	No	No	No	Yes
DC	No	No	Yes[d]	No
Delaware	No	No	No	No
Florida	No	No	No	No
Georgia	No	No	No	No
Hawaii	No	No	No	No
Idaho	No	Yes[a]	No	Yes
Illinois	No	No	No	Yes
Indiana	No	No	No	Yes
Iowa	No	No	No	Yes
Kansas	No	No	No	Yes
Kentucky	No	No	No	Yes
Louisiana	No	No	No	Yes
Maine	Yes[c]	No	No	No
Maryland	No	No	No	Yes
Massachusetts	Yes[c]	No	No	No

Michigan	No	Yes[b]	Yes[d]	No
Minnesota	No	No	No	Yes
Mississippi	No	No	No	Yes
Missouri	No	No	No	Yes
Montana	No	No	No	Yes
Nebraska	No	No	No	Yes
Nevada	No	No	No	No
New Hampshire	Yes[c]	No	No	Yes
New Jersey	No	No	No	No
New Mexico	Yes[c]	No	No	Yes
New York	No	No	No	No
North Carolina	No	No	Yes[d]	No
North Dakota	No	No	No	Yes
Ohio	No	Yes[b]	No	No
Oklahoma	No	No	No	Yes
Oregon	No	Yes[a]	Yes[d]	Yes
Pennsylvania	No	No	Yes[d]	No
Rhode Island	No	Yes[a]	Yes[d]	No
South Carolina	No	No	No	Yes
South Dakota	No	No	No	Yes
Tennessee	No	No	No	Yes
Texas	No	No	No	Yes
Utah	No	Yes	No	Yes
Vermont	Yes[c]	No	No	No
Virginia	No	No	Yes[d]	No
Washington	Yes[c]	No	No	Yes
West Virginia	No	Yes[b]	No	Yes

State	All insurers must guaranteed issue all products (6 states)	All insurers must guaranteed issue some products (8 States)	Insurers of last Resort (6 states)	High-risk pool for medically eligible (31 states)
Wisconsin	No	No	No	Yes
Wyoming	No	No	No	Yes

NOTE: Not applicable to individuals who are eligible for coverage under the Health Insurance Portability and Accountability Act (HIPAA). In several states, including New York, all individual health insurance policies must be offered to all residents on a guaranteed-issue basis year-round. In others, including Ohio, only certain insurers must offer guaranteed-issue policies. If health insurance must be sold on a guaranteed-issue basis, applicants cannot be turned down because of their health or risk status.

[a] Continuously for some individuals.

[b] Periodically for some plans for all individuals.

[c] Continuous for all individuals.

[d] The local or regional Blue Cross Blue Shield Association plan makes coverage available.

Data as of December 2007. Data compiled through review of state laws and regulations and interviews with state health insurance regulatory staff. For more detailed information on consumer protections in any state see Georgetown University's "Consumer Guides for Getting and Keeping Health Insurance" available at http://www.healthinsuranceinfo.net/.

This information was reprinted with permission from the Henry J. Kaiser Family Foundation. The Kaiser Family Foundation is a nonprofit private operating foundation, based in Menlo Park, California, dedicated to producing and communicating the best possible information, research, and analysis on health issues.

REFERENCE

Henry J. Kaiser Family Foundation. 2008. State health facts: Individual market guaranteed issue (not applicable to HIPAA eligible individuals) 2007, http://www.statehealthfacts.org/comparetable.jsp?cat=7&ind=353 (accessed September 23, 2008).

Appendix D

Recent Studies of the Impacts of Health Insurance for Children: Summary Tables

Five tables summarizing the evidence since 2002 on the impacts of health insurance for children are presented in this appendix. These tables were originally presented in a literature review commissioned by the Institute of Medicine Committee on Health Insurance Status and Its Consequences in 2008 titled *Health and Access Consequences of Uninsurance Among Children in the United States: An Update*, by Genevieve M. Kenney, Ph.D., and Embry Howell, Ph.D., The Urban Institute.

- Table D-1: General Health Care: Impacts of Health Insurance on Children's Access and Use of Care
- Table D-2: Dental Services: Impacts of Health Insurance on Children's Access and Use of Dental Services
- Table D-3: Immunizations: Impacts of Health Insurance on Children's Immunizations
- Table D-4: Impacts of Health Insurance on Special Populations of Children
- Table D-5: Impacts of Health Insurance on Children's Health Status and Related Outcomes

Several abbreviations are used frequently in the tables:

- ACSC = ambulatory care sensitive condition
- ADHD = Attention Deficit Hyperactivity Disorder
- CHI = children's health initiatives
- CSHCN = children with special health care needs

143

- D-D = difference-in-difference
- IR = incidence ratio
- MEPS = Medical Expenditure Panel Survey
- NHANES = National Health and Nutrition Examination Survey
- NHIS = National Health Interview Survey
- NSAF = National Survey of America's Families
- NSCH = National Survey of Children's Health
- OLS = ordinary least squares
- Rx = prescription
- SCHIP = State Children's Health Insurance Program

Changes are statistically significant unless otherwise noted as "not significant" ("NS"). N/A indicates that the study in question did not examine the specified outcome.

TABLE D-1 General Health Care: Impacts of Health Insurance on Children's Access and Use of Care

Citation	Location and Time Period of Analysis	Data Sources	Methodology
National Studies			
Banthin and Selden (2003) The ABCs of children's health care: How the Medicaid expansions affected access, burdens, and coverage between 1987 and 1996	United States, 1987 and 1996	National Medical Expenditure Survey (1987) and MEPS (1996)	D-D approach: change between 1987 and 1996 for poverty-related children less change over same time period for slightly higher-income children: Children made eligible for Medicaid under the poverty-related expansions in the 1980s are the treatment group and children with slightly higher income levels—defined as those in the income groups ultimately made eligible for SCHIP as of 2000—are the primary comparison group; controls included a variety of sociodemographic characteristics, as well as income and health status. Service use refers to previous 12 months.
Currie et al. (2008) Has public health insurance for older children reduced disparities in access to care and health outcomes?	United States, 1986 to 2005	NHIS (N = 548,789)	Examine impacts of Medicaid/ SCHIP eligibility expansions on probability of an ambulatory visit and reported health status using a simulated eligibility indicator to address potential endogeny of eligibility. Medicaid/SCHIP generosity index generated by applying state eligibility rules to a sample of children for each state and year. Control variables include interaction terms and age and year dummies. Look at concurrent and lagged effects. Still potentially biased and concerns about appropriateness of simulated eligibility measure in studies of all kids. Service use refers to previous 12 months.

Findings

Usual Source of Care	Any Ambulatory Visit	Any Preventive Visit	Any Unmet Need	Specific Unmet Needs
2.1 percentage point increase (NS)	9.3 percentage point increase	N/A	N/A	N/A
N/A	Eligible children 6.8 percentage points more likely to have ambulatory visit in past year; children ages 9-17 who were eligible as younger children are 3.9 to 8.9 percentage points more likely to have doctor's visit; find positive lagged eligibility effects	N/A	N/A	N/A

Continued

TABLE D-1 Continued

Citation	Location and Time Period of Analysis	Data Sources	Methodology
Davidoff et al. (2005) Effects of the State Children's Health Insurance Program expansions on children with chronic health conditions	United States, 1997, 2000, 2001	NHIS core data source supplemented with state data on policy changes, local data on private premiums	D-D approach: two treatment groups—children in the income group made newly eligible under SCHIP and children already eligible for Medicaid under the poverty-related expansions; comparison group: children with incomes slightly above the SCHIP eligibility thresholds; wide-ranging control variables to address possible confounding changes occurring over the same period. Service use refers to previous 12 months. Sample is restricted to children with chronic health conditions.
Selden and Hudson (2006) Access to care and utilization among children: Estimating the effects of public and private coverage	United States, 1996-2002	MEPS supplemented with state-level Medicaid/SCHIP eligibility and private premiums information; N = 49,003	Children uninsured for full year compared to children with private coverage only and to children with any public coverage. Two-stage least squares with instrumental variables used to address selection bias (estimates reported here are from the model using family instruments). Found that OLS estimates understate positive effects of coverage. Service use refers to previous 12 months.

Findings

Usual Source of Care	Any Ambulatory Visit	Any Preventive Visit	Any Unmet Need	Specific Unmet Needs
N/A	2.4 percentage point increase (NS)	N/A	8.6 percentage point decrease	Rx: 3.7 percentage point decrease
38.5 (public) and 39.7 (private) percentage points more likely than uninsured	32.7 (public) and 30.1 (private) percentage points more likely than uninsured	33.5 (public) and 26.8 (private) percentage points more likely to comply with well-visit guidelines	N/A	N/A

Continued

TABLE D-1 Continued

Citation	Location and Time Period of Analysis	Data Sources	Methodology
State Studies			
Damiano et al. (2003) The impact of the Iowa S-SCHIP program on access, health status, and family environment	Iowa, 1999-2000	Two-wave mail survey (with telephone followup) of parents of new enrollees in Hawk-I (SCHIP) and 1 year later; (N = 463) response rate = 80% for baseline and 72% for followup	Pre-post cohort/longitudinal design. Outcomes for new enrollees compared to outcomes for the same enrollees 1 year later; no information provided on prior coverage of new enrollees. Service use refers to previous 12 months.
Dick et al. (2004) SCHIP's impact in three states: How do the most vulnerable children fare?	Kansas, Florida, and New York. Baseline between June 2000 and March 2001; Followup interviews were conducted 1 year later	Surveys of enrollees in State Children's Health Insurance Programs; adolescents only in FL. KS: N = 434, response rate = 35% FL: N = 944, response rate = 30% NY: N = 2,290, response rate = 55%	Pre-post cohort/longitudinal design. Included children who had disenrolled from SCHIP. Provide separate estimates for children who were previously uninsured.
Feinberg et al. (2002) Family income and the impact of a children's health insurance program on reported need for health services and unmet health need	Massachusetts, 1998-1999	One-wave telephone survey of parents of children in enrolled in Mass. Children's Medical Security Plan, a precursor to SCHIP, that included children of all incomes. (N = 877 primary sample plus 119 Spanish oversample); response rate = 62%	Compared experiences of children before and after enrollment, which parents were asked to recall.

Findings

Usual Source of Care	Any Ambulatory Visit	Any Preventive Visit	Any Unmet Need	Specific Unmet Needs
Increased from 81% to 89%	N/A	N/A	Decreased from 27% to 9% (medical need)	Specialty: Decreased from 40% to 13%; Vision: Decreased from 46% to 12%; Behavioral/Emotional: Decreased from 42% to 18%; Rx: Decreased from 21% to 13%
NY: Increased from 78% to 97%	N/A	KS: Increased from 51% to 66% (NS); NY: increased from 67% to 80%	KS: Decreased from 53% to 20%; NY: decreased from 32% to 21%	N/A
N/A	N/A	N/A	Excluding dental: Declined from 12% before enrollment to 7% after	Rx: Declined from 4% to 3%; Vision: Declined from 30% to 17% (NS); Mental: Declined from 33% to 17% (NS)

Continued

TABLE D-1 Continued

Citation	Location and Time Period of Analysis	Data Sources	Methodology
Fox et al. (2003) Changes in reported health status and unmet need for children enrolling in the Kansas children's health insurance program	Kansas, 1999-2000	Two-wave survey of parents of children enrolled in the program in its first 6 months and of the same parents 1 year later; (N = 1,955), response rate = 60% (Wave 2)	Pre-post cohort/longitudinal design. Responses for children just after enrollment compared to responses for same children 1 year later. Service use refers to previous 12 months.
Kempe et al. (2005) Changes in access, utilization, and quality of care after enrollment into a state child health insurance plan	Colorado, 1999-2001	Survey of enrollees in Colorado's Child Health Plus Program; Baseline survey during 1999 and 2000; follow up survey 1 year later. (N = 480). Response rate = 77% for baseline and 68% for followup	Pre-post cohort/longitudinal design, controlling for race/ethnicity, age, prior insurance status; no separate results reported for the kids who had been uninsured prior to enrolling in SCHIP. Report IR for post- versus pre-enrollment.
Kenney (2007) The impacts of the state children's health insurance program on children who enroll: Findings from 10 states	10 states (CA, CO, FL, IL, LA, MO, NC, NJ, NY, TX), 2002	One-wave survey of parents of children newly enrolled in SCHIP or enrolled for 1 year; response rate = 75-80% depending on state; N = 16,700; data pooled across states. Primary sample consists of 5,394 established enrollees and 3,106 recent enrollees	Compare pre-SCHIP experiences of uninsured children to SCHIP experiences of SCHIP enrollees; regression adjustment for demographic characteristics and income; sensitivity analyses to examine selection. Service use refers to previous 6 months.

Findings

Usual Source of Care	Any Ambulatory Visit	Any Preventive Visit	Any Unmet Need	Specific Unmet Needs
Increased from 91.9% to 95.6%	N/A	Increased from 60.5% to 76.7%	Share who received all care needed increased from 48.9% to 83.5%	Mental health: Decreased from 4.2% to 1.1%; Vision: Decreased from 17.0% to 4.0%; Rx: Decreased from 14.1% to 2.3%
Usual source of preventive care IR = 1.02 (NS)	N/A	Routine visit: IR = 1.39	N/A	Rx: IR = .38; Mental: IR = .63; Dental: IR = .59; Routine care: IR = .17; Sick care: IR = .27; Eyeglasses: IR = .44
21 percentage point increase	7 percentage points increase	11 percentage point increase	13 percentage point decrease	Rx: 6 percentage point decrease; Specialist: 6 percentage point decrease; Hospital care: 6 percentage point decrease

Continued

TABLE D-1 Continued

Citation	Location and Time Period of Analysis	Data Sources	Methodology
Kenney et al. (2007) Medicaid and SCHIP coverage: Evidence from California and North Carolina	California and North Carolina, 2002	Survey of parents of Medicaid enrollees in two states (N = 1,162; 830 established enrollees and 332 recent Medicaid enrollees). Response rate = 41% for CA and 60% for NC	Compared pre-Medicaid experiences when uninsured to Medicaid experiences; regression adjustment for demographic characteristics, income, health status, and parent's attitudes regarding efficacy of medical care. Service use refers to previous 6 months.
Moreno and Hoag (2001) Covering the uninsured through TennCare: Does it make a difference?	Tennessee, 1998 and 1999	Five-state household survey, Random Digit Dial component from TN reported in study; 1,376 completed interviews (1,061 adults and 315 children; response rate = 72% for 1998 and 76% for 1999	Compared kids enrolled in TennCare under the expansion category (treatment group) to uninsured children (comparison group); controls include standard variables related to sociodemographic characteristics and health status and also included controls for differences in health care beliefs; small sample sizes for analyses on children—162 in the treatment group and 153 in the comparison group; regression-adjusted means were computed and compared for the treatment and the comparison group.
Slifkin et al. (2002) Effect of the North Carolina State Children's Health Insurance Program on beneficiary access to care	North Carolina, Summer 1999 for baseline and Summer 2000 for followup	Survey of children enrolled in NC Health Choice; N = 987; response rate = 75% for baseline and 74% for followup	Pre-post longitudinal/cohort study; also analyzed a fresh sample of new enrollees at followup to assess possible secular trends; pre period includes insured and uninsured kids and the uninsured sample is quite small (N = 32). Service use refers to previous 12 months.

Findings

Usual Source of Care	Any Ambulatory Visit	Any Preventive Visit	Any Unmet Need	Specific Unmet Needs
29 percentage points more likely with Medicaid	8 percentage points more likely	8 percentage points more likely	13 percentage points less likely	Rx: 3 percentage points more likely (NS); Specialist: 3 percentage points more likely (NS); Hospital: 4 percentage points more likely
Medicaid: 98.3%; Uninsured: 73.7%	N/A	Received on schedule: Medicaid: nearly 75% percent Uninsured: 55%	Estimates not given, but "similar" to adult estimates of Medicaid: 63.8%; Uninsured: 33.6%	N/A
"Had provider for checkups" 0-5y: Increased from 86% to 96% (NS); 6-11y: Increased from 68% to 93%	N/A	0-5y: Increased from 48% to 61% (NS); 6-11y: Increased from 16% to 41%	Medical: 0-5y: Decreased from 29% to 0%; 6-11y: Decreased from 62% to 2%	N/A

Continued

TABLE D-1 Continued

Citation	Location and Time Period of Analysis	Data Sources	Methodology
Szilagyi et al. (2004) Improved asthma care after enrollment in the State Children's Health Insurance program in New York	New York State, 2001-2002	Two-wave telephone survey of parents of children enrolled in Child Health Plus (SCHIP) for 4-6 months and about 1 year after enrollment; N = 2,290; response rate = 87% for followup	Outcomes for newly enrolled children compared to outcomes for the same children 1 year later. Pre period includes insured and uninsured kids, but 80 percent uninsured for part of the year. Service use refers to previous 12 months.
Local Studies			
Eisert and Gabow (2002) Effect of Child Health Insurance Plan enrollment on the utilization of health care services by children using a public safety net system	Denver, CO, 1998-2000	SCHIP enrollment data from Denver County merged with Denver Health Medical Plan dental utilization data (N = 748 before enrollment and 757 after)	Service use for children enrolled in the Denver Health Medical Plan for a year prior to SCHIP enrollment compared to during 12 months after. Only 14% of children were uninsured before enrollment. Service use refers to previous 12 months.
Howell et al. (2008a) The impact of the Los Angeles Health Kids Program on access to care, use of services, and health status	San Mateo County, CA, 2006-2007	One-wave survey of parents of primarily undocumented children newly enrolled in Healthy Kids insurance and enrolled for 1 year; (N = 1,404) response rate = 77%	Newly enrolled children compared to children enrolled for 1 year; regression adjustment for demographic characteristics, income, and medical and dental need. Service use refers to previous 6 months.

Findings

Usual Source of Care	Any Ambulatory Visit	Any Preventive Visit	Any Unmet Need	Specific Unmet Needs
11.6 percentage point increase	6.2 percentage point increase	8.9 percentage point increase	13.8 percentage point decrease	Specialty: 3.5 percentage point decrease; Preventive: 9.6 percentage point decrease; Rx: 4.1 percentage point decrease; Vision: 3.6 percentage point decrease
N/A	N/A	Increased from 31.0% to 42.0%	N/A	N/A
New: 59.4% Established: 89.1%	New: 40.7% Established: 58.6%	New: 36.7% Established: 54.3%	New: 28.5% Established: 16.0%	Delay in vision: New: 5.5% Established: 1.7%

Continued

TABLE D-1 Continued

Citation	Location and Time Period of Analysis	Data Sources	Methodology
Howell et al. (2008b) Final report of the evaluation of the San Mateo County Children's Health Initiative	Los Angeles County, CA, 2005-2007	Two-wave survey of parents of primarily undocumented children ages 1-5 enrolled in Healthy Kids insurance (N = 975); response rate to both waves = 77%	D-D; changes over a year for children who had been enrolled for a year in Wave 1 compared to changes for newly enrolled children; regression adjustment for demographic characteristics, income, and medical and dental need. Service use refers to previous 6 months.
Trenholm et al. (2005) The Santa Clara County Healthy Kids Program: Impacts on children's medical, dental, and vision care. Final report submitted to the Lucille and David Packard Foundation	Santa Clara County, CA, 2003-2004	Survey of parents of undocumented children enrolled in Healthy Kids insurance; (N = 1,235) response rate = 89%	Newly enrolled children compared to children enrolled for 1 year (established); 63% of new enrollees were uninsured for all 6 months prior to enrollment; regression adjustment for demographic characteristics, income, and medical and dental need. Service use refers to previous 6 months.

NOTE: Changes are statistically significant unless otherwise noted as "not significant" ("NS"). N/A indicates the study did not examine that outcome. D-D = difference-in-difference; IR = incidence ratio; MEPS = Medical Expenditure Panel Survey; OLS = ordinary least squares; SCHIP = State Children's Health Insurance Program; Rx = prescription.

Findings

Usual Source of Care	Any Ambulatory Visit	Any Preventive Visit	Any Unmet Need	Specific Unmet Needs
New enrollees increased from 79.5% to 94.0% while established remained unchanged at 93.6% and 94.2%	No significant changes for new enrollees (69.5-72.0%) or established enrollees (76.2-71.6%), but D-D is significant	No significant changes for new enrollees (65.1-67.6%) or established enrollees (69.9-69.0%). D-D not significant	N/A	Preventive: New enrollees decreased from 22.7% to 8.8%, D-D significant; Specialty: New enrollees decreased from 10.0% to 2.8%, D-D is significant
New: 49% Established: 89%	New: 32% Established: 54%	New: 25% Established: 43%	New: 24% Established: 10%	Specialist: New: 7% Established: 3%; Rx: New: 6% Established 1%; Preventive: New 18% Established 5%; Delay in vision: New 8% Established 2%

TABLE D-2 Dental Services: Impacts of Health Insurance on Children's Access and Use of Dental Services

Citation	Location and Time Period of Analysis	Data Sources	Methodology
Banthin and Selden (2003) The ABCs of children's health care: How the Medicaid expansions affected access, burdens, and coverage between 1987 and 1996	United States, 1987 and 1996	National Medical Expenditure Survey (1987) and MEPS (1996)	D-D approach—change between 1987 and 1996 for poverty-related children less change over same time period for slightly higher-income children: Children made eligible for Medicaid under the poverty-related expansions in the 1980s are the treatment group and children with slightly higher income levels (defined as those in the income groups ultimately made eligible for SCHIP as of 2000) are the primary comparison group; controls included a variety of sociodemographic characteristics, as well as income and health status. Service use refers to previous 12 months.
Damiano et al. (2003) The impact of the Iowa S-SCHIP program on access, health status, and family environment	Iowa, 1999-2000	Two-wave mail survey (with telephone followup) of parents of new enrollees in Hawk-I (SCHIP) and 1 year later; (N = 463) response rate = 80% for baseline and 72% for followup	Pre-post cohort/longitudinal design. Outcomes for new enrollees compared to outcomes for the same enrollees 1 year later; no information provided on prior coverage of new enrollees. Service use refers to previous 12 months.

Findings

Has Usual Source of Dental Care	Any Dental Use	Preventive Use	Unmet Dental Need
N/A	5.1 percentage point increase (NS, but D-D without controls is significant)	N/A	N/A
Increased from 82% to 87%	Increased from 48% to 69%	N/A	Decreased from 30% to 10%

Continued

TABLE D-2 Continued

Citation	Location and Time Period of Analysis	Data Sources	Methodology
Davidoff et al. (2005) Effects of the State Children's Health Insurance Program expansions on children with chronic health conditions	United States, 1997, 2000, 2001	NHIS core data source supplemented with state data on policy changes, local data on private premiums	D-D approach: two treatment groups—children in the income group made newly eligible under SCHIP and children already eligible for Medicaid under the poverty-related expansions; comparison group: children with incomes slightly above the SCHIP eligibility thresholds; wide-ranging control variables to address possible confounding changes occurring over the same period. Service use refers to previous 12 months. Sample is restricted to children with chronic health conditions.
Eisert and Gabow (2002) Effect of Child Health Insurance Plan enrollment on the utilization of health care services by children using a public safety net system	Denver, CO, 1998-2000	SCHIP enrollment data from Denver County merged with Denver Health Medical Plan dental utilization data (N = 748 before enrollment and 757 after)	Service use for children enrolled in the Denver Health Medical Plan for a year prior to SCHIP enrollment compared to during 12 months after. Only 14% of children were uninsured before enrollment. Service use refers to previous 12 months.
Feinberg et al. (2002) Family income and the impact of a children's health insurance program on reported need for health services and unmet health need	Massachusetts, 1998-1999	One-wave telephone survey of parents of children in enrolled in Mass. Children's Medical Security Plan, a precursor to SCHIP, that included children of all incomes. (N = 877 primary sample plus 119 Spanish oversample); response rate = 62%	Compared experiences of children before and after enrollment, which parents were asked to recall.

Findings

Has Usual Source of Dental Care	Any Dental Use	Preventive Use	Unmet Dental Need
N/A	4.5 percentage point increase (NS)	N/A	7.4 percentage point decrease
N/A	(NS)	N/A	N/A
N/A	N/A	N/A	Declined from 31% before enrollment to 27% after

Continued

TABLE D-2 Continued

Citation	Location and Time Period of Analysis	Data Sources	Methodology
Fox et al. (2003) Changes in reported health status and unmet need for children enrolling in the Kansas children's health insurance program	Kansas, 1999-2000	Two-wave survey of parents of children enrolled in the program in its first six months and of the same parents 1 year later; (N = 1,955) response rate = 60% (Wave Two)	Pre-post cohort/longitudinal design. Responses for children just after enrollment compared to responses for same children 1 year later. Service use refers to previous 12 months.
Howell et al. (2008a) Final report of the evaluation of the San Mateo County Children's Health Initiative	San Mateo County, CA, 2006-2007	One-wave survey of parents of primarily undocumented children newly enrolled in Healthy Kids insurance and enrolled for 1 year; (N = 1,404) response rate = 77%	Newly enrolled children compared to children enrolled for 1 year; regression adjustment for demographic characteristics, income, and medical and dental need. Service use refers to previous 6 months.
Howell et al. (2008b) The impact of the Los Angeles Health Kids Program on access to care, use of services, and health status	Los Angeles County, CA, 2005-2007	Two-wave survey of parents of primarily undocumented children ages 1-5 enrolled in Healthy Kids insurance (N = 975); Response Rate = 86% (Wave 1) and 77% (Wave 2)	D-D; changes over a year for children who had been enrolled for a year in Wave 1 compared to changes for newly enrolled children; regression adjustment for demographic characteristics, income, and medical and dental need. Service use refers to previous 6 months.

Findings

Has Usual Source of Dental Care	Any Dental Use	Preventive Use	Unmet Dental Need
N/A	Increased from 48.2% to 70.7%	N/A	Decreased from 40.1% to 11.5%
New: 41.9%; Established: 86.6%	New: 26.5%; Established: 67.3%	New: 24.9%; Established: 65.2%	New: 21.9%; Established: 11.2%
New enrollees increased from 41.0% to 69.1% while established remained unchanged at 68.7%; D-D is significant	New enrollees increased from 37.6% to 53.8% while established enrollees remained unchanged (46.6-48.2%). D-D is significant	N/A	Decreased from 24.5% to 12.8% for new enrollees. D-D is significant

Continued

TABLE D-2 Continued

Citation	Location and Time Period of Analysis	Data Sources	Methodology
Kempe et al. (2005) Changes in access, utilization, and quality of care after enrollment into a state child health insurance plan	Colorado, 1999-2001	Survey of enrollees in Colorado's Child Health Plus Program; Baseline survey during 1999 and 2000; follow up survey 1 year later. (N = 480). Response rate = 77% for baseline and 68% for followup	Pre-post cohort/longitudinal design, controlling for race/ethnicity, age, prior insurance status; no separate results reported for the kids who had been uninsured prior to enrolling in SCHIP. Report IR for post- versus pre-enrollment.
Kenney (2007) The impacts of the State Children's Health Insurance Program on children who enroll: Findings from 10 states	10 states (CA, CO, FL, IL, LA, MO, NC, NJ, NY, TX), 2002	One-wave survey of parents of children newly enrolled in SCHIP or enrolled for 1 year; response rate = 75-80% depending on state; N = 16,700; data pooled across states. Primary sample consists of 5,394 established enrollees and 3,106 recent enrollees	Compare pre-SCHIP experiences of uninsured children to SCHIP experiences of SCHIP enrollees; regression adjustment for demographic characteristics and income; sensitivity analyses to examine selection. Service use refers to previous 6 months.
Kenney et al. (2007) Medicaid and SCHIP coverage: Evidence from California and North Carolina	California and North Carolina, 2002	Survey of parents of Medicaid enrollees in 2 states (N = 1,162; 830 established enrollees and 332 recent Medicaid enrollees). Response rate = 41% for CA and 60% for NC	Compared pre-Medicaid experiences when uninsured to Medicaid experiences; regression adjustment for demographic characteristics, income, health status, and parent's attitudes regarding efficacy of medical care. Service use refers to previous 6 months.

Findings

Has Usual Source of Dental Care	Any Dental Use	Preventive Use	Unmet Dental Need
N/A	N/A	N/A	IR = .59
31 percentage point increase	N/A	25 percentage point increase	11 percentage point decrease
22 percentage points more likely with Medicaid	N/A	16 percentage points more likely with Medicaid	11 percentage points less likely with Medicaid

Continued

TABLE D-2 Continued

Citation	Location and Time Period of Analysis	Data Sources	Methodology
Lave et al. (2002) The impact of dental benefits on the utilization of dental services by low-income children in western Pennsylvania	Western Pennsylvania, 1995-1996	Three wave telephone survey with families of newly enrolled children in Pa. CHIP (a precursor to SCHIP); response rate = 88% (Wave 1), 84% (combined Waves 2 and 3); N = 750	Pre-post cohort/longitudinal design, with separate sample comparison group. Outcomes for newly enrolled children were compared to outcomes for the same children 6 months and 1 year later and to separate sample. Service use refers to previous 6 months.
Lewis et al. (2007) Preventive dental care for children in the United States: A national perspective	United States, 2003-2004	NSCH (N = 102,353)	Children without any dental insurance compared to children with insurance; regression adjustment controlled for differences in demographic characteristics, having a personal doctor, and income. Service use refers to previous 12 months.
McBroome et al. (2005) Impact of the Iowa S-SCHIP program on access to dental care for adolescents	Iowa, 2000-2001	Two-wave mail survey with telephone followup for parents of newly enrolled school-aged children in SCHIP; (N = 1,399) overall response rate = 39%	Pre-post cohort/longitudinal design. Outcomes for newly enrolled children were compared to outcomes for the same children 1 year later.

Findings

Has Usual Source of Dental Care	Any Dental Use	Preventive Use	Unmet Dental Need
Increased from 60% at enrollment to 85% at 12 months	Increased from 40% at enrollment to 60% at 6 months to 65% at 12 months	Increased from 34% at enrollment to 56% at 6 months to 62% at 12 months	Decreased from 43% at enrollment to 15% at 6 months to 10% at 12 months (includes unmet or delayed need)
N/A	N/A	Insured: 77.2%; Uninsured: 57.0% (Adjusted odds ratio for uninsured: 0.41)	N/A
Increased from 81% to 88%	N/A	N/A	Decreased from 23% to 9%

Continued

TABLE D-2 Continued

Citation	Location and Time Period of Analysis	Data Sources	Methodology
Mofidi et al. (2002) The impact of a state children's health insurance program on access to dental care	North Carolina, 1999-2000	Two-wave mail survey with telephone followup for parents of newly enrolled school aged children in NC Health Choice (SCHIP); (N = 639) response rate = 75% at baseline and 74% of those at followup	Pre-post cohort/longitudinal design. Outcomes for newly enrolled children compared to outcomes for the same children 1 year later. Service use refers to previous 12 months.
Selden and Hudson (2006) Access to care and utilization among children: Estimating the effects of public and private coverage	United States, 1996-2002	MEPS supplemented with state-level Medicaid/SCHIP eligibility and private premiums information; N = 49,003	Children uninsured for full year compared to children with private coverage only and to children with any public coverage. Two-stage least squares with Instrumental Variables used to address selection bias (estimates reported here are from the model using family instruments). Found that OLS estimates understate positive effects of coverage. Service use refers to previous 12 months.
Szilagyi et al. (2004) Improved access and quality of care after enrollment in the New York State children's health insurance program	New York State, 2001-2002	Two-wave telephone survey of parents of children enrolled in Child Health Plus (SCHIP) for 4-6 months and about 1 year after enrollment; N = 2,290; response rate = 87% for followup	Outcomes for newly enrolled children compared to outcomes for the same children 1 year later. Pre period includes insured and uninsured kids, but 80 percent uninsured for part of the year. Service use refers to previous 12 months.

Findings

Has Usual Source of Dental Care	Any Dental Use	Preventive Use	Unmet Dental Need
Increased from 77% to 90%	Increased from 48% to 65%.	N/A	Decreased from 43% to 18%
N/A	19.1 (public) and 22.6 (private) percentage points more likely than uninsured	N/A	N/A
N/A	(NS)	N/A	6.7 percentage point decline

Continued

TABLE D-2 Continued

Citation	Location and Time Period of Analysis	Data Sources	Methodology
Trenholm et al. (2005) The Santa Clara County Healthy Kids Program: Impacts on children's medical, dental, and vision care	Santa Clara County, CA, 2003-2004	Survey of parents of undocumented children enrolled in Healthy Kids insurance; (N = 1,235) response rate = 89%	Newly enrolled children compared to children enrolled for 1 year ("established"); 63% of new enrollees were uninsured for all 6 months prior to enrollment; regression adjustment for demographic characteristics, income, and medical and dental need. Service use refers to previous 6 months.
Wang et al. (2007) Effects of the State Children's Health Insurance Program on access to dental care and use of dental services	United States, 1997-2002	NHIS (N = 21,295) SCHIP-eligible children ages 2-17	Children in states with implemented SCHIP programs compared to children in states without programs; regression adjustment controlled for differences in demographic characteristics and income; two-staged least squares controlled for selection.

NOTE: Changes are statistically significant unless otherwise noted as "not significant" ("NS"). N/A indicates the study did not examine that outcome. MEPS = Medical Expenditure Panel Survey; NHIS = National Health Interview Survey; NSCH = National Survey of Children's Health; SCHIP = State Children's Health Insurance Program.

Findings

Has Usual Source of Dental Care	Any Dental Use	Preventive Use	Unmet Dental Need
New: 30%; Established: 81%	N/A	New: 22%; Established: 61%	New: 21%; Established: 9%
N/A	Publicly insured low-income children 16.6 percentage points more likely than uninsured to have visit within 6 months and 22.6 percentage points more likely within 12 months	N/A	Publicly insured low-income children 7.9 percentage points less likely than uninsured

TABLE D-3 Immunizations: Impacts of Health Insurance on
Children's Immunizations

Citation	Place and Time Period of Findings	Data Sources
Allred et al. (2007) The association of health insurance and continuous primary care in the medical home on vaccination coverage for 19- to 35-month-old children	United States, 2003	NSCH linked to National Immunization Survey (N = 5,400)
Dombkowski et al. (2004a) Role of health insurance and a usual source of medical care in age-appropriate vaccination	United States, 1993-1996	NHIS, immunization and health insurance supplements
Dombkowski et al. (2004b) Risk factors for delay in age-appropriate vaccination	United States, 1992-1996	NHIS, immunization supplement
Henderson et al. (2006) Immunization initiation among infants in the Oregon Health Plan	Oregon, 2000-2001	Infant Oregon Health Plan records linked to Alert Immunization Registry (N = 39,708; 81% match between two sources)
Joyce and Racine (2005) CHIP shots: Association between the State Children's Health Insurance Programs and immunization rates	United States, 1995-2002	National Immunization Survey; Between 73% and 82% have complete vaccine data (N = 264,214)
Santoli et al. (2004) Insurance status and vaccination coverage among US preschool children	United States, 2000	Linked National Immunization Survey and National Survey of Early Childhood Health (N = 735)

Methodology	Findings
Uninsured children ages 19-35 months compared to continuously insured privately insured children; regression adjustment controlled for continuous primary care, demographic characteristics and WIC status.	Uninsured children significantly less likely to be up to date on 4:3:1:3:3 series immunizations (Odds ratio: .45 [unadjusted] and .38 [adjusted, marginally significant] for children continuously uninsured during past year).
Simulations of percentage of children with age-appropriate DTP4, Polio3, and MMR1 vaccinations based on whether the child had health insurance and/or a usual source of care.	Having health insurance and having a usual source of care were both very important for DTP4 and Polio3, but health insurance was much more important for having an age-appropriate single MMR1 vaccination.
Uninsured children ages 25-72 months compared to insured children; multivariate regression adjustment for demographic characteristics and urbanicity.	Insured children less likely to experience a 7 or more months delay in being up to date on 4:3:1 series immunizations (odds ratio: .50).
Children enrolled in the first month of life compared to children enrolled later in first year.	Infants enrolled in first month were significantly more likely to start any immunizations within first 3 months (odds ratio: 2.1).
Changes in the proportion of poor and near-poor children ages 19-35 months that is up-to-date for the 4:3:1 and 4:3:1:3:3 series compared to changes for nonpoor children following SCHIP implementation. Regression analysis controls for demographic and area characteristics, timing of SCHIP implementation and income.	The probability that poor or near-poor children are up-to-date for 4:3:1:3:3 series increased by 10.9 and 12.1 percentage points, respectively, during the SCHIP implementation period, but there were similar increases for nonpoor children. For the varicella vaccine, however, increases for poor and near-poor children were 12.3 and 8.0 percentage points more than for nonpoor children, respectively. Increases were greatest in areas with more uninsured children.
Uninsured children ages 19-35 months compared to insured children; multivariate regression adjustment for demographic characteristics, income, WIC participation, and site of well-child care.	While uninsured children had a lower rate of coverage for the 4:3:1:3:3 series, the difference from privately insured children was not statistically significant (odds ratio = .5) while Medicaid children had significantly lower rates than privately insured children (odds ratio = .3).

Continued

TABLE D-3 Continued

Citation	Place and Time Period of Findings	Data Sources
Zhao et al. (2004) Impact of health insurance status on vaccination coverage in children 19-35 months old, United States, 1993-1996	United States, 1993-1996	NHIS, immunization and health insurance supplements (N = 7,535)

NOTE: Changes are statistically significant unless otherwise noted as "not significant" ("NS"). N/A indicates the study did not examine that outcome. MEPS = Medical Expenditure Panel Survey; NHIS = National Health Interview Survey; NSCH = National Survey of Children's Health; SCHIP = State Children's Health Insurance Program.

Methodology	Findings
Uninsured children ages 19-35 months compared to insured children; multivariate regression adjustment for demographic characteristics.	Uninsured children significantly less likely than insured children to be up-to-date on 4:3:1:3 series immunizations (odds ratio: .76).

TABLE D-4 Impacts of Health Insurance on Special Populations of Children

Citation	Place and Time Period of Findings	Data Sources
Adolescents		
Dick et al. (2004) SCHIP's impact in three states: How do the most vulnerable children fare?	Kansas, Florida, and New York. Baseline between June 2000 and March 2001; followup interviews conducted 1 year later	Surveys of enrollees in state children's health insurance programs; adolescents in FL (N = 796) and NY (N = 710) only
Kenney (2007) (Appendix Table) The impacts of the State Children's Health Insurance Program on children who enroll: Findings from 10 states	10 states (CA, CO, FL, IL, LA, MO, NC, NJ, NY, TX), 2002	One-wave survey of parents of children newly enrolled in SCHIP or enrolled for 1 year; response rate = 75-80% depending on state; N = 16,700; data pooled across states. Adolescents aged 13-18: N = 1,769
Klein et al. (2007) Impact of the State Children's Health Insurance Program on adolescents in New York	New York State, 2001-2002	Two-wave telephone survey of newly enrolled adolescents (ages 12-18) in Child Health Plus (SCHIP) (N = 970)
Probst et al. (2005) Update: Health insurance and utilization of care among rural adolescents	United States, 1999-2000	NHIS (N = 8,503 adolescents)

Methodology	Findings
Pre-post cohort/longitudinal design. Included children who had disenrolled from SCHIP. Provide separate estimates for children who were previously uninsured.	Usual source of care: increased from 81% to 89% in FL and 71% to 95% in NY; any preventive use increased from 72% to 79% in FL and 60% to 73% in NY; unmet need decreased from 28% to 21% in FL and 38% to 22% in NY following enrollment in public health insurance.
Compare pre-SCHIP experiences of uninsured adolescents to SCHIP experiences of SCHIP enrollees; regression adjustment for demographic characteristics and income; sensitivity analyses to examine selection. Service use refers to previous 6 months.	Found statistically significant increases in the likelihood of having a usual source of care, an ambulatory care visit, a preventive visit, a dental visit, and a specialist visit for adolescents after enrolling in SCHIP. In addition, adolescents were significantly less likely to experience unmet health needs for medical, specialist, hospital, dental, and any type of care after enrolling in SCHIP and were more likely than other age groups to gain a usual source of care following enrollment in SCHIP.
Pre-post cohort/longitudinal design. Responses for the newly enrolled adolescents compared to responses for the same youth 1 year later.	Significant increases in the proportion with a usual source of care, significant reductions in unmet need, and significantly more adolescents reported being able to speak privately with their provider. However, there was no reduction in unmet need for mental health or reproductive health care.
Uninsured adolescents (ages 12-17) compared to privately insured adolescents; regression adjustment for demographic characteristics and income.	Uninsured adolescents significantly less likely to have a usual source of care (odds ratio = .18); a medical visit in the past year (odds ratio = .40); or a preventive visit in past year (odds ratio = .42).

Continued

TABLE D-4 Continued

Citation	Place and Time Period of Findings	Data Sources
Slifkin et al. (2002) Effect of the North Carolina State Children's Health Insurance Program on beneficiary access to care	North Carolina, summer 1999 for baseline and summer 2000 for followup	Survey of children enrolled in NC Health Choice; (N = 987) response rate = 75% for baseline and 74% for followup

Children with Asthma

Citation	Place and Time Period of Findings	Data Sources
Halterman et al. (2008) The impact of health insurance gaps on access to care among children with asthma in the United States	United States, 2003-2004	NSCH (N = 8,097)
Szilagyi et al. (2006) Improved asthma care after enrollment in the state children's health insurance program in New York	New York State, 2001-2002	Two-wave telephone survey of parents of children with asthma in Child Health Plus—SCHIP (N = 334 at baseline and 364 at followup)
Wood et al. (2002) Relationships between welfare status, health insurance status, and health and medical care among children with asthma	San Antonio, TX, 2001	Parents of children ages 2-12 with asthma were interviewed in person (N = 386)

Methodology	Findings
Pre-post longitudinal/cohort study; also analyzed a fresh sample of new enrollees at followup to assess possible secular trends; pre period includes insured and uninsured kids and the uninsured sample is quite small (N = 32). 87% of adolescents had previously been enrolled in Medicaid at some time in their life. Service use refers to previous 12 months.	Among those uninsured at the time of enrollment, usual source of care increased from 59 to 93%; checkup in last year increased from 25 to 54%; unmet medical need decreased from 51 to 2%.
Children uninsured in the past year or intermittently insured (gained or lost insurance) compared to continuously privately insured children; regression adjustment for demographic characteristics, income, and severity of condition.	All three groups of uninsured children with asthma significantly more likely to have unmet medical and medication need, to lack a personal doctor, and to have no preventive care from a personal doctor.
Responses for parents of newly enrolled children compared to responses for the same parents 1 year later.	After 1 year of enrollment, parents report significantly fewer problems getting help and advice from a usual source of care for their child's asthma and greater continuity of care. They rated the quality of care significantly higher than before enrollment.
Uninsured compared to privately insured adolescents; regression adjustment for demographic characteristics and experience with welfare system (no income adjustment).	There was no significant difference in asthma symptom score between privately insured and uninsured children with asthma, yet uninsured children had significantly fewer asthma care visits in the past year.

Continued

TABLE D-4 Continued

Citation	Place and Time Period of Findings	Data Sources
Children with Other Special Health Care Needs		
Busch and Horwitz (2004) Access to mental health services: Are uninsured children falling behind?	United States, 1997 and 1999	NSAF (N = 37,012)
Davidoff et al. (2005) Effects of the state children's health insurance program expansions on children with chronic health conditions	United States, 1997, 2000, 2001	NHIS core data source supplemented with state data on policy changes, local data on private premiums, etc.
Dick et al. (2004) SCHIP's impact in three states: How do the most vulnerable children fare?	Kansas, Florida, and New York. Baseline surveys between June 2000 and March 2001; followup interviews conducted 1 year later	Surveys of enrollees in state children's health insurance programs; adolescents only in FL. KS: N = 434, response rate = 35% FL: N = 944, response rate = 30% NY: N = 2,290, response rate = 55%
Jeffrey and Newacheck (2006) Role of insurance for children with special health care needs: A synthesis of the evidence	United States, 1990s and early 2000s	Multiple sources

Methodology	Findings
Uninsured children compared to privately insured children; regression adjustment for demographic characteristics, income, and mental health need.	In 1997, there were no significant differences between the two groups in the probability of a mental health visit, but by 1999 uninsured children were less likely to have a visit.
D-D approach: two treatment groups—children in the income group made newly eligible under SCHIP and children already eligible for Medicaid under the poverty-related expansions; comparison group: children with incomes slightly above the SCHIP eligibility thresholds; wide-ranging control variables to address possible confounding changes occurring over the same period. Service use refers to previous 12 months. Sample is restricted to children with chronic health conditions.	Reduction in unmet need 8.6 percentage points greater among children with chronic conditions eligible for SCHIP than among those just above the SCHIP income level. Reduction in unmet need greater among children with chronic conditions than without chronic conditions. No significant impacts on use of services or out-of-pocket expenses.
Pre-post cohort/longitudinal design. Included children who had disenrolled from SCHIP.	There were fewer significant changes among CSHCN than among other children, and results were inconsistent across states; levels of effects were similar between the CSHCN and other children.
Comprehensive literature review of 35 studies addressing insurance effects for CSHCN in published articles from 1995-2005.	Results consistently show uninsured CSHCN to have poorer access to care across multiple measures and much higher out-of-pocket costs when adjusted for family income.

Continued

TABLE D-4 Continued

Citation	Place and Time Period of Findings	Data Sources
Kenney (2007) The impacts of the State Children's Health Insurance Program on children who enroll: Findings from 10 states	10 states (CA, CO, FL, IL, LA, MO, NC, NJ, NY, TX), 2002	One-wave survey of parents of children newly enrolled in SCHIP or enrolled for 1 year; response rate = 75-80% depending on state; N = 16,700; data pooled across states. For children with special health care needs, N = 1,291
Mayer et al. (2004) Unmet need for routine and specialty care: Data from the National Survey of Children with Special Health Care Needs	United States, 2001	National Survey of Children with Special Health Care Needs (N = 38,866)
Porterfield and McBride (2007) The effect of poverty and caregiver education on perceived need and access to health services among children with special health care needs	United States, 2001	National Survey of Children with Special Health Care Needs (N = 38,866)
Wang and Watts (2007) Genetic counseling, insurance status, and elements of medical home: Analysis of the national survey of children with special health care needs	United States, 2001	National Survey of Children with Special Health Care Needs (N = 38,866)

Methodology	Findings
Compare pre-SCHIP experiences of uninsured children to SCHIP experiences of SCHIP enrollees; regression adjustment for demographic characteristics and income; sensitivity analyses to examine selection. Service use refers to previous 6 months.	Found that children with special health care needs were significantly more likely to have a preventive visit, a dental visit, and a usual source of care, and significantly less likely to experience unmet health needs for medical, prescription drug, specialist, hospital, dental, and any type of care following enrollment in SCHIP. The largest improvements in unmet needs were for children with special health care needs.
CSHCN ever uninsured in the year compared to privately insured CSHCN; regression adjustment for demographic and area characteristics, income and severity of condition.	Among all children with a need, uninsured children were significantly more likely to have an unmet need for routine care (odds ratio = 7.51) or specialty care (odds ratio = 4.29).
Two-stage probit model predicting first need for specialist services and then use of services; adjustment for demographic characteristics and income.	After adjusting for need for services, CSHCN with at least 1 uninsured month significantly less likely to receive specialist services.
CSHCN ever uninsured in the year compared to continuously insured CSHCN; regression adjustment for demographic characteristics and severity of condition (but not income).	CSHCN with interrupted insurance coverage or with no coverage were significantly less likely to receive genetic counseling (odds ratios .43 and .20, respectively).

Continued

TABLE D-4 Continued

Citation	Place and Time Period of Findings	Data Sources
Yu et al. (2006) Role of SCHIP in serving children with special health care needs	United States, 2001	National Survey of Children with Special Health Care Needs (N = 38,866)

NOTE: Changes are statistically significant unless otherwise noted as "not significant" ("NS"). N/A indicates the study did not examine that outcome. CHSCN = children with special health care needs; MEPS = Medical Expenditure Panel Survey; NHIS = National Health Interview Survey; NSAF = National Survey of America's Families; NSCH = National Survey of Children's Health; SCHIP = State Children's Health Insurance Program.

Methodology	Findings
CSHCN eligible for SCHIP but uninsured compared to CSHCN enrolled in SCHIP; regression adjustment for demographic characteristics and income.	Uninsured children significantly more likely to have unmet health care needs (odds ratio = 5.92).

TABLE D-5 Impacts of Health Insurance on Children's Health Status and Related Outcomes

Citation	Place and Time Period of Analysis	Data Sources
Late Diagnosis		
Froehlich et al. (2007) Prevalence, recognition, and treatment of attention-deficit/ hyper-activity disorder in a national sample of U.S. children	United States, 2001-2004	Children ages 8-15 in the NHANES who were screened for and identified with ADHD (N = 222)
Maniatis et al. (2005) Increased incidence and severity of diabetic ketoacidosis among uninsured children with newly diagnosed type 1 diabetes mellitus	Barbara Davis Center for Childhood Diabetes, University of Colorado Health Sciences Center, 2002-2003	Medical record review for all children with Type 1 diabetes (N = 383)
Preventable Hospitalization		
Aizer (2007) Public health insurance, program take-up, and child health	California, 1996-2000	Zip code–level/race/ethnicity level quarterly data on: Medicaid enrollment, ACSC hospitalizations, and child population counts from Medicaid enrollment files, state hospital discharge files from California's Office of Statewide Planning and Human Development, and U.S. census
Bermudez and Baker (2005) The relationship between SCHIP enrollment and hospitalizations for ambulatory care sensitive conditions in California	California, 1996-2000	County-level monthly data on: SCHIP enrollment, ACSC hospitalizations, and child population counts from SCHIP enrollment files, state hospital discharge files from California's Office of Statewide Planning and Human Development, and U.S. census

Methodology	Findings
Uninsured children with ADHD compared to insured children with ADHD; regression adjustment for differences in demographic characteristics and income.	Uninsured children less likely to have previously received a diagnosis of ADHD at the time of the examination (odds ratio = .1).
Uninsured children compared to privately insured children; no regression adjustment differences in characteristics.	Uninsured children were significantly more likely to present with diabetic ketoacidosis (odds ratio = 6.19) and severed diabetic ketoacidosis (odds ratio = 6.09).
Two-stage instrumental variable regression analysis predicting first the rate of Medicaid enrollment using placement and timing of outreach investments (e.g., application assistors and advertising campaigns), and then the rate of ACSC admissions, controlling for zip code characteristics including income and county fixed effects. Uses alternative instruments and also explored possible effects on length of stay.	Higher Medicaid enrollment rate is associated with a lower ACSC admission rate. A 10 percent increase in Medicaid enrollment leads to a 2.3 to 3.4% decrease in Medicaid ACS hospitalizations. Similar range found under alternative specifications. The OLS estimates were smaller in absolute value.
A regression model predicted the rate of ACSC hospitalization per child ages 1-18, controlling for the rate of SCHIP enrollment in the county (lagged by 1 year), county-level demographics (including income), pediatric provider supply, and county fixed effects. As a control, test whether SCHIP enrollment affected ACSCs among adults ages 19 to 29 or admission for appendicitis, which is not an ACSC.	A 1 percentage point increase in SCHIP enrollment was associated with a reduction of .86 ACSC hospitalizations per 100,000 children, a significant but small effect compared to a mean of 28.9. There was no significant change for young adults. Appendicitis hospitalization rates also declined significantly, but at a much lower level.

Continued

TABLE D-5 Continued

Citation	Place and Time Period of Analysis	Data Sources
Cousineau et al. (2008) Preventable hospitalizations among children in California counties after child health insurance expansion initiatives	9 counties in California that implemented CHIs to cover uninsured children, 2000-2005	Quarterly hospital discharge data on ACSCs
Szilagyi et al. (2006) Improved asthma care after enrollment in the state children's health insurance program in New York	New York State, 2001-2002	Two-wave telephone survey of parents of children with asthma in Child Health Plus—SCHIP (N = 334 at baseline and 364 at followup)

Perceived Health Status/Missed School Days/Other

Currie et al. (2008) Has public health insurance for older children reduced disparities in access to care and health outcomes?	United States, 1986 to 2005	NHIS (N = 548,789)

Methodology	Findings
ACSC rates are modeled as a function of CHI implementation, time, county, and insurance. Changes in ACSC rates for children who are either publicly insured or self-pay in each of the nine CHIs are compared to changes occurring among other children.	The rate of hospitalization for ACSCs declines following CHI implementation for lower-income children, while there is no change for higher-income children.
Responses for parents of newly enrolled children compared to responses for the same parents 1 year later.	After 1 year enrolled in SCHIP, the percentage of children hospitalized for asthma in the past year declined significantly from 11.1 to 3.4%. There were also significant reductions in emergency room visits and other health care visits for asthma.
Examine impacts of Medicaid/SCHIP eligibility expansions on probability of a physician visit and reported health status using a simulated eligibility indicator to address potential endogeneity of eligibility. Medicaid/SCHIP generosity index generated by applying state eligibility rules to a sample of children for each state and year. Control variables include interaction terms and age and year dummies. Look at concurrent and lagged effects. Still potentially biased and concerns about appropriateness of simulated eligibility measure in studies of all kids. Service use refers to previous 12 months.	No statistically significant concurrent effects on perceived health status. Statistically significant, positive effects of eligibility for children ages 2, 3, and 4 on health status of children ages 9 to 17, suggesting that the effects of insurance coverage on perceived health do not show up immediately.

Continued

TABLE D-5 Continued

Citation	Place and Time Period of Analysis	Data Sources
Damiano et al. (2003) The impact of the Iowa S-SCHIP program on access, health status, and family environment	Iowa, 1999-2000	Two-wave mail survey (with telephone followup) of parents of new enrollees in Hawk-I (SCHIP) and 1 year later; (N = 463) response rate = 80% for baseline and 72% for followup
Fox et al. (2003) Changes in reported health status and unmet need for children enrolling in the Kansas children's health insurance program	Kansas, 1999-2000	Two-wave survey of parents of children enrolled in the program in its first six months and of the same parents 1 year later; N = 1,955, response rate = 60% (Wave 2)
Howell and Trenholm (2007) The effect of new insurance coverage on the health status of low-income children in Santa Clara County	Santa Clara County, CA, 2003-2004	Survey of parents of undocumented children enrolled in Healthy Kids insurance; (N = 1,235) response rate = 89%
Howell et al. (2008a) Final report of the evaluation of the San Mateo County Children's Health Initiative	San Mateo County, CA, 2006-2007	One-wave survey of parents of primarily undocumented children newly enrolled in Healthy Kids insurance and enrolled for 1 year; (N = 1,404), response rate = 77%

Methodology	Findings
Pre-post cohort/longitudinal design. Outcomes for new enrollees compared to outcomes for the same enrollees 1 year later; no information provided on prior coverage of new enrollees. Service use refers to previous 12 months.	The proportion of children identified as being in excellent or very good health by their parents increases significantly from 79% to 82%. The proportion of children who missed 5 or more days of school due to illness or injury declined significantly from 35% to 25%.
Pre-post cohort/longitudinal design. Responses for children just after enrollment compared to responses for same children 1 year later. Service use refers to previous 12 months.	The proportion of children identified as being in excellent or very good health by their parents increases significantly from 71.2% to 75.7%. The proportion of parents who reported that their child's health is better now than it was a year ago also increased significantly from 11.6% to 20.0%.
Newly enrolled children compared to children enrolled for 1 year (established); regression adjustment for demographic characteristics, income, and medical and dental need.	Percent in fair/poor health reduced by 13.0 percentage points; significant change for both those who enroll and do not enroll for medical reasons; percent with more than 3 school days missed in month is reduced by 5.8 percentage points among those not enrolling for a medical reason.
Newly enrolled children compared to children enrolled for 1 year; regression adjustment for demographic characteristics, income, and medical and dental need. Service use refers to previous 6 months.	No significant effect on perceived health status. Significant reduction in percentage of children with missed school days in past 4 weeks, from 47.5% to 40.8%.

Continued

TABLE D-5 Continued

Citation	Place and Time Period of Analysis	Data Sources
Howell et al. (2008b) The impact of the Los Angeles Health Kids Program on access to care, use of services, and health status	Los Angeles County, CA, 2005-2007	Two-wave survey of parents of primarily undocumented children ages 1-5 enrolled in Healthy Kids insurance (N = 975); response rate = 86% (Wave 1) and 77% (Wave 2)
Szilagyi et al. (2004) Improved access and quality of care after enrollment in the New York state children's health insurance program	New York State, 2001-2002	Two-wave telephone survey of parents of children enrolled in Child Health Plus (SCHIP) for 4-6 months and about 1 year after enrollment; N = 2,290; response rate = 87% for followup

NOTE: Changes are statistically significant unless otherwise noted as "not significant" ("NS"). N/A indicates the study did not examine that outcome. ACSC = ambulatory care sensitive condition; CHI = children's health initiatives; MEPS = Medical Expenditure Panel Survey; NHANES = National Health and Nutrition Examination Survey; NHIS = National Health Interview Survey; NSCH = National Survey of Children's Health; OLS = ordinary least squares; SCHIP = State Children's Health Insurance Program.

Methodology	Findings
D-D; changes over a year for children who had been enrolled for a year in Wave 1 compared to changes for newly enrolled children; regression adjustment for demographic characteristics, income, and medical and dental need. Service use refers to previous 6 months.	D-D for percentage in excellent/very good health not significant; however both new and established enrollees improve significantly from Wave 1 to Wave 2.
Outcomes for newly enrolled children compared to outcomes for the same children 1 year later. Pre period includes insured and uninsured kids, but 80% uninsured for part of the year.	No significant effect on perceived health status.

Appendix E

Recent Studies of the Impacts of Health Insurance for Adults: Summary Table

A table summarizing quasi-experimental studies since 2002 on the impacts of health insurance on health outcomes of adults in the United States is presented in this appendix. The table was originally presented in a literature review commissioned by the Institute of Medicine Committee on Health Insurance Status and Its Consequences in 2008 titled *Health Consequences of Uninsurance Among Adults in the United States: An Update*, by J. Michael McWilliams, M.D., Ph.D., Harvard Medical School.

Several abbreviations are used in the tables:

- HRS = Health and Retirement Study
- MEPS = Medical Expenditure Panel Survey
- NCHS = National Center for Health Statistics
- NHIS = National Health Interview Survey
- NIS = National Inpatient Sample
- NPHS = National Population Health Survey
- SEER = Surveillance, Epidemiology, and End Results
- SSA = Social Security Administration

TABLE E-1 Recent Quasi-Experimental Studies of the Effects of Health Insurance Coverage on Adults' Health Outcomes, 2002-2008

Study	Data	Methodological Approach
Card et al. (2004) The impact of nearly universal coverage on health care utilization and health: Evidence from Medicare	Cross-sectional survey data from the 1992-2001 NHIS; mortality data from NCHS Multiple Cause of Death files	Regression discontinuity analysis of general health status by age
Card et al. (2007) Does Medicare save lives?	Cross-sectional state hospital discharge data from California from 1992-2002	Regression discontinuity analysis of mortality by age among acutely ill adults hospitalized for non-deferrable conditions
Decker and Rapaport (2002) Medicare and inequalities in health outcomes: The case of breast cancer	SEER cancer registry data from 1980-1994 with followup mortality data	Difference-in-differences comparisons of stage of diagnosis and survival for white and black women with breast cancer before and after age 65
Decker (2005) Medicare and the health of women with breast cancer	SEER cancer registry data from 1980-2001 with followup mortality data	Difference-in-differences comparisons of stage of diagnosis and survival for white, black, and Hispanic women with breast cancer before and after age 65
Decker and Remler (2004) How much might universal health insurance reduce socioeconomic disparities in health?	Cross-sectional survey data from the 1997-1998 NHIS and the 1996-1997 NPHS	Difference-in-differences-in-differences comparison of general health status by age in the United States and Canada

Principal Findings*	Limitations
Medicare eligibility after age 65 associated with significant 12% reduction in sociodemographic disparity in general health status but no evidence of deceleration in mortality rates at age 65	Comparisons by prior insurance status or pre-existing conditions not possible with cross-sectional data; only one self-reported general health outcome assessed; differential changes in health trends not assessed; regression discontinuity design not suited for identification of delayed mortality effects in general population
Medicare eligibility after age 65 associated with abrupt absolute decrease in 7-day mortality of 1% (20% relative reduction) that persisted for at least 2 years after admission	Comparisons by prior insurance status not possible with cross-sectional data; alternative explanations for survival gains could not be tested directly
Medicare eligibility after age 65 associated with significant decrease in probability of late detection for white women but not black women; coverage estimated to increase 5-year survival rate for both black and white women diagnosed with early stage disease, but differential effect for black women not significant	Comparisons by prior insurance status not possible; persistent racial and ethnic disparities in outcomes among insured adults may have reduced differential effects; outcomes assessed for breast cancer only
Medicare eligibility after age 65 associated with absolute decrease of 3.4% in probability of late detection for Hispanic women and 1.8% decrease for white women, but differential effect not significant; 11% relative reduction in mortality risk after age 65 did not differ by race or ethnicity	Comparisons by prior insurance status not possible; persistent racial and ethnic disparities in outcomes among insured adults may have reduced differential effects; outcomes assessed for breast cancer only
Medicare eligibility after age 65 associated with a significant differential reduction of 4.0 percentage points (se = 1.9) in probability of fair or poor health for low-income U.S. adults; socioeconomic disparity in general health among nonelderly adults reduced by more than half	

Continued

TABLE E-1 Continued

Study	Data	Methodological Approach
Dor et al. (2006) The effect of private insurance on the health of older, working age adults: Evidence from the Health and Retirement Study	Longitudinal survey data from the 1992-1998 HRS	Instrumental variables analysis using state-level marginal tax rates, unemployment rates, and unionization rates as instruments for health insurance coverage
Finkelstein and McKnight (2005) What did Medicare do (and was it worth it)?	Mortality data from NCHS Multiple Cause of Death files	Difference-in-differences comparisons of mortality before and after 1965 by age (young elderly who became covered by Medicare vs. near-elderly who did not) and by geographic variation in insurance rates prior to 1965
Hadley and Waidmann (2006) Health insurance and health at age 65: Implications for medical care spending on new Medicare beneficiaries	Longitudinal survey data from the 1992-1998 HRS	Instrumental variables analysis using spouse's prior union status, immigrant status and years in the Unied States, and involuntary job loss as instruments for health insurance coverage
Lichtenberg (2002) The effects of Medicare on health care utilization and outcomes	Cross-sectional survey data from the 1987-1991 NHIS; vital status data from SSA life tables	Regression discontinuity analyses of disability and mortality by age

Principal Findings*	Limitations
Having private insurance at baseline associated with significantly better health scores for a summary index of five general and physical health measures	
No discernable impact of the introduction of Medicare in 1965 on overall mortality for elderly adults	
Continuous insurance coverage associated with significantly fewer deaths among the near-elderly prior to age 65 (2.8% absolute decrease in death rate) and significant upward shift in distribution of general health states among those who survived (3.3% and 4.1% absolute increases in probability of excellent and very good health, respectively)	Validity of results depend on the validity of the instruments used; self-reported health outcomes
13% relative reduction in bed days and 5.1 percentage point decrease in 10-year mortality risk associated with Medicare eligibility after age 65	Effects not disaggregated by predictors of insurance status; comparisons by prior insurance status not possible with cross-sectional data; potentially spurious results due to data limitations of SSA life tables; formal testing of effects not consistently conducted; alternative explanations not addressed

Continued

TABLE E-1 Continued

Study	Data	Methodological Approach
McWilliams et al. (2007) Health of previously uninsured adults after acquiring Medicare coverage	Longitudinal survey data from the 1992-2004 HRS	Comparison of health trend changes at age 65 by prior insurance status
Pauly (2005) Effects of insurance coverage on use of care and health outcomes for non-poor young women	Cross-sectional survey data from the 1996 MEPS	Instrumental variables analysis using firm size and marital status as instruments for health insurance status
Polsky et al. (2006) The health effects of Medicare for the near-elderly uninsured	Longitudinal survey data from the 1992-2004 HRS	Comparison of health trend changes at age 65 by prior insurance status
Volpp et al. (2003) Market reform in New Jersey and the effect on mortality from acute myocardial infarction	Cross-sectional state and national hospital discharge data from New Jersey, New York, and the NIS from 1990-1996	Difference-in-differences comparisons of mortality rates for hospitalized patients with acute myocardial infarction in New Jersey and New York before and after state reforms in New Jersey reduced subsidies for hospital care for the uninsured and introduced price competition

Principal Findings*	Limitations
Medicare eligibility after age 65 associated with differentially improved health trends for previously uninsured with cardiovascular disease or diabetes in summary health (p = .006), change in general health (p = .03), mobility (p = .05), agility (p = .003), and adverse cardiovascular outcomes (p = 0.02); differential improvement also significant for depressive symptoms (p = .002) but not summary health (p = 0.17) for previously uninsured without these conditions	Self-reported health outcomes; subject to bias from differential mortality among previously uninsured or coincidental changes in time-varying predictors of health between comparison groups
Associations between insurance coverage and probability of fair or poor health not significant in either naïve or instrumental variables analyses	Validity of results depend on the validity of the instruments used; imprecise estimates; only one self-reported general health outcome assessed
Medicare eligibility after age 65 associated with significant improvements in health trajectories for both previously insured and previously uninsured adults; differential increase in probability of being in excellent or very good health after age 65 not significant for previously uninsured adults (+1.8%; 95% CI: −2.6,7.0)	Only one self-reported general health outcome assessed; subject to bias from differential mortality among previously uninsured or coincidental changes in time-varying predictors of health between comparison groups
New Jersey health care reform associated with no significant changes in mortality for insured patients in New Jersey relative to New York or the nation, but with a significant differential increase of 3.7 to 5.2 percentage points in mortality rates for uninsured patients in New Jersey	Subject to bias from coincidental changes in state-specific predictors of mortality in insured and uninsured populations; mortality for only one conditions assessed; analysis limited to one state and may not generalize to national population of uninsured

Continued

TABLE E-1 Continued

Study	Data	Methodological Approach
Volpp et al. (2005) The effects of price competition and reduced subsidies for uncompensated care on hospital mortality	Cross-sectional state hospital discharge data from New Jersey and New York from 1990-1996	Difference-in-differences comparisons of mortality rates for hospitalized patients with 6 other acute conditions in New Jersey and New York before and after state reforms in New Jersey reduced subsidies for hospital care for the uninsured and introduced price competition

NOTE: HRS = Health and Retirement Study; MEPS = Medical Expenditure Panel Survey; NCHS = National Center for Health Statistics; NHIS = National Health Interview Survey; NIS = Nationwide Inpatient Sample; NPHS = National Population Health Survey; SEER = Surveillance, Epidemiology, and End Results; SSA = Social Security Administration.
*Point estimates, standard errors (se), 95% confidence intervals (CI), or P-values presented as reported in original articles.

Principal Findings*	Limitations
New Jersey health care reform associated with relative increases in mortality for uninsured New Jersey patients with congestive heart failure ($p < .05$) and stroke ($p > .05$) compared to uninsured New York patients; mortality trends similar in New Jersey and New York for patients with other conditions, regardless of insurance status	Subject to bias from coincidental changes in state-specific predictors of mortality in insured and uninsured populations; analysis limited to one state and may not generalize to national population of uninsured

Appendix F

Committee Biographies

Lawrence S. Lewin, M.B.A. (*Chair*) founded the Lewin Group in 1970 and remained its president and chief executive officer until 1999. He has directed a wide range of projects in health policy and finance, public health, academic medicine, public and private health insurance, technology and market assessment of medical devices and pharmaceutical products, strategic visioning and planning, and health systems management and governance. He has conducted nearly 100 workshops and strategic planning conferences for a wide variety of health care executives and organizations. He left the Lewin Group in December 1999 and currently is an executive consultant assisting senior health care executives, foundations, and organizations in strategic decision making, program improvement, and executive coaching. Mr. Lewin was elected to the Institute of Medicine (IOM) in 1984, served 8 years as an elected member of the IOM Council, and in 2004 was awarded the IOM's Adam Yarmolinsky Medal for Distinguished Service. He has served on several IOM committees. He was a founding member of the Association for Health Services Research (now AcademyHealth) and is currently a member of the National Commission on Prevention Priorities. Mr. Lewin holds an A.B. from Princeton University's Woodrow Wilson School of Public and International Affairs and an M.B.A. from the Harvard Business School, where he was a Baker Scholar. Mr. Lewin served as an officer in the U.S. Marine Corps.

Jack Ebeler, M.P.A. (*Vice Chair*) is a consultant in health care policy, focusing on federal policy and the changing health care marketplace. Previously, he served as president and chief executive officer of the Alliance of Community

Health Plans. Prior to that, Mr. Ebeler was senior vice president and director of the health care group at the Robert Wood Johnson Foundation, where he focused on the uninsured, health care quality, and chronic care issues. Mr. Ebeler served as deputy assistant secretary for planning and evaluation for health and as acting assistant secretary for planning and evaluation at the U.S. Department of Health and Human Services. Over the years, he has also held positions in the health care industry and on Capitol Hill. Mr. Ebeler serves as a commissioner on the Medicare Payment Advisory Commission; the Health Care Services board of the Institute of Medicine; the board of trustees of Inova Health System in Virginia, where he chairs the board of health care services; and the board of directors of Families USA. Mr. Ebeler holds an M.P.A. from the John F. Kennedy School of Government at Harvard University, and his undergraduate degree is from Dickinson College. Mr. Ebeler chaired the IOM Committee on the Review of the Adoption and Implementation of Health IT Standards of the Office of the National Coordinator for Health Information Technology within the U.S. Department of Health and Human Services. He was a member of the IOM Subcommittee on Strategies and Models for Providing Health Insurance, as well as other IOM committees and planning groups.

John Z. Ayanian, M.D., M.P.P., is a professor of medicine and health care policy at Harvard Medical School and professor of health policy and management at the Harvard School of Public Health. He is the director of the General Internal Medicine Fellowship and medical director of the Center for Surgery and Public Health at Brigham and Women's Hospital. He is also a practicing general internist in the Division of General Medicine at Brigham and Women's Hospital, where he sees patients and teaches medical residents. Dr. Ayanian's research focuses on the effect of patients' race, ethnicity, gender, insurance coverage, and socioeconomic characteristics on access to care and clinical outcomes, as well as on the impact of physicians' specialty and organizational characteristics on the quality of care. He is the principal investigator of the Harvard/Northern California research team in the Cancer Care Outcomes Research and Surveillance Consortium. In Dr. Ayanian's recent research, he has studied trends in quality of care and racial disparities in Medicare managed care plans, the effect of Medicare coverage on previously uninsured adults, the impact of ambulatory care from primary care physicians and cardiologists on the outcomes of Medicare beneficiaries who have survived a heart attack, and the quality of cancer care by race, ethnicity, and language. Dr. Ayanian received his B.A. degree summa cum laude from Duke University, his M.D. degree from Harvard Medical School, and his M.P.P. degree from the Harvard Kennedy School of Government, with a concentration in health policy. Dr. Ayanian was a member of the IOM Committee on Cancer Survivorship and the Committee on the Consequences of Uninsurance. He has received numerous awards for his research.

Katherine Baicker, Ph.D., is professor of health economics in the Department of Health Policy and Management at the Harvard School of Public Health. She received her B.A. in economics from Yale in 1993 and her Ph.D. in economics from Harvard in 1998. She is a research associate at the National Bureau of Economic Research. She has served on the faculty of the Economics Department at Dartmouth College, the Center for the Evaluative Clinical Sciences and the Department of Community and Family Medicine at Dartmouth Medical School, and in the School of Public Affairs at the University of California, Los Angeles. From 2005 to 2007, Dr. Baicker served as a Senate-confirmed member of the President's Council of Economic Advisers. Dr. Baicker's research interests include health economics, welfare, and public finance, with a particular focus on the financing of health insurance, spending on public programs, and fiscal federalism. Her research has been published in journals such as the *American Economic Review, Health Affairs, Journal of Public Economics,* and *Quarterly Journal of Economics*, and has been featured in the *New York Times, Wall Street Journal, Business Week*, and on National Public Radio.

Christine Ferguson, J.D., is a research professor at the George Washington School of Public Health and Health Services. Ms. Ferguson has been engaged in the development of an educational program in state health policy and concentrates her research on health reform, health services for vulnerable populations, overweight and obesity, and health systems reform. From 1981 to 1995, Ms. Ferguson served as counsel and deputy chief of staff to the late U.S. Senator John H. Chafee (R-RI). In this role, Ms. Ferguson served as lead staff negotiator for the Mainstream Senators in their 1993-1994 attempt to develop a bipartisan health reform proposal. Ferguson served as secretary of the Rhode Island Department of Human Services from 1995 to 2001, under Governor Lincoln Almonds' two-term administration. As commissioner of the Massachusetts Department of Public Health under Governor Mitt Romney from 2003 to 2005, Ms. Ferguson led the Administration's efforts in the areas of emergency preparedness, substance abuse services, medical errors reduction, and early childhood education and child care. Most recently, Ferguson served as president of First Focus, a special initiative funded by the David and Lucile Packard Foundation and the Atlantic Philanthropies. A graduate of the University of Michigan and the Washington College of Law at American University, Ms. Ferguson is a member of the Board on Children, Youth, and Families of the National Academy of Sciences and the Board of the Neighborhood Health Plan of

Rhode Island. She has also served in a leadership capacity at the National Academy for State Health Policy and other organizations.

Robert S. Galvin, M.D., M.B.A., is the director of Global Health Care for General Electric (GE). He is in charge of the design and performance of GE's health programs, totaling over $3 billion annually, and oversees the 1 million patient encounters that take place in GE's 220 medical clinics in more than 20 countries. Drawing on his clinical expertise and training in Six Sigma, Dr. Galvin has been an advocate and leader in extending the benefits of this methodology to health care. Dr. Galvin has focused on issues of market-based health policy and financing, with a special interest in quality improvement, payment reform, and the assessment of medical innovations. He was recently appointed to the National Advisory Council for Healthcare Research and Quality, which provides advice and recommendations to the director of the Agency for Healthcare Research and Quality and to the Secretary of Health and Human Services on priorities for a national health services research agenda. He is also on the board of the National Committee for Quality Assurance and was a member of the Task Force on the Future of Military Health Care. He is a cofounder of the Leapfrog Group and is the founder of Bridges to Excellence, one of the first pay-for-performance initiatives. Dr. Galvin is widely published on issues affecting the purchaser side of health care, and is professor adjunct of medicine and health policy at Yale University, where he directs the seminar series on the private sector for the Robert Wood Johnson Clinical Scholars fellowship. He is a fellow of the American College of Physicians. Dr. Galvin has served on numerous IOM committees.

Paul Ginsburg, Ph.D., is president of the Center for Studying Health System Change (HSC). Founded in 1995 by Dr. Ginsburg, HSC conducts research to inform policy makers and other audiences about changes in organization of financing and delivery of care and their effects on people. HSC is widely known for the objectivity and technical quality of its research and its success in communicating it to policy makers and the media, as well as to the research community. Dr. Ginsburg is particularly known for his understanding of health care markets and health care costs. In 2007, for the fifth time, he was named by *Modern Healthcare* as one of the 100 most powerful persons in health care. Dr. Ginsburg served as the founding executive director of the predecessor to the Medicare Payment Advisory Commission. Widely regarded as highly influential, the commission developed the Medicare physician payment reform proposal that was enacted by the Congress in 1989. Dr. Ginsburg was a senior economist at RAND and served as deputy assistant director at the Congressional Budget Office. Before serving in that capacity, he served on the faculties of Duke and Michigan State Universities. Dr. Ginsburg earned his doctorate in economics from Harvard University.

Leon L. Haley, Jr., M.D., M.H.S.A., FACEP, CPE, is currently the deputy chief of staff and deputy senior vice-president of medical affairs for the Grady Health System. Dr. Haley holds the additional titles of chief of service, emergency medicine for the Grady Health System, medical director of the Emergency Care Center at Grady Memorial Hospital and vice-chairman, clinical affairs, Grady Health System and associate professor of emergency medicine at Emory University and The Emory Clinic. Dr. Haley has interests and publications in health administration, operations and strategic management, and diversity as it relates to health care and emergency medicine in particular. Dr. Haley serves on or chairs various hospital, university, and national committees including the Board of Directors for the Society for Academic Emergency Medicine. He is a member of several national organizations, including the American College of Emergency Physicians, the American College of Healthcare Executives, and the American College of Physician Executives. Dr. Haley is also an oral board examiner for the American Board of Emergency Medicine. Dr. Haley is board-certified in emergency medicine and a fellow of the American College of Emergency Physicians. Dr. Haley has additionally completed the Woodruff Leadership Program at Emory University and a fellowship for the National Association of Public Hospital Program. Dr. Haley has been funded by the Robert Wood Johnson Foundation and the Healthcare Foundation of Georgia. Dr. Haley is a member of the State of Georgia's Trauma Network Commission as an appointee of the Lt. Governor. A native of Pittsburgh, Pennsylvania, Dr. Haley received his undergraduate degree from Brown University, his medical degree from the University of Pittsburgh, and his master's degree in health services administration from the University of Michigan. Dr. Haley completed his residency in emergency medicine, including a year as chief resident, at the Henry Ford Health System in Detroit, Michigan. Prior to holding positions at Grady and Emory, Dr. Haley was a senior staff physician at the Henry Ford Health System and a member of the Henry Ford Medical Group.

Catherine McLaughlin, Ph.D., is a senior fellow at Mathematica Policy Research, Inc., and the director of research for Mathematica's new office in Ann Arbor, Michigan. She is also a professor in the Department of Health Management and Policy and the director of the Economic Research Initiative on the Uninsured (ERIU) at the University of Michigan. ERIU, an initiative funded by the Robert Wood Johnson Foundation, conducts and disseminates research aimed at increasing our understanding of the interaction between health and labor market dynamics and the uninsured.

Dr. McLaughlin is on the board of trustees of the American Hospital Association's Health Research and Educational Trust, the treasurer of the American Society of Health Economists, and a member of the Council on Health Care Economics and Policy. She is on the editorial board of *Health Services Research*. Her current research interests are focused on the uninsured, managed care, market competition, and employer and employee benefit choice. She has published numerous articles including research on the working uninsured. Professor McLaughlin received her Ph.D. in economics from the University of Wisconsin. Dr. McLaughlin was appointed to the Institute of Medicine in 2006.

James J. Mongan, M.D., is president and chief executive officer of Partners HealthCare System. He is also professor of health care policy and professor of social medicine at Harvard Medical School and chairs the Commonwealth Fund Commission on a High Performance Health System. From 1996-2002, Dr. Mongan served as president of Massachusetts General Hospital. Earlier in his career, Dr. Mongan was the executive director of the Truman Medical Center in Kansas City and dean of the University of Missouri-Kansas City School of Medicine. He was also staff to the Senate Committee on Finance, a deputy assistant secretary for health in the U.S. Department of Health and Human Services, and an associate director of the Carter White House domestic policy staff. Dr. Mongan is a member of the Institute of Medicine (IOM) and has served on numerous boards of trustees, including those of the American Hospital Association and the Kaiser Family Foundation. Dr. Mongan earned his medical degree from Stanford University Medical School. He was a member of the IOM Committee on the Consequences of Uninsurance and has served on the IOM Council, the National Research Council's Governing Board, and other IOM committees.

Robert D. Reischauer, Ph.D., is the president of The Urban Institute. Previously, he was a senior fellow with the Brookings Institution, and from 1989 to 1995, he was the director of the Congressional Budget Office. He is vice chair of the Medicare Payment Advisory Commission. He also currently serves on the boards of the Center on Budget and Policy Priorities, AcademyHealth, the Committee for a Responsible Federal Budget, and Harvard University (the Corporation). Dr. Reischauer is a member of the Institute of Medicine and the National Academy of Public Administration and is a founding member of the National Academy of Social Insurance. Dr. Reischauer received his A.B. degree from Harvard College and his M.I.A. and Ph.D. from Columbia University.

William J. Scanlon, Ph.D., is a senior policy advisor with Health Policy R&D. He is a consultant to the National Health Policy Forum and is an affiliated faculty member with the Institute for Policy Studies, The Johns Hopkins University. He was the managing director of health care issues at the U.S. General Accounting Office (GAO) (now the U.S. Government Accountability Office) until 2004. At GAO, he oversaw congressionally requested studies of Medicare, Medicaid, the private insurance market and health delivery systems, public health, and the military and veterans' health care systems. Prior to joining GAO in 1993, he was the co-director of the Center for Health Policy Studies and an associate professor in the Department of Family Medicine at Georgetown University. Also, Dr. Scanlon was a principal research associate in Health Policy at the Urban Institute. Currently, Dr. Scanlon is a member of the Medicare Payment Advisory Commission and the National Committee on Vital and Health Statistics. Dr. Scanlon has published extensively and has served as a frequent consultant to federal agencies, state Medicaid programs, and private foundations. He earned his doctoral degree in economics from the University of Wisconsin-Madison.

Antonia Villarruel, Ph.D., is professor and associate dean for research at the University of Michigan School of Nursing. She was elected to the Institute of Medicine in 2007. Dr. Villarruel has an extensive background in health promotion and health disparities research and practice. Her research focuses on the development and testing of behavioral interventions to reduce HIV sexual risk behaviors among Mexican and Latino youth. Dr. Villarruel's research integrates a community participatory approach. Dr. Villarruel is vice president and a founding member of the National Coalition of Ethnic Minority Nursing Associations and past president of the National Association of Hispanic Nurses. She was co-chair of the Diversity Working Group of the National Advisory Council for Nursing Education and Practice, U.S. Department of Health and Human Services. Dr. Villarruel has received numerous honors and awards including recognition in the Michigan Nurses Hall of Fame. She is a fellow of the American Academy of Nursing.

Lawrence Wallack, Dr.P.H., is the dean of the College of Urban and Public Affairs at Portland State University and Emeritus Professor of Public Health, University of California, Berkeley. Dr. Wallack was a founding senior fellow and first President of the Rockridge Institute, a California-based think tank. He is also a senior fellow at the Longview Institute. Dr. Wallack is the founding director of the Prevention Research Center, the first federally funded national alcohol research center with a primary emphasis on prevention. He is a founding director of the Berkeley Media Studies Group, an organization conducting research and training in the use of media to promote healthy public policies. Dr. Wallack is one of the primary architects of media advocacy—an innovative approach to working with mass media to advance social and public health issues. He has published extensively and lectures frequently on the news media and public health policy issues. Dr. Wallack has been honored with several awards including the Robert Wood Johnson Foundation Innovators Award for lifetime achievement and innovation in the area of prevention. He earned his doctoral degree in health education from the University of California, Berkeley. Dr. Wallack was a member of the Institute of Medicine Committee on the Consequences of Uninsurance.